Building
ANTIQUE MODEL
CARS
in Wood

William Reeves

Sterling Publishing Co., Inc. New York
A Sterling/Tamos Book

A Sterling/Tamos Book
© 2003 William Reeves

Sterling Publishing Co., Inc.
387 Park Avenue South
New York, NY 10016-8810

Tamos Books Inc.
300 Wales Avenue
Winnipeg, MB Canada R2M 2S9

10 9 8 7 6 5 4 3 2 1

Distributed in Canada by Sterling Publishing Co., Inc.
C/o Canadian Manda Group, One Atlantic Avenue, Suite 105
Toronto, Ontario, Canada M6K 3E7
Distributed in Great Britain by Chrysalis Books
64 Brewery Road, London N7 9NT, England
Distributed in Australia by Capricorn Link (Australia) Pty Ltd.
P.O. Box 704, Windsor, NSW 2756 Australia

Design A. Crawford
Photography Jerry Grajewski, Grajewski Fotograph Inc.,
Winnipeg, Canada

Printed in China

National Library of Canada Cataloging in Publication Data
Reeves, William, 1957-
  Building antique model cars in wood / William Reeves.

"A Sterling/Tamos book".
Includes index
ISBN 1-895569-51-6

1. Antique and classic cars--Models--Design and construction. 2.
Automobiles--Models--Design and construction. I. Title.
TL237.R43 2003   629.22'12   C2003-910579-2

      Library of Congress Cataloging-in-Publication Data

Reeves, William, 1944-
  Building antique model cars in wood / William Reeves ; photography by
Jerry Grajewski.
    p. cm.
  "A Sterling/Tamos Book."
  Includes index.
  ISBN 1-895569-51-6
  1. Automobiles--Models--Design and construction. 2. Woodwork. I.
Title.
TL237.R42 2003
629.22'1--dc21
                        2003006886

Tamos Books Inc. acknowledges the financial support of the Government of Canada
through the Book Publishing Development Program (BPIDP) for our publishing activities.

Note   If you prefer to work in metric measurements, to convert inches to millimeters
multiply by 25.4.

ISBN 1-895569-51-6

About the Author

William Reeves was born in Winnipeg, Canada. His
father was in the military and his interest in history
and woodworking was passed on to William, who
developed a passion for all things wood and for the
pioneer years when airplanes and automobiles were
being tested. He built radio-controlled airplanes and
plastic models and at age 36 turned his attention
to model cars. Since he couldn't find ready-
made wood kits of pioneer automobiles he
decided to build his own from pictures. His
research has continued and now he is an
authority on antique cars. Recently he won
first place in the Canadian Woodworking
Show for one of his antique car models.

William Reeves lives in Winnipeg with his
wife and daughter. He holds the title of
Journeyman Sheet Metal but works as a
welder fitter and runs CNC machinery.

Acknowledgements

I am indebted to many people for helping me make
this book a reality. In particular, many thanks to my
co-worker and friend, Gerald R. Chabot, for believing
in me and encouraging me to share my projects with
woodworking and car enthusiasts and to the staff of
Windsor Plywood who liked my work and supplied
me with wonderful exotic woods that made it
possible to build these model cars. I am more than
fortunate that my eight-year old daughter Angela
made me supper and snacks and stapled my pages
together during the writing stages of this book and
always assured me that my model cars were "cool".
My wife Donna turned my scrambled notes into
sentences and paragraphs and offered practical
suggestions on materials for some of the model car
parts. Without her input this project would not have
succeeded.

Table of Contents

Projects

Introduction

The automobile dates back to 1769 when Nicolas-Joseph Cugnet of France built the first self-propelled steam-powered vehicle that traveled for twenty minutes at 2.25 miles per hour. This vehicle was noisy, smelly, and potentially dangerous because its boiler could blow up; nevertheless, people rode in it and in Britain such a vehicle was used as a form of public transportation in the early eighteen hundreds. Steam and electricity seemed to be the preferred power source for these motorcars until the beginning of the twentieth century even though the gasoline-driven 4-stroke engine had been developed in Germany as early as 1876. However, gasoline-powered engines eventually prevailed. They could travel farther faster and this was important to the automobile's future.

Not many cars were made in the early years and those that were available were costly. Motorcar driving was predominately a rich man's hobby. In Germany Daimler and Benz made cars in the 1880s and in the United States Ramon Eli Olds and Alexander and James Packard built automobiles. By 1908 there were 241 companies in the automobile manufacturing business. Generally it was a slow process and not many cars were produced. All this changed when Henry Ford that same year introduced assembly-line production and brought out his model T car that was inexpensive, easy to maintain, and easy to operate. This made cars available to the middle class and by the 1920s automobiles became commonplace in society.

There were several different models of cars built in those early days and I am fascinated with all of them — their history, how they were built, how they operated, and the importance they played in the development of our social and economic structures. Each model was amazing. Did you know that the Stanley steam car required only three minutes from the time the boiler was started to reach running pressure? Or that the Locomobile was a luxury car and manufactured only until 1929? Both cars were built in the United States. The 1903 Ford launched one of the greatest car builders in North America, the Mercedes gave the industry the first front-mounted engine and rear wheel drive, while the Bouton was the first car with both back wheels turning, having individual drive shafts to each wheel turned by a single drive shaft from the engine, a technology that is still used today.

Each of these old cars was important in its own way and I wanted to own all of them. Since this was impossible I decided to build my own miniatures, and that's how my model building began. My cars are designed from photographs of the original and details learned about the construction from the manufacturer's specifications that I studied to gain historic accuracy. I start each car with finding out the wheel base and distance between the tires which are common to all cars. Although the work requires only basic woodworking skills I am careful to keep all edges square and straight so that building can proceed smoothly. I use natural wood for the body and brass for the trim, as it was used to enhance the original car. Different woods provide the variation of color one finds in the original models. The dash of the assembled model, also made of wood, looks the same as it would look if you sat on the seat of the real car and looked at the dash in front of you. In some cars I have included the engine (built of wood) and the hood is open to show this. Other models do not include the engine and are easier to build. I try to make the cars replicas of the originals. I use basic woodworking tools and I have adapted some tools in my shop to accommodate the small size of the parts. The construction is fairly straight-forward and requires patience more than anything else. The cars can be made with as much detail and personal touches as you wish. This is in character since the historic cars often had details that reflected the tastes of their owners.

Most of the materials used to make these cars can be found at your neighborhood wood supply store. Each car requires only a minimum amount of wood which is not costly. It is best to choose different types of wood for the color, to provide contrast for the different parts of the car. An old door frame made of walnut or mahogany purchased at a secondhand shop is ideal because it is aged to a deep woodgrain color and is already dry. The brass material can be found at a metal supply store or radio control or hobby shop. Only a very small amount is required. I have supplied all patterns and measurements in this book. Step-by-step instructions guide you through every phase of the construction process.

Each model is a pleasure to build and the finished piece looks like the real car. Some models such as the Stanley Steamer or Cadillac are very easy to build, others are more detailed and a bit more difficult. I suggest beginning with either the Stanley or the Cadillac. The Locomobile and De Dion-Bouton are more complex. The finished cars attract a lot of attention and you can display them in clear glass cases, which makes them easy to transport.

Choosing Suitable Woods

Since these model cars are not painted it is important to choose wood for its color and grain so that it will represent the real car. I try to select wood that is used to make furniture, tool handles, and musical instruments. These woods hold their shape better than soft woods. The dealer can usually be helpful in recommending and selecting suitable wood. The grain of the wood is also important. Use fine grain for special effects and contrast fine grain and coarse grain for different parts.

Many suitable woods can be found at used building material stores. This wood is well seasoned, is usually solid wood, and comes from the fittings of old buildings such as doors, door frames, and cabinet doors. These are ideal. Try not to choose plywoods because they do not carry the grain through the thickness of the wood.

Safety

Dust is always a major safety problem with any woodworking project. When wood comes into contact with tools for cutting and sanding, large and small wood particles are released into the air. Larger chips are easily cleaned up with a good shop vacuum but finer particles can pose a health hazard if breathed in. You can protect yourself by wearing a quality dust respirator. SInce the parts for these car projects are so small a full dust collection system is not necessary, but placing the shop vacuum in a position to suck up the dust coming off the cutter or sander works well. Please be sure not to wear loose clothing as it can get caught in moving machinery parts and wear safety glasses to protect your eyes. Remove pencils and pens from shirt pockets so they do not fall into spinning machines. Also remove rings before beginning work with any machines. Using common sense and obeying all rules outlined in power tool manuals will make woodworking a pleasurable experience.

Patterns

Some of the patterns for car parts in this book are actual size and can be used as photocopied directly from the page. If patterns need to be enlarged, photocopy them to size.

Transferring Patterns

Method 1

1   From a drafting supply store purchase a small roll of white, 50% clear drafting vellum.
2   Place the vellum over the required drawing and trace the pattern with a fine tipped pen.
3   Wrap a piece of black carbon paper around the wood and tape it securely to the back of the piece of wood with masking tape.
4   Place the vellum pattern on top of the carbon paper and tape it in place.
5   Trace over pattern. Use a small straightedge to draw all straight lines.
6   The pattern will be outlined on the wood ready to cut out.

Method 2

1   Repeat steps 1 and 2 at left.
2   Place the carbon paper over thin cardboard then cover with the vellum and trace over lines on vellum.
3   Cut out the cardboard pattern to use as a template.
4   Place template on wood and trace around it with fine pen on light wood or use white spray-on stencil ink on dark wood.
5   Cut out. Remove ink by sanding. Save template for future use.

Read from top
1   Assemble materials to transfer pattern. Trace pattern on vellum
2   Place carbon paper over wood
3   Place pattern over carbon paper
4   Tape vellum in place
5   Draw over pattern, use a straightedge for straight lines
6   Lift off pattern & carbon. Pattern is on wood

Tools

These model car replicas can be built with ordinary woodworking tools that you have in your home workshop. Most of the model pieces are quite small and require some patience in cutting, shaping, and fitting. You can adapt some of the tools you have to make it easier to work with the small pieces and purchase or build only a minimum of special tools. These are the tools I have at hand for making these model cars.

Band Saw   A 10-in tabletop band saw is adequate. It is used for cutting out the larger pieces, cutting angles, and cutting the wood into thin pieces for the small car parts that are required. Use it with different width blades to cut different size circles, to notch side rails of cars for the cross members, and to cut different sizes of square wood to make smaller parts.

Scroll Saw   Use this single speed saw to cut out center sections of wood, between wheel spokes and chassis rails for the different cars. A scroll saw with a tilting table makes it easier to cut out curved fenders. This saw can cut thin pieces of wood but is limited to the size of wood being cut by the total height between top and table. I keep a set of blades on hand with different numbers of teeth per inch to help in cutting different types of wood. The softer the wood the more teeth per inch needed to give a better cut.

Hole Saws   These cutters make the round parts for the projects. Since there are so many different sizes of round parts it is practical to own a set of these saws. If you don't have a lathe you can make most of the round parts with hole saws.

Miniature Hacksaw   A small 6-in hacksaw is used to rough-cut brass rods to a workable length to place them in the metal lathe for machining. This tool can also be used to cut brass tubing but doesn't do as good a job as the tube cutter. I also use a hacksaw for cutting grooves in wood while the piece is spinning in the lathe.

Small Table Saw   A small table saw is useful for building these miniature cars, although a large one is fine. If you don't have a small one, building your own is not difficult (to order pattern, see p96). I have had good use from my homemade saw (at right) for 16 years. This saw is powerful and cuts through ¾ in board with the blade sticking out the top plate as far as it can go.

Miniature Tube Cutter   This tool is used to cut brass tubes to make lights. It cuts square to the ends and leaves a nice finish. It cuts all the different sizes including aluminum tubes. Available at most hardware stores, not expensive.

Calipers   Use for measuring the tiny parts.

Tin Snips   Use to cut the cross pieces for steering wheels.

Needle Files   A set of needle files offers different shapes for different operations on wood and brass. Use them for cutting some of the small grooves and shaping the brass handles on the brake levers.

Automatic Center Punch   This tool is used for marking the center of holes in metal and wood and making dimples in metal. Purchase the small one so the force of the spring will not be too strong. To use, place the sharp end of the punch on the mark and push down on tool. Remove tool and a dimple is left in the material.

Read from top
1 10-in band saw
2 Set of hole saws can cut
   out different sizes of
   round parts
3 Miniature hacksaw
4 Calipers & small traightedge
5 Tin snips
6 Automatic center punch

Lathe A Sherline lathe turns both wood and metal. I chose this one because the head can be turned to machine tapers. The lathe also has a tailstock that is used to hold a drill chuck, which in turn holds drill bits to drill holes in the center of the parts. The travel bed on this lathe is very rigid and does not flex which is important. Attachments and parts are available and you can make your own repairs from instructions provided with any purchased replacement parts from Sherline. *Note* When you purchase the lathe include a book called *The Home Machinist's Handbook* which shows how to perform different operations on this lathe such as boring, drilling, parting, and general machining as well as some good projects to build from metal.

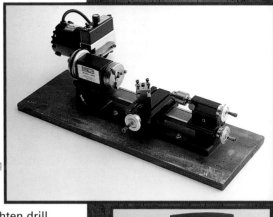

Tools for Lathe A parting tool is used to cut small grooves and remove machined parts. A T-wrench is used to tighten tools. A chuck key is used to tighten drill bits into drill chuck. Center drills are used to locate the center of a round object on a lathe and can make a pilot hole for drilling larger holes in the center of round object.

Dremel Tool This important tool is required for shaping and carving some of the car parts. Different types of cutters, grindstones, a small drum sander, and small wire brushes can be chucked in the dremel making them easier to use. If you purchase resharpened electronic carbide drill bits in surplus stores, these bits can be used in a dremel. The dremel is also used to cut small grooves and for drilling some of the holes required for mounting individual parts to the car. A 3-speed dremel is sufficient.

These tools can be used in a dremel

Read from top clockwise **T wrench, chuck key, boring tool, machining tool, center drills, parting tool**

Dremel Tool with Cutter
Carbide cutters are used for carving some of the small parts

Carbide Drills
Use these in a dremel to drill tiny holes. Bits have ⅛ in shaft

Wire Brushes
Wire brushes are used for polishing brass parts

Microtorch Use a butane refillable microtorch for soldering the brass parts together for these cars because a soldering gun (even dual heat) will not generate enough heat. To tell if the parts are hot enough, listen to the flux hissing, then touch the parts with the solder until it melts and flows into the joint. Allow to cool, then use a small amount of rubbing alcohol to clean the excess flux off the joint. Polish the joint with a wire wheel in a dremel at medium speed. *Remember to wear safety glasses to protect the eyes from wires that might come off the wire wheel while performing this operation.* If there is too much solder on the joint use a needle file or x-acto knife to file or scrape off the excess, then polish. If the metal has turned a different color while soldering, the discoloring will disappear when polished. Tin and brass can be soldered together, nonferrous metals such as aluminum cannot be soldered. To adhere brass together use a 60 - 40 solder width .025 in diameter. This small size is important so that excess solder is not left on parts. Also if solder diameter is too large it requires more heat to melt it.

Soldering Paste Use a rosin flux purchased in a tin. Solder comes with a flux inside but extra is needed to clean the metal while soldering. While soldering use fine steel wool to clean brass where it will be joined. Use the third hand to hold the parts in place while soldering.

Drill Press   Use drill press to make holes in thick pieces of wood or to shape small round pieces of wood by placing them in the drill chuck and spinning the wood, shaping with a needle file as the wood spins. This is also a safe way to drill holes in brass. Clamp the brass piece in a drill press vice, clamp the vice to the table on the drill press, and drill the holes. The drill press allows the operator to use both hands when using a drum sander and to drill tiny holes with less chance of breaking the drill bit. A flex shaft used in the drill press allows the use of larger cutters that won't fit in a dremel. The drill press spins the cutters at a slower speed with more torque than a dremel, making it ideal for polishing brass and smoothing wood surfaces. I use a small bench-top 3-speed model that I purchased at a secondhand store. You will need high-speed drill bits from $\frac{1}{16}$ in to $\frac{1}{2}$ in with $\frac{1}{32}$ in drill bits in between.

Drill Bits   I prefer to have all the number, letter, and standard fraction drill bits. This way if any machined brass parts are not quite right I know there is a drill bit that will match the size. Buying a full set of drill bits can be expensive but makes it easier to match parts to holes.

Drum Sanders   A set of these sanders (shown at left) chucked into a drill press provides different sizes for sanding edges, small curves, and inside circles.

Belt Sander   A 3 in x 22 in belt sander is used to sand the faces, edges, and thicknesses of wood. It can also sand aluminum to the right width seen on some of the cars. Since the belt of the sander travels in only one direction it is easier to sand wood in the same direction as the grain and to remove saw tooth marks. The sanding belt is 220 grit which works well for a finished surface on the cars.

Disk Sander   If you don't own a disk sander it is easy to make one. I made this sander with an old oil furnace motor (great because it has no cooling vents so dust cannot get inside the motor). The disk that holds the sandpaper is made from an 8-in diameter aluminum plate. I turned the plate in a lathe and drilled a hole the same size as the shaft in the center. I machined a small step in the back of the plate to allow a set screw to hold the plate to the shaft while spinning the plate. The stand is made from a 3-in-square tube $\frac{3}{16}$ in thick wall with plates welded to the top and bottom. The top plate holds the motor and the bottom plate is mounted to the floor. This tool rough sands the parts. Finish sanding is done on a belt sander.

Disk Sander Top View

sanding support

aluminum disk

motor

adjustment bolt

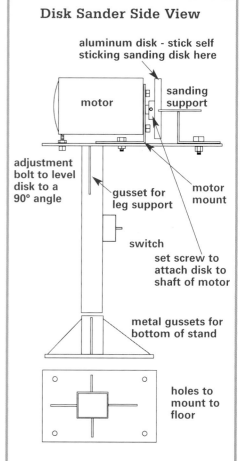

Disk Sander Side View

aluminum disk - stick self sticking sanding disk here

sanding support

motor

adjustment bolt to level disk to a 90° angle

gusset for leg support

motor mount

switch

set screw to attach disk to shaft of motor

metal gussets for bottom of stand

holes to mount to floor

Read from top
1 3-speed drill press
2 Drill bits
3 Belt sander
4 Drum sanders

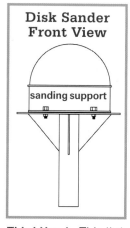

Disk Sander Front View

sanding support

The tool works well for sanding car seats to their final shape. I use 8-in-diameter 120-grit self-sticking sanding disk on this disk sander. Since the disk turns in a circle it can sand across the grain if the piece is large, making it necessary to sand the piece again to remove the marks. An alternative is to purchase a belt and disk sander combination which makes it easier to sand the floor and dash of these cars to the proper thickness.

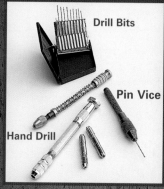

Drill Bits

Pin Vice

Hand Drill

Third Hand   This little tool (shown at far top right) is indispensable for holding small parts together while soldering.

Pin Vices and Miniature Hand Drill   A pin vice that comes with different size collets can hold larger drill bits up to $\frac{1}{16}$ in diameter. This hand drill allows you to hold the tiny drill bits, (ranging from no. 50 to no. 80) which might break in a power tool, shown at right.

Hollow Punches   Use to punch out plastic and vinyl disks for the lens or lights on the cars. Most common sizes of punches are $\frac{1}{2}$, $\frac{1}{4}$, $\frac{5}{8}$, $\frac{3}{8}$ in (at right). Purchase in individual packages or sets at most hardware and tool supply stores. Or make your own from small metal pipes ground on one end to a bevel.

Miniature Pliers   The tiny pliers used by hobbyists can be purchased in sets at any tool store. They are used to form different bends in brass wire and cut brass wire to different lengths. Tiny needle nose pliers help place tiny parts into the cars.

Small Clamps   Use these to clamp parts while the glue dries. The clamps shown are "C" type clamp and spring clamp. Spring clamps have the right amount of pressure to hold the parts together without marking the wood surfaces. They are also cheaper than screw-type clamps and come in many different sizes.

"C" Clamps

Spring Clamps

Other miscellaneous items such as wax paper, carbon paper, rubbing alcohol, masking tape, pins, brushes, compass, glue, fine chain, 5-minute & 24-hour epoxy, cardboard, and steel wool are used to make the cars

Chain   Fine chain (no larger than $\frac{1}{8}$ in diameter) is used to represent the chain drive on each car. Purchase at any fabric store.

Note   The router is dangerous to use and I do not recommend it for any of the small parts. I have used it only for the side panels on the Ford but only woodworkers who are experienced with the tool should use it. I do not recommend using it for the wheels.

Jigs

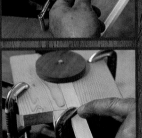

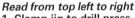

Sanding Jig

diagram half size

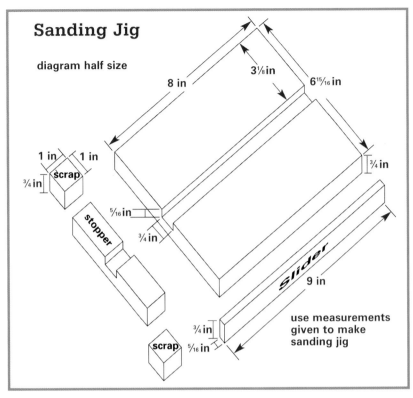

8 in

3⅛ in

6¹⁵⁄₁₆ in

¾ in

1 in   1 in

scrap

¾ in

⁵⁄₁₆ in

stopper

¾ in

Slider

9 in

use measurements given to make sanding jig

¾ in

scrap ⁵⁄₁₆ in

Finished Sanding Jig
This finished sanding jig is helpful when handling small pieces. The finished sanding jig is shown in the photo, bottom left.

Assembled Sanding Jig

diagram not to size

place dowel ½ in from end of slider

cut out half circle if you are using a drum sander

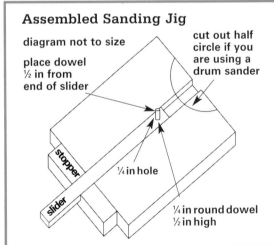

stopper

slider

¼ in hole

¼ in round dowel ½ in high

Read from top left to right
1 Clamp jig to drill press
2 Insert slider into jig
3 Place wheel disk on slider
4 Place stopper on slider
5 Clamp stopper in place
6 Push disk against drum sander
7 Turn disk to shape it

Sanding Jig

To build this jig use any scrap wood 9 in x 7¼ in x ¾ in thick.

1 Cut a square groove, as shown.

2 Cut a ⁵⁄₁₆ in strip off the long side to make the slider. Check that the piece fits the groove and is flush with the top surface of the jig to move more easily.

3 Drill a ¼ in hole in the piece ½ in from one end and glue in a ¼ in dowel ½ in long. This is the pivot pin.

4 Using the piece of wood with the groove in it, cut off a 1 in piece leaving a base of 7 in x 8 in.

5 Cut off a 1 in piece on either side of the groove making a stopper.

Wheel and Spoke Jig

Build this jig from scrap wood.

1. Cut a piece of scrap wood 4¾ in x 4¾ in x ¾ in thick. Draw a line corner to corner forming a center X.
2. Using a compass draw a 4 in diameter circle from the center of the X, as shown.
3. Divide the circle into 12 spaces and mark. Using a center punch or nail, pierce each mark, including the center of the circle.
4. With ¼ in drill bit, drill the center all the way through.
5. With ⅛ in drill bit, drill the 12 indented marks all the way through.
6. Glue ¼ in dowel 1 in long into center hole flush with the bottom.
7. Glue twelve, ⅛ in dowels 1¼ in long, into the 12 holes, flush with the bottom.

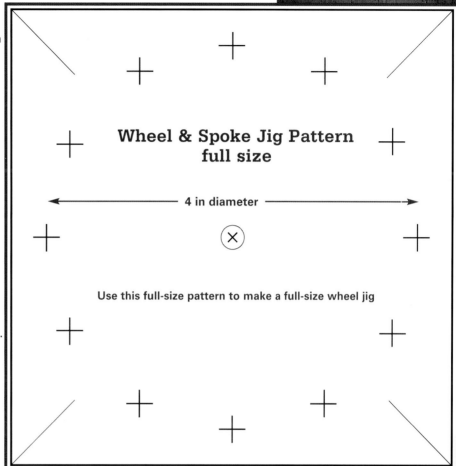

Wheel & Spoke Jig Pattern full size

← 4 in diameter →

⊗

Use this full-size pattern to make a full-size wheel jig

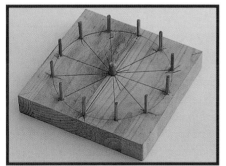

Finished Wheel & Spoke Jig
This jig is used to make the spokes on the wheel disk for cutting

Making Wheels

Model car building is easier if you begin with the wheels. Getting this part right helps to make the rest of the building proceed smoothly. The same method of construction for the wheels is used for every car model in this book. The patterns and dimensions given here are for the Ford Model A car. To make the wheels for other cars, use the dimensions given with the instructions for each car and follow these instructions.

Inside Wheel

The inside wheel is made from a piece of bloodwood 13 in x 3 in x ¼ in thick.

1. Draw a line across the center and measure in 1½ in from both ends. Divide remaining line segment into four 2½ in segments. Draw four 2½ in circles.
2. Draw 2¼ in circles inside the 2½ in circles. Smaller circles provide a reference line for sanding the outside diameter of disks.
3. Place a 2½ in hole saw in a drill press and cut out disks.
4. When disk is removed from the inside of hole saw it will be 2⅜ in diameter with a ¼ in hole in the center.

An alternative method is to use a wheel cutter to make these disks. *Note* This method is not recommended for inexperienced woodworkers.

1. Set wheel cutter for 2¼ in diameter circle. Place cutter in drill press. Using slowest speed and a piece of ¼ in scrap wood, cut out disk.
2. Fit in tire to test fit. Then cut the ¼ in thick bloodwood.
3. Change diameter of cutting setting to ⅛ in smaller.
4. Hold wheel in drill press and etch line on both sides wheel for rim line. This can be done after this is glued in place. Use just enough pressure in vice to hold piece from spinning.
5. Feed cutter slowly into wood just deep enough to mark the circle.

Inside Wheel Pattern half size

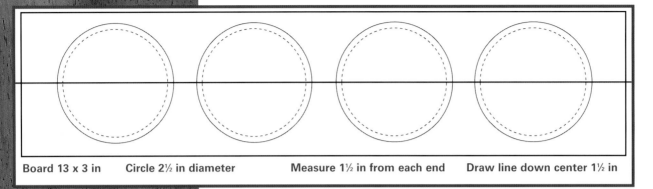

| Board 13 x 3 in | Circle 2½ in diameter | Measure 1½ in from each end | Draw line down center 1½ in |

Tire Pattern half size

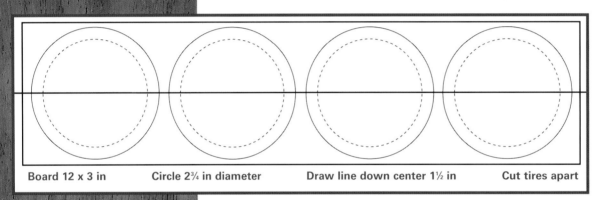

| Board 12 x 3 in | Circle 2¾ in diameter | Draw line down center 1½ in | Cut tires apart |

Cutout of wheel and tire

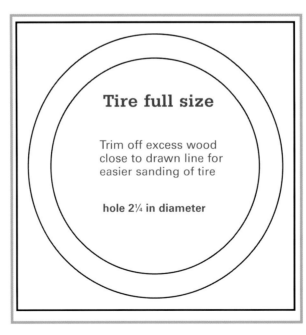

Tire full size

Trim off excess wood close to drawn line for easier sanding of tire

hole 2¼ in diameter

Tire

The tires are made from a piece of African blackwood 12 in x 3 in x ⅜ in thick, as shown.

1 Draw a line across the center. Divide the line into four 3 in segments.

2 In each segment draw a 2¾ in circle, leaving enough space between circles to cut them apart.

3 Place a 2¼ in hole saw in drill press and cut out all the inside of the 2¾ in circles you've drawn.

4 Cut circles apart. Trim off corners next to drawn lines to make sanding easier, as shown.

5 Bloodwood wheel will eventually fit into blackwood tire.

Sanding the Wheels

Sand carefully so inside wheel will fit into outside tire.

1   Mount sanding jig on table of belt sander or drill press, as shown p10.

2   Cut curved line shown on drawing so the drum of the sander will be inside the edge of the sanding jig, as shown p10.

3   Mount the bloodwood disk with the 2¼-in circle on the slider pivot pin of the sanding jig and place slider in jig groove.

4   Turn on machine and slowly push disk into sander until you hit outside of drawn line. Turn off machine.

5   Push disk against sander at the same point and clamp stopper and slider, as shown (p10), to hold disk at correct radius while sanding the diameter.

6   Turn machine on, begin sanding outside diameter, try first disk in all four tires and check for fit. Disk must slide into blackwood tires without force or pressure. Proceed with all bloodwood pieces.

7   Glue (use 24-hour epoxy) bloodwood wheels into blackwood tire pieces. Wipe off excess. Allow to dry.

8   Place pieces one at a time back on sanding jig and sand the tire to finished diameter of 2¾ in. Repeat as above to set jig for this operation.

9   Sand outer edge of tires, rounding off the edge. If unsure of shape, look at bicycle tires which have same shape as these old tires.

Tire & Wheel Assembly

2⅜ in spoke disk is sanded down to fit inside the tire

hole inside diameter of tire after cut is 2¼ in

tire

this line for hub

¾ in diameter

tire

spoke

hole ⅜ in diameter

rim line is drawn later

cut-away of tire & disk showing alignment of parts

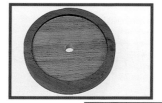

Making Spokes

1   Using the spoke jig, place wheel on center pin. Mark center of pin with ball point pen. See p14.

2   Use a compass to draw a circle ⅛ in from inside tire edge to mark location of rim.

3   Draw ¾ in circle from the same center point for the location of the hub as specified for each car. Repeat for all 4 wheels.

4   With a small ruler that fits between the pegs, draw the spokes on both sides of pegs between hub line and rim line.

5   Drill holes between spokes to insert a fine tooth scroll saw blade. Cut out pieces towards the center, stopping at outside hub line. Cut along rim line to take out piece between spokes.

6   Using a dremel tool with a fine cutter, round edges of spokes on both sides of wheel. Apply pressure carefully so spokes don't break. Repeat for all 4 wheels.

7   Glue wooden hubs to wheels making sure center holes line up with each other. Allow to dry.

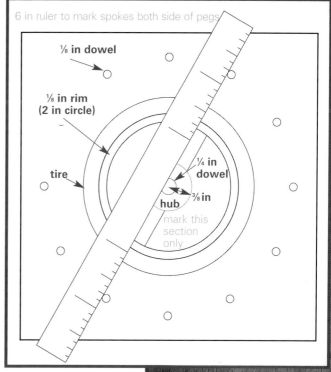

6 in ruler to mark spokes both side of pegs

⅛ in dowel

⅛ in rim (2 in circle)

tire

¼ in dowel

⅜ in

hub

mark this section only

Making Hub Bolts

1 Place the wheel back in the spoke jig.

2 Use a miniature drill bit the diameter of a tack pin and drill in a piece of scrap wood. Check to see that pin fits tightly.

3 Drill holes in every second spoke in the middle of the hub on all 4 wheels, on one side only. Choose best side for drilling. It will be outside of wheel.

4 Then cut the pins short enough so heads touch the hubs. *Note* Pins do not need to be glued. Pressure holds them in place.

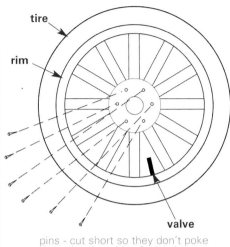

Location of Pins & Valve

tire
rim
valve

pins - cut short so they don't poke through other side of wheel (give appearance of wheel bolts)

Making Tire Valve

1 Use a piece of black electronic wire $\frac{1}{16}$ in diameter or smaller or small wires inside a phone or cable cord.

2 Match a drill bit to the wire diameter.

3 Drill at a slight angle on outside of tire through the rim, deep enough to hold the wire. *Note* Leave the wire $\frac{1}{2}$ in long and glue it in the hole with 5-minute epoxy. When dry, trim wire to $\frac{1}{4}$ in protruding out of the rim.

Machining Brass To Shape

The brass parts for these cars are very small and machining them to shape can be awkward. Although light dimensions vary with different cars the procedure for making brass lights is the same.

1 Use a brass rod the same size as largest diameter of the part being made.

2 Shape end of rod on lathe. Machine the smallest diameter parts first then the larger parts. When complete, separate the parts from the brass rod with a parting tool. These parts pictured were made on a $\frac{3}{16}$ in diameter brass rod long enough to be held in lathe chuck while machining.

Wheel with Spokes
full size

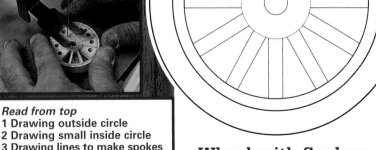

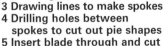

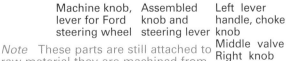

Machine knob, lever for Ford steering wheel

Assembled knob and steering lever

Left lever handle, choke knob
Middle valve
Right knob

Note These parts are still attached to raw material they are machined from

Finishing

When the car is built and completely assembled note any excessive glue and move a wire brush in a dremel back and forth carefully over excess glue to remove it. Fill any holes in the wood with 5-minute epoxy. Using a vacuum with small brush attachment carefully dust car. Then dust with a new paintbrush. Put one coat of urethane clear gloss over the entire car including the brass fittings. Use a soft brush that doesn't leave hairs on the car. Dry first coat overnight.

Add a second coat to the underside of the car. Wait one hour and add another coat. While underside coats are drying add a second coat to the rest of the car. Dry for one hour, add another coat, and dry overnight. For more than three coats, repeat this procedure. My cars have six coats. *Note* Spray-on coatings produce overspray that takes the shine off the coating on the other parts and leaves the surface rough. Not recommended.

Optional Since people ask questions about the make and model of the car some answers can be provided by a small thin wood sign. I include price of car, year it was built, speed, horsepower, and country of origin. If you display your car you will find that people are very interested in all aspects of the car's history.

Making Display Case

My cases are built from pieces of wood and glass purchased from a secondhand building supply store. Cut old windows to size. Make bottom board ¾ in thick and large enough to hold car with 2 in space around it. Make small lip to hold in glass. Cover bottom with colored foam or glass mirror glued on with rubber cement. Purchase oak or maple floor trim to finish the edge. Cut corners at a 45° angle.

The top frame should be the same size as the bottom frame with grooves matching. Frames require one groove for the glass. The corner posts require two grooves so side and end glasses are held together. Grooves must be in line with grooves in top and bottom frames so glass will stay in place. To determine the length and side pieces of glass, place corner post on the frame and measure the distance between the posts and add the depth of grooves in the top and bottom frames and add this to the length to the corner pieces. Subtract ¹⁄₁₆ in from this length of the glass. This will allow the wood to expand and shrink with moisture. Glass must protrude past top corner posts so glass will fit into the groove of the top frame.

Assemble glass cover and glue (24-hour epoxy) corner post to bottom frame, top frame to top of corner post. Put masking tape around entire cover to hold in place until dry. Cut glass for the top leaving ¼ in space from edge of wood to glass all around the top. Make small L-shape frame to hold glass in place. The notch cut from one side must be deep enough to allow for the thickness of the glass and hang over the edge of glass no wider than the frame. Cut corners on frame at 45° angle and glue with white carpenter's glue in place over the glass. Dry and use sandpaper to finish.

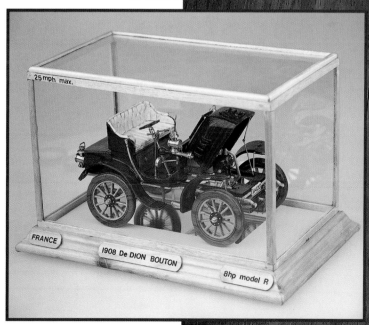

Stanley Steamer

Francis Edgar and Freelan O. Stanley, twin brothers, believed that the future of the automobile lay with the steam engine. Its invention in 1769 by Nicolas-Joseph Cugnot led these two American inventors to build an early version of their Stanley Steamer in 1897. The brothers had been successful in building and selling graphic plates and sewing machines, but when they saw an early imported steam car at a fair they decided to build one of their own. They bought an old bicycle factory and began developing steam-powered cars. The Stanley Motor Company was born.

Many of the models were very successful. The cars competed in racing events from 1902 - 09, frequently beating larger gasoline-powered cars. In 1906 one of their steam cars set a world's record for the fastest mile in 28.2 seconds corresponding to a speed of 127 miles (205 km) per hour. They also set several hill climbing records. By this time they were the most famous car builders in America and in 1911 designed a car with no clutch or gears with a horse power of 20 - 30 and a speed of 50 miles per hour. The brothers set themselves a goal to build many cars. In 1918 they sold about 10,000 at a price of $1,500 each car. The car in this book is one of their more famous touring cars, but after 1925 these cars were no longer built.

The steam car had progressed rapidly after 1900 because of the adoption of the flash boiler which raised steam quickly. Steam cars were easy to operate and did not require an elaborate transmission. However, it was expensive to build an engine light enough to be practical. By 1910 most steam vehicle manufacturers had turned to gasoline power. The Stanleys were the only hold-outs.

1911 Stanley Steamer

Car Parts List

Note Exact sizes are given here; however, some parts will require a larger piece of material to hold while cutting the parts.

Car Part	Material	Size	Pieces
Wheels	maple	10 in x 3 in x ¼ in	1
	walnut	13½ in x 3½ in x ⅜ in	1
	black wire	¹⁄₁₆ in x ¼ in long	4
Main Floor	purple heart	10¼ in x ³⁄₁₆ in x ¼ in	1
Side Panel	purple heart	7½ in x 2 in x ⅜ in	2
	purple heart	2¹¹⁄₁₆ in x ½ in x ¼ in	2
	purple heart	2¹¹⁄₁₆ in x 1 in x ¼ in	2
Springs	maple	3½ in x 1 in x ½ in	2
	maple dowel	¼ in x ¼ in long	4
Axles	maple dowel	¼ in x 6 in long	2
	maple	½ in sq. ¼ in thick	2
Dash	purple heart	3⅛ in x 1¾ in x ¼ in	1
Engine	maple dowel	⅛ in x 1 in long	2
	walnut	1¼ in x 1 in x ⅛ in	1
	walnut	2⅛ in x 1³⁄₁₆ in x ⅛ in	2
	walnut	1 in x 1½ in x ⅛ in	1
	walnut dowel	¾ in x 1 in long	1
	walnut dowel	⅞ in x 1¼ in long	1
	walnut dowel	⅝ in x ¾ in long	1
Pedal Board	maple	⅜ in x ⅛ in x ⅛ in	2
	maple dowel	¹⁄₁₆ in x ½ in long	2
	mahogany	⅝ in sq. 2¹¹⁄₁₆ in	1
Braking Rod	maple dowel	⅛ in x 3¼ in long	1
	maple	⅜ in x ³⁄₁₆ in x ⅛ in	2
	brass tack pins		2
Hubs	mahogany dowel	⅛ in x 1 in long	2
Axle Supports	bamboo skewers	⅛ in diameter	2
Torsion Bar	OD aluminum tube	⅛ in x 5 in long	1
Horn	African blackwood	dowel ⅜ in x 1 in long	1
	brass rod	⁵⁄₁₆ in x ¼ in long	1
	brass rod	⅛ in x 2 in long	1
Fender Floor Mats	African blackwood	4 in x ¾ in x ⅛ in	2
	African blackwood	1 in x ¾ in x ⅛ in	2
Front Seat Rail	brass rod	¹⁄₁₆ in x 3 in long	1
	brass rod	¹⁄₁₆ in x 1 in long	2
Fenders	purple heart	12 in x 5 in x ¾ in	1
	brass tube	⅛ x 1 in long	4

Car Part	Material	Size	Pieces
Boiler Block	purple heart	2¹¹⁄₁₆ in x 2⁷⁄₁₆ in x 1⁵⁄₁₆ in	1
	purple heart	2⁷⁄₁₆ in x 1³⁄₁₆ in x ⅛ in	1
	purple heart	2⅜ in x 1⅜ in x ⅛ in	1
	purple heart	⅞ in x ³⁄₁₆ in x ¹⁄₁₆ in	10
	purple heart dowel	⅛ in x ¼ in long	1
Steering Wheel	maple	1¹⁄₁₆ in sq ¹⁄₁₆ in thick	1
	maple dowel	⅛ in x 3 in long	1
	maple dowel	⅛ in x ⅜ in long	2
	maple dowel	¼ in x ⅛ in thick	2
	mahogany dowel	1¼ in x ½ long	1
	brass rod	¹⁄₃₂ in x 3 in long	2
Dash Levers	maple dowel	⅛ in x ¾ in long	1
	maple dowel	⅛ in x ⅝ in long	1
	maple dowel	⅛ in x ⅜ in long	1
	maple dowel	¹⁄₁₆ in x ¼ in long	3
Floor Shifters	maple dowel	³⁄₁₆ in x 1¾ in long	1
	maple dowel	³⁄₁₆ in x ⅝ in long	1
Brake Lever	maple	2⅜ in x ¼ in x ⅛ in	1
Lights	maple dowel	1 in x ⅝ in long	2
	maple	¼ in x ³⁄₁₆ in x ¼ in	2
	maple	⅜ in x ³⁄₁₆ in x ³⁄₁₆ in	2
	brass rod	¹⁄₁₆ in x 4 in long	2
Front Seat	purple heart	3 in x 1¾ in x ⁵⁄₁₆ in	1
	purple heart	3⅝ in x 1¾ in x ⅛ in	1
	purple heart	1¾ in x 1¾ in x ⁵⁄₁₆ in	2
Seat Cushions	African blackwood	*4 in x 3¾ in x ⅛ in	1
Rear Seat	purple heart	3½ in x 1⅜ in x ¾ in	1
	purple heart	3 in x ½ in x ⅛ in	1
Rear Seat Cushion	African blackwood	3 in x 1 in x ¼ in	1
	brass rod	¹⁄₁₆ in x 14 in long	1
Tool Box	purple heart	1 in x ¾ in x ⅝ in	1
Hasp and Lock	as per drawing		
Pressure Tank	maple dowel	½ in x 1⅞ in long	1
	black wire	¹⁄₁₆ in x 5 in long	1

*Approximately

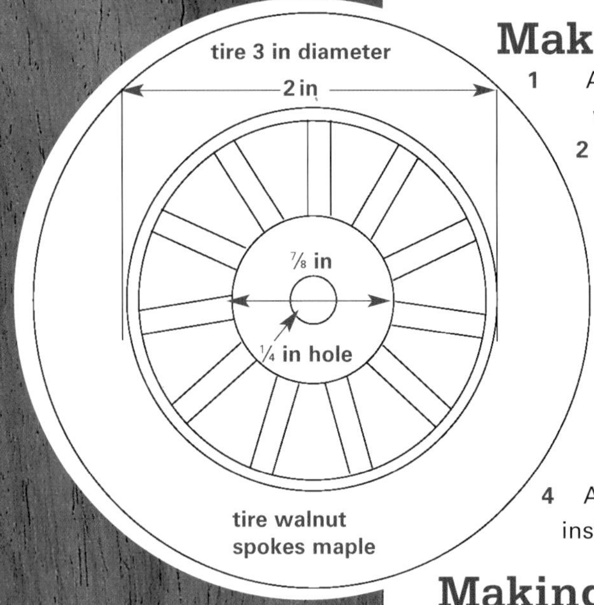
tire 3 in diameter
2 in
7/8 in
1/4 in hole
tire walnut
spokes maple

Making Wheels

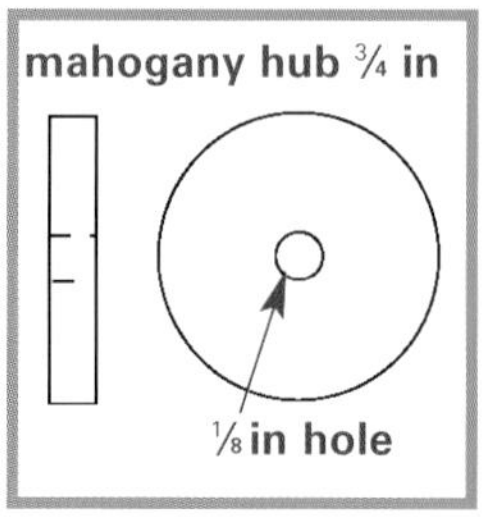
mahogany hub 3/4 in
1/8 in hole

1. Adjust dimensions and use pattern (p12) to build wheels according to instruction method given on p11.
2. Use walnut $13\frac{1}{2}$ in x $3\frac{1}{2}$ in x $\frac{3}{8}$ in to make 4 tires, cutting spoke disks with $2\frac{1}{4}$ in hole saw. Use plug from hole saw. Make center holes with 2 in hole saw.
3. Mark the first piece of maple with a 2 in diameter circle for reference when sanding. Draw this circle from the center mark of one of the disks before cutting. Use maple 10 in x 3 in x $\frac{1}{4}$ in to make spokes.

   Note Check the fit of the first disk in all the tires to make sure the sanding jig is set accurately.
4. Assemble parts and saw cut final parts, as shown in the general instructions p12.

Making Main Floor

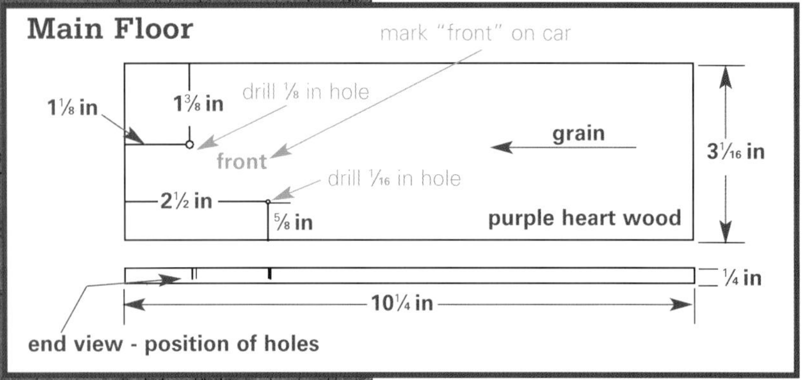
Main Floor
mark "front" on car
1 1/8 in
1 3/8 in
drill 1/8 in hole
front
grain
3 1/16 in
drill 1/16 in hole
2 1/2 in
5/8 in
purple heart wood
1/4 in
10 1/4 in
end view - position of holes

1. Cut piece of purple heart $10\frac{1}{4}$ in x $3\frac{1}{16}$ in x $\frac{1}{4}$ in thick. *Note* This piece must be perfectly square and flat to ensure that the finished car sits level. The car is built around it. Check grain direction on diagram.
2. Holes are drilled to the front of car, which will be shown on final assembly of car.

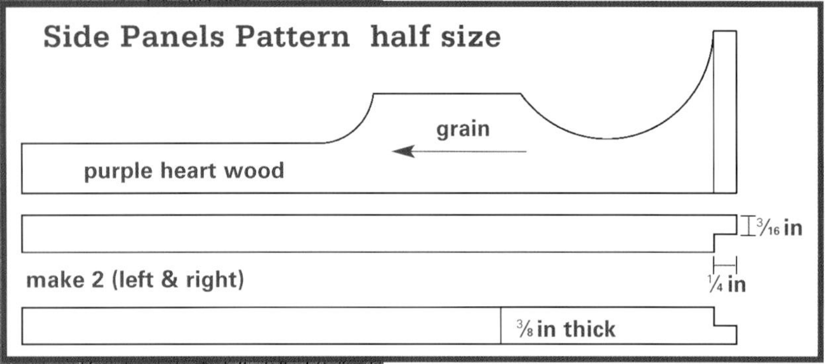
Side Panels Pattern half size
grain
purple heart wood
3/16 in
make 2 (left & right)
1/4 in
3/8 in thick

Making Side Panels

1. Transfer (p5) pattern at left to piece of purple heart $\frac{3}{8}$ in thick and large enough to make 2 panels (left & right).
2. Cut the joint first (used to mount the dash to the side panels) then cut the parts to shape on a scroll or band saw.
3. Sand edges of parts sharp on drum sander at medium speed. Do not sand the edges round.
4. Cut 4 pieces of purple heart, as shown for the car body main frame assembly. Two pieces $2\frac{11}{16}$ in long x $\frac{1}{2}$ in wide x $\frac{1}{4}$ in thick are for back seat mounts. Two pieces $2\frac{11}{16}$ in long x 1 in wide x $\frac{1}{4}$ in thick are for front seat mounts.
5. Sand smooth and set aside for final assembly.

   Note Keep all pieces square and even on all edges.

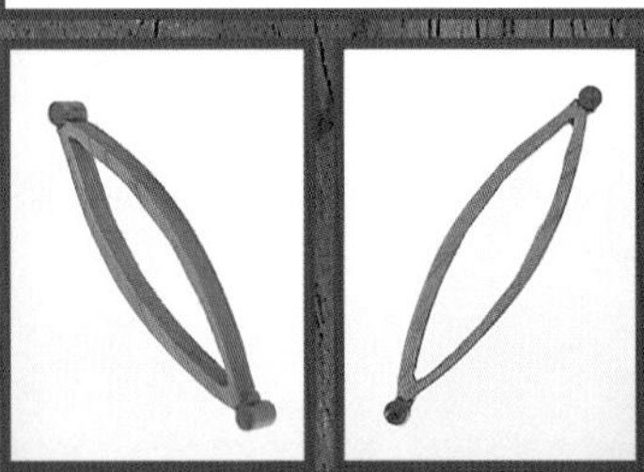

These springs are for the Stanley Steamer and show the general shape of the assembled springs

Making Springs

1. Transfer (p5) pattern (p19) to 2 pieces of maple $3\frac{1}{2}$ in x 1 in x $\frac{1}{2}$ in.
2. Make springs the same as described, p19. This car requires 4 springs the same size.
3. To finish the ends of the springs, glue with 5-minute epoxy 4 pieces of maple dowel $\frac{1}{4}$ in diameter and $\frac{1}{4}$ in long to each end after cutting out springs. Sand smooth and set aside for final assembly.

Making Axles

1. Cut 2 maple dowels 6 in long.
2. Cut 4 small blocks of scrap wood $\frac{1}{2}$ in square and $\frac{1}{4}$ in thick.
3. Drill $\frac{1}{4}$ in hole through center of blocks.
4. Mark dimensions on dowels using the center line as a reference.
5. Place blocks on a flat table and glue to ends of dowels keeping them level with each other.
6. On a scroll or band saw set a stop on each side of blade that allows $\frac{1}{8}$ in deep cut into the dowel. Remember to add the width of the blocks to the stop so the saw will cut into the axle $\frac{1}{8}$ in deep.
7. Cut out notches on axle. Keep notches aligned with each other.
8. Using drill press, drill 2 holes $\frac{1}{8}$ in diameter in back axle. Do not drill all the way through.
9. Measure axles $2\frac{1}{2}$ in from either side of center lines and mark. Cutting on these marks through the axles leaves an axle 5 in long. When cutting, place a spacer under the axle thick enough to raise the blocks off the table to keep the cuts straight.

Making Dash

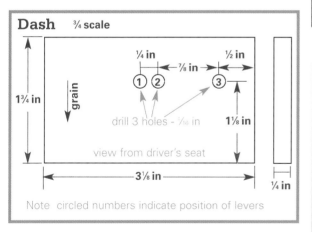

Dash ¾ scale

drill 3 holes - $\frac{1}{16}$ in

view from driver's seat

grain

$1\frac{3}{4}$ in

$\frac{1}{4}$ in

$\frac{7}{8}$ in

$\frac{1}{2}$ in

$1\frac{1}{8}$ in

$3\frac{1}{8}$ in

$\frac{1}{4}$ in

Note circled numbers indicate position of levers

1. Use piece of purple heart $3\frac{1}{8}$ in x $1\frac{3}{4}$ in x $\frac{1}{4}$ in that is square and flat. Note the direction of grain. Drill 3 holes $\frac{1}{16}$ in diameter, as shown.
2. Countersink each hole with holes facing the same way, as shown in diagram.
   Note Numbers on diagrams are used to show where each lever fits into dash.
3. Sand smooth on all sides and set aside for final assembly.

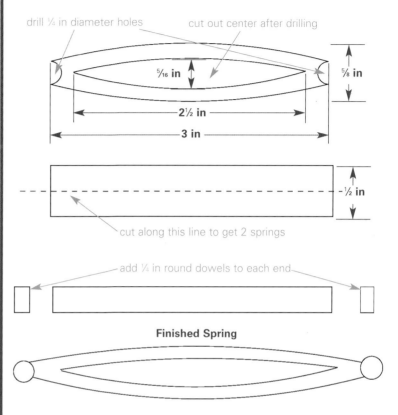

Front & Back Springs Pattern full size

drill $\frac{1}{4}$ in diameter holes

cut out center after drilling

$\frac{5}{16}$ in

$\frac{5}{8}$ in

$2\frac{1}{2}$ in

3 in

$\frac{1}{2}$ in

cut along this line to get 2 springs

add $\frac{1}{4}$ in round dowels to each end

Finished Spring

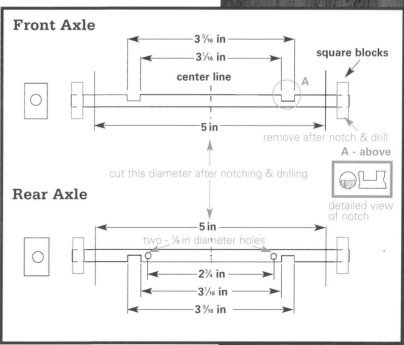

Front Axle

$3\frac{9}{16}$ in

$3\frac{1}{16}$ in

center line

square blocks

A

5 in

remove after notch & drill

A - above

detailed view of notch

cut this diameter after notching & drilling

Rear Axle

5 in

two - $\frac{1}{8}$ in diameter holes

$2\frac{3}{4}$ in

$3\frac{1}{16}$ in

$3\frac{9}{16}$ in

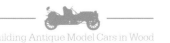

Making Engine

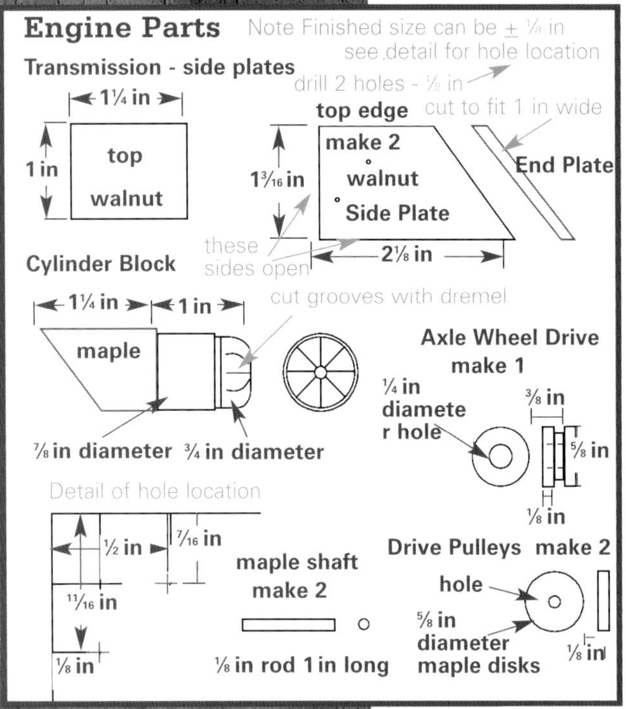
Engine Parts
Note Finished size can be ± 1/8 in
see detail for hole location
Transmission - side plates
drill 2 holes - 1/8 in
1 1/4 in
1 in
top
walnut
top edge
cut to fit 1 in wide
make 2
walnut
Side Plate
End Plate
1 3/16 in
these sides open
2 1/8 in
Cylinder Block
cut grooves with dremel
1 1/4 in
1 in
maple
7/8 in diameter
3/4 in diameter
Axle Wheel Drive
make 1
1/4 in diameter hole
3/8 in
5/8 in
1/8 in
Detail of hole location
1/2 in
7/16 in
11/16 in
1/8 in
maple shaft
make 2
1/8 in rod 1 in long
Drive Pulleys make 2
hole
5/8 in diameter maple disks
1/8 in

1 See diagram. Clamp together 2 side pieces of 1/8 in thick walnut keeping edges even. Drill two 1/8 in diameter holes.

2 Cut out top piece and end piece which should fit on sloped end of side pieces. Glue pieces together (5-minute epoxy). The top piece fits on the top edge. Allow to dry.

3 Push shafts through the hole, sliding the disks onto the shaft before going through hole on opposite side plate. Check fit, glue (5-minute epoxy).

4 Make cylinder from 7/8 in diameter dowel turned to shape.

5 With dremel and small cutter, cut grooves on end of cylinder. Cut larger diameter to match slope of end plate, as shown on diagram.

6 Glue (5-minute epoxy) cylinder to transmission, as shown below. Sand smooth and set aside for final assembly.

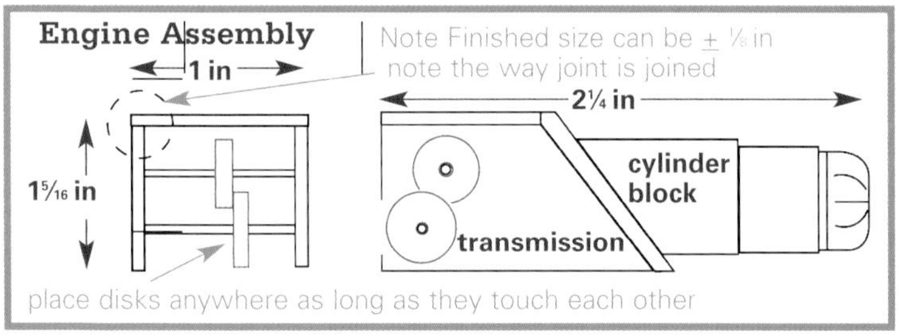
Engine Assembly
Note Finished size can be ± 1/8 in
note the way joint is joined
1 in
2 1/4 in
1 5/16 in
cylinder block
transmission
place disks anywhere as long as they touch each other

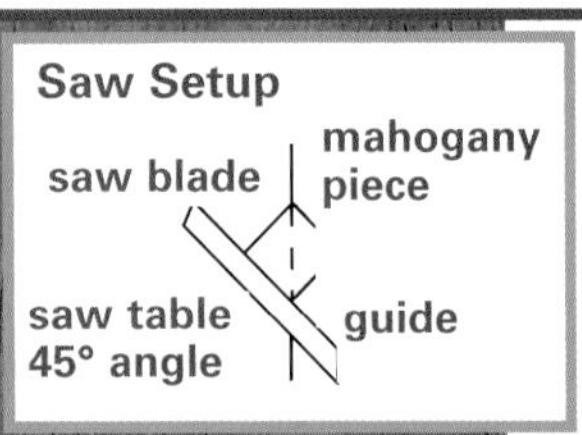
Saw Setup
saw blade
mahogany piece
saw table 45° angle
guide

Note Cylinder can also be built from 2 pieces of dowel, one 7/8 in diameter and the other 3/4 in diameter. Before gluing together, cut a groove in the 3/4 in diameter dowel by spinning the piece in band saw with a stop behind the blade. Glue piece together with 5-minute epoxy. Place a small dowel in the middle to hold them.

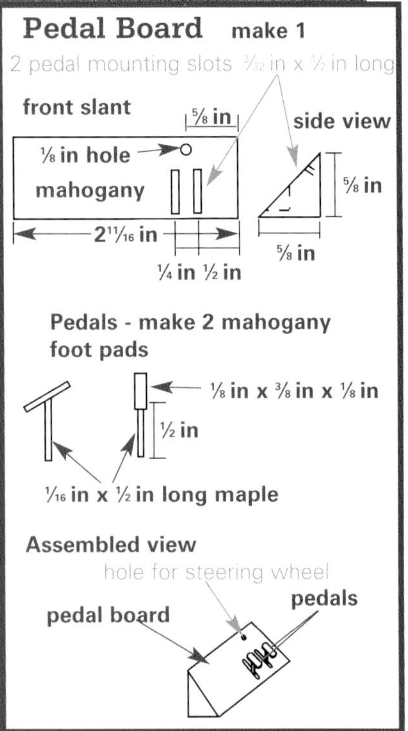
Pedal Board make 1
2 pedal mounting slots 3/32 in x 1/2 in long
front slant
5/8 in
side view
1/8 in hole
mahogany
5/8 in
2 11/16 in
1/4 in 1/2 in
5/8 in
Pedals - make 2 mahogany foot pads
1/8 in x 3/8 in x 1/8 in
1/2 in
1/16 in x 1/2 in long maple
Assembled view
hole for steering wheel
pedals
pedal board

Making Pedal Board

1 Use piece of mahogany 5/8 in sq and 2 11/16 in long. Cut in half from corner to corner by setting band or scroll saw table to a 45° angle. Set a guide on table to run the piece along to keep cut straight. Use dremel with a small 3/32 in diameter cutter and cut out two slots. Do not go through the edge of piece.

2 Drill 1/8 in hole straight with the sloping side of piece. Angle doesn't have to be perfect as the steering wheel angle can be adjusted on assembly.

3 For pedal pads cut a piece of maple 3/8 in wide x 3/16 in thick and long enough to hold. Cut two 1/8 in thick pieces off one end (3/16 in x 3/8 in x 1/8 in).

4 Mount pedals with round toothpicks cut to length.

5 Use 5-minute epoxy to glue rods into the slots. Allow to dry. Glue pedals to rods.

Making Brake Rod

1 Use 1/8 in diameter rod 3 1/4 in long. Drill hole in each end to completely insert sewing tack pins. Make levers from maple 4 to 5 in long for easier handling and 1/8 in thick.

2 Drill two 1/32 in holes 1/4 in apart 1/8 in from the edge of wood (staying in middle of wood. See diagram p21). Use dremel with small round cutter to cut curved notch on each side between holes.

3 Round off ends of wood. Hold levers with small needle nose pliers and separate levers from wood piece with band or scroll saw. Hold piece with needle nose pliers and sand on a belt sander.

4   Repeat to cut the lever from the opposite end of wood. When assembling this part, the pins hold everything together. Glue with 5-minute epoxy. Place on flat surface to keep levers level.

Making Hubs

1   For back wheel hubs slice 1 in mahogany dowel into 2 disks ⅛ in thick. Use drill press to drill ¼ in hole in center of disk. Use pin vice and 1/32 in drill bit, drill hole by hand, close to edge of ⅛ in disks.

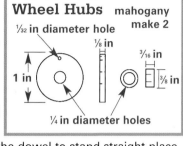

Wheel Hubs mahogany **make 2**
1/32 in diameter hole
⅛ in
3/16 in
1 in
⅜ in
¼ in diameter holes

2   For front hub, clamp ⅜ in diameter mahogany dowel 3 in long in drill press vice. Use ¼ in drill bit to drill hole ½ in deep in end of dowel in the center. To get the dowel to stand straight place dowel in vice, lower the drill bit down beside the dowel. Push dowel against drill bit then tighten vice to hold dowel straight, then raise the drill bit, slide dowel under drill bit, and drill through center of dowel.

Note   To drill hole put ⅜ in dowel into a lathe chuck, center drill, finish with ¼ in drill, and cut disk to proper length with band saw.

Making Axle Supports

Make these parts from bamboo barbecue skewers. Length will be determined on assembly. Leave the bamboo at full length until final assembly.

Making Torsion Bar

Use ⅛ in outside diameter aluminum tube 5 in long. Length determined on assembly.

Making Horn

1   Turn long brass rod equal to largest diameter of the bell on metal lathe and shape bell at end of rod with file as metal spins. Remove part.

2   Make curled part of horn by curling ⅛ in diameter brass rod around tip of small needle nose pliers. Hold with another pair of pliers. Cut to length after forming.

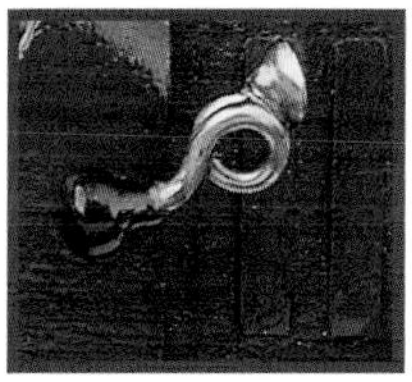

3   Make bulb of horn from African blackwood using the same method as forming the bell.

4   Drill ⅛ in diameter hole in end to insert curled part of horn before shaping the bulb. Use third hand and solder bell to curled part of horn. Polish with wire wheel in dremel.

5   Glue bulb to horn with 5-minute epoxy. Allow to dry. Drill 1/16 in diameter hole in bulb. Drill on proper side of horn bulb so that horn can be mounted to car (using small round toothpick) on driver side of car. *Note* Do not drill all the way through bulb.

Making Fender and Floor Mats

1   Make fender mats 4 in long and floor mats 1 in long from African blackwood ¾ in wide x ⅛ in thick. Texture surface of mats using dremel with a small saw blade at slow speed. Cut grooves lightly so saw blade doesn't cut through wood. *Note*   Cut two mats from one piece of wood to keep pattern the same.

2   Use a wire brush in dremel to buff grooves removing any burrs. Set aside.

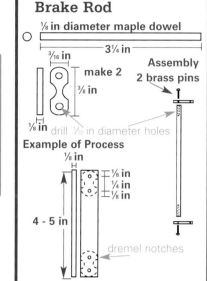

Brake Rod
⅛ in diameter maple dowel
3¼ in
3/16 in
make 2
⅜ in
Assembly
2 brass pins
⅛ in drill ½ in diameter holes
Example of Process
⅛ in
⅛ in
¼ in
⅛ in
4 - 5 in
dremel notches

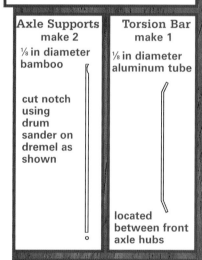

Axle Supports
make 2
⅛ in diameter bamboo
cut notch using drum sander on dremel as shown

Torsion Bar
make 1
⅛ in diameter aluminum tube
located between front axle hubs

Horn Assembled

Horn   African blackwood
⅜ in diameter
Brass Construction
⅛ in brass rod
¼ in
⅛ in
5/16 in

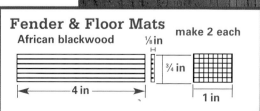

Fender & Floor Mats   **make 2 each**
African blackwood   ⅛ in
¾ in
4 in
1 in

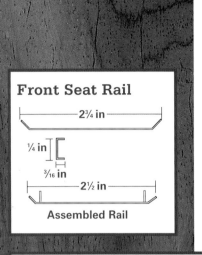

Front Seat Rail

2¾ in

¼ in

³⁄₁₆ in

2½ in

Assembled Rail

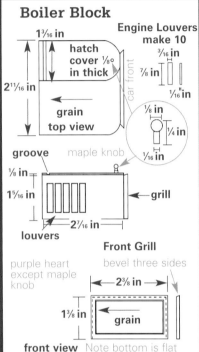

Boiler Block

1³⁄₁₆ in

hatch cover ⅛° in thick

2¹¹⁄₁₆ in

grain top view

Engine Louvers make 10

³⁄₁₆ in

⅞ in

¹⁄₁₆ in

⅛ in

¼ in

¹⁄₁₆ in

maple knob

car front

groove

⅛ in

1⁵⁄₁₆ in

grill

2⁷⁄₁₆ in

louvers

Front Grill

purple heart except maple knob

bevel three sides

2⅜ in

1⅜ in

grain

front view Note bottom is flat

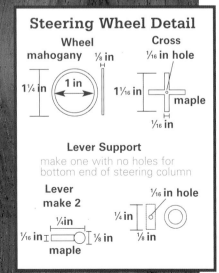

Steering Wheel Detail

Wheel mahogany

⅛ in

1¼ in 1 in

Cross ¹⁄₁₆ in hole

1¹⁄₁₆ in

maple

¹⁄₁₆ in

Lever Support

make one with no holes for bottom end of steering column

Lever make 2

¹⁄₁₆ in hole

¼ in

¼ in

¹⁄₁₆ in ⅛ in

⅛ in

maple

Making Front Seat Rail

1 Cut ¹⁄₁₆ in diameter brass rod 2¾ in long. Bend ¼ in from each end on slight angle. Ensure bends are aligned with each other.

2 Make 2 "C" shaped parts, as shown, using a pair of pliers. Make sure there is no twist in the ends.

3 Using third hand, solder the two "C" pieces to rail beside the bends.

4 Using dremel with a wire brush, polish the rail. Mount on back of front seat ½ in from top of seat and even on both sides. *Note* To mount rail, hold rail against back after front seat is made, and mark 4 holes. Drill same size as rods but not through back of seat. Glue rail in place with 5-minute epoxy. Set aside for final assembly.

Making Boiler Block

1 Cut out main block from a solid piece of purple heart or glue (5-minute epoxy) thin pieces of purple heart to a different type of wood; however, make sure purple heart is thick enough to sand to required shape.

2 Make front grill from purple heart. Check grain direction and cut apart. Sand to shape on belt sander. Check angle of top and side edges as the edges slope towards the boiler block. Bottom edge remains flat. With dremel, cut groove around edge of front grill for decoration.

3 Make louvers from purple heart ⅞ in x ³⁄₁₆ in, as shown. Piece should be long enough to cut 10 pieces ¹⁄₁₆ in thick on a band or scroll saw.

4 Make hatch cover from piece of purple heart 2⁷⁄₁₆ in x 1³⁄₁₆ in x ⅛ in thick. Use band or small handsaw to cut groove in one end. After cutting, glue hatch to top of boiler block, as shown. *Make sure hatch is glued to proper side on top of boiler block.*

5 Drill ¹⁄₁₆ in diameter hole for hatch knob. Make knob from ⅛ in maple dowel spun in drill press shaped with a needle file or turning ⅛ in dowel in small lathe.

6 Glue all parts to block except knob. Sand lightly. Attach knob to hatch door. Set aside.

Making Steering Wheel

1 Use ⅛ in maple dowel 3 in long. On one end of dowel, turn down to ¹⁄₁₆ in diameter and ⅛ in long stub. Use lathe or spin a long dowel on edge of disk or belt sander. Cut to proper length, as shown. Maple levers can be turned on drill press by placing a short ⅛ in diameter dowel in a drill chuck and shaping with a needle file. Sand smooth while spinning in drill press.

2 Make small lever support from ¼ in diameter dowel long enough to handle. Measure ¹⁄₁₆ in from one end and drill through the ¼ in dowel. Drill ⅛ in diameter hole in the end past the ¹⁄₁₆ in hole. Cut wood dowel to ⅛ in length leaving a piece with ⅛ in hole into center and ¹⁄₁₆ in hole. This is the lever support. Glue (5-minute epoxy) lever support to shaft, keeping it level with bottom of ¹⁄₁₆ in diameter pin on one end, and glue the other one with no hole ¼ in from other end of steering column.

3 Glue levers into the small holes on the lever support, across from each other.

4 Bend one end of ¹⁄₃₂ in brass wire 3 in long to 90° angle ⅛ in long. Make 2.

5 Drill ¹⁄₃₂ in diameter hole through lever support shaft between levers.

6 Insert brass wire in the hole on both sides. Trim these wires to ¼ in from end of steering wheel shaft so they will not interfere with mounting steering wheel shaft to pedal board. Glue brass wires with 5-minute epoxy.

7 Draw shape of cross piece of steering wheel on a piece of mahogany ¹⁄₁₆ in thick and large enough to handle. Drill center hole ¹⁄₁₆ in diameter. Check that steering shaft fits

into hole. On this piece cut out the cross on scroll saw with a thin piece underneath to help support the cross while cutting out. Use dremel with a small cutter and round all edges, being careful cross doesn't break.

8 Use mahogany piece 1¼ in diameter, ⅛ in thick and round off edge with belt sander or dremel. Use compass to mark 1 in diameter circle from center of 1¼ in disk, and drill ⅜ in hole through center. Use dremel with a small cutter to cut out the center section. When cut out is big enough to fit a small sanding drum into it, stop cutting. Change dremel to a small drum sander and finish inside diameter at slow speed.

9 Drill hole in piece of scrap wood big enough to insert steering shaft. This will hold it upright for assembly of parts.

10 Glue cross to 1/16 in stub in steering shaft, at the same time glue wheel to the cross, keeping everything centered. Set aside for final assembly.

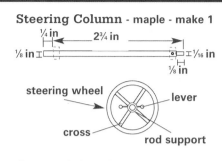

Steering Column - maple - make 1

Steering Wheel Assembly

Making Dash Levers

1 On 3/16 in diameter maple dowel mark hole locations. Leave room between parts. Turn dowel in lathe using holes as a guide for where to machine parts to different diameters. If using drill press to shape levers cut them as individual pieces and drill holes last. See diagram.

2 Sand round toothpicks on belt sander until they fit into the 1/16 in holes.

Note Lever 1 and 2 have the pins protruding from both sides. Lever 3 has pin on one side only.

3 Cut pins ¼ in long and glue pins to levers with 5-minute epoxy.

wood dowel

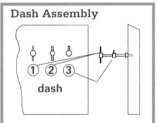

Dash Assembly

dash

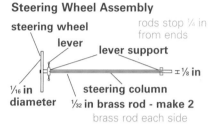

Dash Levers

Lever Layout on 3/16 in Dowel - quarter size
place marks in dowel for matching, repeat for each lever

drill these holes first

Making Floor Shifters

1 Spin 3/16 in diameter dowel in small lathe and shape, as shown or use round toothpicks as shaft for the shifter. Drill a hole in end of dowel to fit toothpicks.

2 Shape dowel on belt sander, cut off part, and glue to shaft. Shifter knobs do not have to be perfectly round but should be the same on each shifter.

3 Cut rings ⅛ in thick with handsaw from 3/16 in dowel after drilling hole in the end to fit a toothpick. Glue ring to the opposite end of shifter knob on shaft, ⅛ in from the end. Set aside for final assembly.

Floor Shifters

Making Brake Lever

1 Make brake lever from maple piece 2¾ in x ¼ in x ⅛ in thick. Piece is longer than required for easier handling. Drill all holes using pin vice to hold the drill bit.

2 Cut a "v" shape at one end and the hand grip at the other end.

3 Cut center section of lever to ⅛ in width and sand smooth. Cut and shape piece of 1/32 in diameter brass wire, as shown on diagram. Glue in place with 5-minute epoxy.

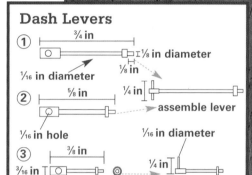

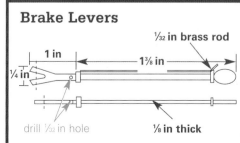

Brake Levers

drill 1/32 in hole   ⅛ in thick

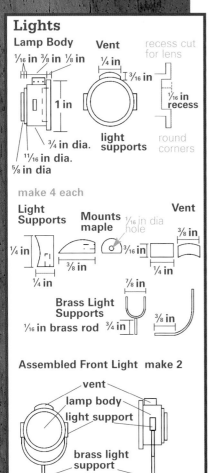

Lights

Lamp Body

Vent

recess cut for lens

$\frac{1}{16}$ in $\frac{3}{8}$ in $\frac{1}{8}$ in

$\frac{1}{4}$ in

$\frac{3}{16}$ in

1 in

$\frac{1}{16}$ in recess

$\frac{3}{4}$ in dia.

light supports

round corners

$\frac{11}{16}$ in dia.

$\frac{5}{8}$ in dia

make 4 each

Light Supports

Vent

Mounts maple

$\frac{1}{16}$ in dia hole

$\frac{3}{8}$ in

$\frac{1}{4}$ in

$\frac{3}{16}$ in

$\frac{3}{8}$ in

$\frac{1}{4}$ in

$\frac{1}{4}$ in

$\frac{3}{8}$ in

$\frac{7}{8}$ in

Brass Light Supports

$\frac{1}{16}$ in brass rod $\frac{3}{4}$ in

$\frac{3}{8}$ in

Assembled Front Light make 2

vent

lamp body

light support

brass light support

mounts

Making Lights

1   Use 1 in maple dowel turned to shape in lathe or different sizes of dowels glued together with 5-minute epoxy. See diagram for dimensions.

2   Make vent, light supports, and mounting blocks from piece of maple $\frac{1}{4}$ in wide and $\frac{3}{16}$ in thick. Keep piece long enough to hold and cut parts from end. Make curves in these pieces with dremel using a small carving bit. Shape one piece at a time on each end and cut off part when sanding is complete.

3   Make supports using same piece of maple and drill $\frac{1}{16}$ in hole in the end, then shape using the same method as above. Make sure 2 parts are the same.

4   Using the same piece of maple, drill the same size holes as above and form the light mounts, as seen on diagram. Glue to lamp body.
    Note Have holes for supports pointing in the same direction and straight. Glue vent on top of the lamp body, opposite to the holes, as shown on diagram.

5   Wrap $\frac{1}{16}$ in diameter long brass rod around $\frac{3}{8}$ in diameter drill bit to get $\frac{1}{2}$ in curve, then cut to proper length. The $\frac{7}{8}$ in diameter curve is done with $\frac{3}{4}$ in diameter rod or dowel. Check shape by sliding brass into light supports into drilled holes. There should be $\frac{1}{8}$ in gap between lamp body and brass support. Make lens, p52.

6   Use third hand to hold pieces together and solder. *Make sure brass pieces are in proper alignment before soldering.* Polish with wire brush in dremel at slow speed.

7   Glue brass support to light body and light mount to stem with 5-minute epoxy.

Making Front Seat

1   Bottom seat is purple heart $3\frac{5}{8}$ in x $1\frac{3}{4}$ in x $\frac{1}{8}$ in.

2   Cut side pieces $1\frac{3}{4}$ in sq and $\frac{5}{16}$ in thick. Make 2, left and right. Note grain direction. Glue together with piece of paper between so they can be separated later.

3   Transfer (p5) pattern for side pieces to wood. Cut (scroll or band saw) along outside of line leaving line. Use drum sander in drill press to sand side pieces to pattern line. Pry pieces apart and sand off excess paper and glue.

4   Cut back part of seat 3 in x $1\frac{3}{4}$ in x $\frac{5}{16}$ in (note grain direction). Glue back piece and side pieces to bottom piece of seat. Allow to dry.

5   Sand back corners round and sand remainder of seat smooth, rounding off all outside edges of seat. Final size of seat $3\frac{3}{8}$ in across back.

6   Make cushions from African blackwood $\frac{3}{16}$ in thick. Make back and bottom seat cushions in one piece. Ensure wood piece is big enough to cover the inside back and bottom of seat. It should be $3\frac{1}{4}$ in wide.

7   Cut grooves (see seat cushion diagram). Use band saw looking from behind the blade cutting $\frac{1}{8}$ in into cushion. Use dremel with a cone shape cutter to cut into the grooves giving squares of the cushion a rounded look, as shown.

8   Side cushions are made from African blackwood $\frac{1}{8}$ in thick. Make pattern from thin cardboard (cereal box). Place on the inside of seat end and draw contour of seat. Do each side separately. Cut cushions to shape and fit inside ends of seat. Cut grooves, as shown. Do not dremel grooves on side panels.

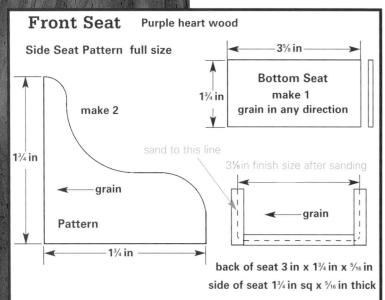

Front Seat   Purple heart wood

Side Seat Pattern full size

make 2

$1\frac{3}{4}$ in

grain

Pattern

$1\frac{3}{4}$ in

sand to this line

$3\frac{5}{8}$ in

Bottom Seat
make 1
grain in any direction

$1\frac{3}{4}$ in

$3\frac{1}{8}$ in finish size after sanding

grain

back of seat 3 in x $1\frac{3}{4}$ in x $\frac{5}{16}$ in

side of seat $1\frac{3}{4}$ in sq x $\frac{5}{16}$ in thick

9   Glue side pieces to front seat. Cut back cushion from grooved piece, leaving piece large enough for bottom of seat. *Note* Make sure bottom is long enough to go past front edge of seat by ⅛ in.

10 Trim width of pieces on each side to fit between side cushions. Glue (5-minute epoxy) cushions in place.

11 Use dremel with cone shape cutter to cut along the bottom edge of seat where cushions join.

12 Round the front edge of seat cushion under driver's legs. Cut grooves to edge giving front of seat a contour that matches grooves shown on assembly diagram. This will give cushions a puffy look where they join together. If a leather look is desired, paint with semi gloss urethane sealer (2 coats on seat cushions and let dry).

13 Use dremel at a low speed with a small wire brush (be sure to use a new one), and buff seat cushions to desired effect. Do not buff purple heart wood. Set aside.

Making Rear Seat

1   Use purple heart 3½ in x 1⅜ in x ¾ in thick. Check grain direction. Drill six 1/16 in holes ⅛ in deep. See diagram.

2   Cut a groove with band or scroll saw ⅛ in down from top edge, same side as holes. To keep groove straight wrap masking tape around the part ⅛ in from top and cut along tape edge. Do not cut too deep, groove is for decoration only.

3   Cut piece of purple heart 3 in x ½ in x ⅛ in thick for back piece of seat rest. Sand smooth.

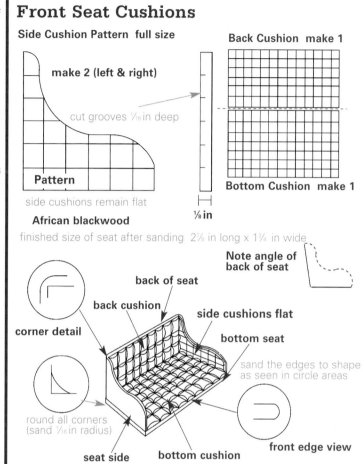

Front Seat Cushions

Side Cushion Pattern full size

make 2 (left & right)

cut grooves 1/16 in deep

Pattern

side cushions remain flat

African blackwood

finished size of seat after sanding 2⅞ in long x 1¾ in wide

Back Cushion make 1

Bottom Cushion make 1

⅛ in

Note angle of back of seat

back of seat

back cushion

side cushions flat

bottom seat

sand the edges to shape as seen in circle areas

corner detail

round all corners (sand 1/16 in radius)

seat side

bottom cushion

front edge view

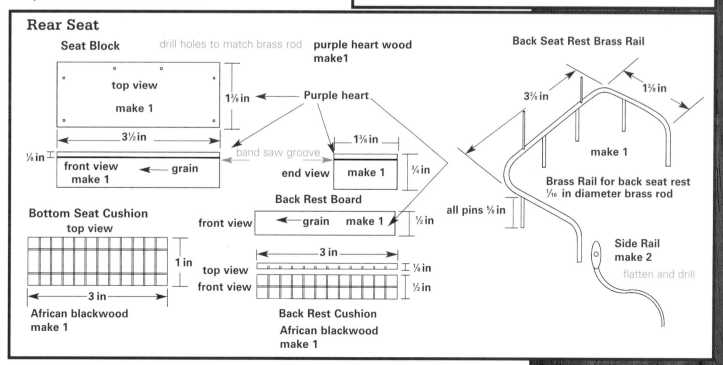

Rear Seat

Seat Block

drill holes to match brass rod   **purple heart wood make1**

top view
make 1

1⅜ in ← Purple heart

3½ in

⅛ in

front view
make 1

← grain

band saw groove

end view   make 1

1⅜ in

¾ in

Back Rest Board

front view   ← grain   make 1

½ in

all pins ⅝ in

Bottom Seat Cushion
top view

1 in

3 in

African blackwood
make 1

top view
front view

3 in

⅛ in
½ in

Back Rest Cushion
African blackwood make 1

Back Seat Rest Brass Rail

3⅜ in

1⅜ in

make 1

Brass Rail for back seat rest
1/16 in diameter brass rod

Side Rail
make 2

flatten and drill

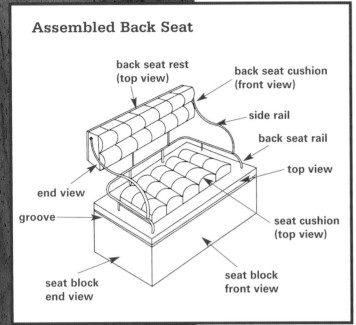

Assembled Back Seat

back seat rest (top view)

back seat cushion (front view)

side rail

back seat rail

top view

end view

groove

seat cushion (top view)

seat block end view

seat block front view

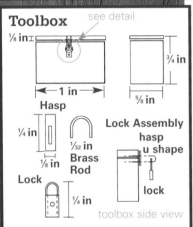

Toolbox

see detail

1/8 in

3/4 in

1 in

5/8 in

toolbox side view

Hasp

1/4 in

1/32 in

1/8 in

Brass Rod

Lock Assembly

hasp

u shape

Lock

1/4 in

lock

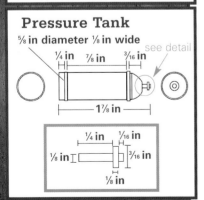

Pressure Tank

5/8 in diameter 1/8 in wide

see detail

1/4 in   7/8 in   3/16 in

1 7/8 in

1/4 in   1/16 in

1/8 in   3/16 in

1/8 in

4   Cut blackwood 3 in x 1 1/2 in x 1/4 in thick to make both seat cushions.

5   Cut shallow grooves into blackwood with a band saw. Dremel to shape, as front seat directions. Use same finish method so both seats will look the same.

6   Cut larger piece in 2 pieces - 3 in x 1 in, and 3 in x 1/2 in.

7   Glue 3 in x 1/2 in piece of blackwood to 3 in x 1/2 in purple heart with 5-minute epoxy.

8   Glue 1 in x 3 in blackwood to seat block. Keep cushion even with front edge.

9   Place cushion in middle so both sides are even from the edges of seat block. Do not cover holes with glue.

10 Build seat rail as shown and assemble on seat.

Making Toolbox

1   On purple heart 1 in x 5/8 in x 3/4 in use band or handsaw to cut slit 1/8 in from top edge to stimulate lid. Make hasp by forming "u" shape with 1/32 in brass wire and trim to 1/4 in long. Mark latch pattern on piece of thin aluminum.

2   Use dremel to make 1/32 in wide slot and long enough to fit "u" shaped wire into. Trim piece as close to size as possible with snips.

3   Hold aluminum hasp with needle nose pliers, sand to final shape on belt sander.

4   Build lock with 1/32 in brass wire and make a "u" shape. Cut aluminum tube 1/4 in long and slide wire through pulling it as far as possible, leaving a loop protruding. With a pair of pliers squeeze the aluminum tube pinching the wire inside tube.

5   Drill a small hole in the middle of tube to give lock a keyhole. Trim wires off lock.

6   Mark slot in middle of toolbox keeping hasp even with top. On "u"wire, mark 2 holes same distance apart as "u" shape and drill holes.

7   Glue slotted metal to box with 5-minute epoxy. At the same time push "u" shape wire through lock through the slot into drilled holes.

Making Pressure Tank

Turn a single piece of 5/8 in maple dowel in a small lathe or cut 1/2 in dowel and 5/8 in dowel into different sizes shown and glue (5-minute epoxy) together, keeping them in the center of each other. Make small valve end by spinning 3/16 in diameter dowel in a drill press and shaping with small needle nose file. Set speed as slow as possible.

First Stage Assembly

1   On flat surface spread with wax paper, glue (24-hour epoxy) main body. Fit seat mounts at proper locations. Use small square against one side and across back, pushing all parts against the square. Dry overnight.

2   Check main body diagram for how to sand corners and top edge of dash. Back edge of car is slightly rounded, and front finished size is 3 1/8 in wide. Top of dash blends into side pieces with slope facing front of car.

3   Drill a hole on driver side of car body same size as hole in brake lever.

4   Glue main floor to main body assembly with 24-hour epoxy. Keep back of car even with back of main body assembly. *Holes in main floor should be at front of car.*

5   Attach boiler block to main floor keeping in center of dash and even on both sides

from main floor edges. Dry overnight. Sand smooth. Glue pedal board in place between side panels against dash and floor.

6   Mount back springs ½ in from back edge of car. Glue to edge of main floor and rest on side pieces protruding past main floor. Make a mark ½ in from back edge and on center of spring and keep springs level. Place scrap wood same height as end of spring between spring and main floor, as a stop to keep springs in straight line. Glue with 5-minute epoxy. Wrap string tight around assembly and dry.

7   Glue front spring ¼ in from front edge of main floor. Kept level same way as for rear springs. Dry overnight. Hold in place with a 4 in "C" clamp.

8   Glue (5-minute epoxy) front axle over front springs with notches fitting onto spring. Mount back axle same as front axle. Before gluing slide the axle drive wheel onto axle, *but do not glue drive wheel to axle.* Drive wheel has to move to be lined up with transmission wheel when mounting engine in place under car.

9   Glue sparingly (5-minute epoxy) brake rod to bottom of car 3⅜ in back from the front edge, straight across bottom of car (see underside assembly diagram, p29) with levers pointing straight up if car is upside down.

10 Mount engine ½ in from edge of car on driver side. Lay engine on bottom of car and line up drive wheel with drive wheel on engine. Wheels should touch. Mark engine location and axle wheel. Glue with 5-minute epoxy.

11 Slide small hub against spring when mounting to front axle. Large hubs go on back axle sliding them against springs also. Small drilled hole must be at the top of hub on the spring side of axle. Mount wheels with valve stem on outside of wheel in different locations.

12 Bend piece of aluminum tube (see diagram) and cut to length. Glue to front axle between the hubs. Bend another piece of aluminum 90° and place in ⅛ in hole under car and join to side of engine.

Making Fenders

1   Use piece of purple heart 12 in x 5 in x ¾ in thick for the fenders.

2   For fender mounts use 4 pieces ⅛ in brass tube 1¼ in long. See fender diagram. Flatten ¼ in of ends of the 4 brass tubes with pliers and squeeze ends together and form to shape at the same time, as shown on page 28.

3   Make a cardboard cutout ⅛ in thick of the fender profile. The radius distance for the curved part of the fenders should match the distance between the wheel centers after the wheels are mounted on car. This measurement is not given, as each person's measurements might be slightly different when assembling the car.

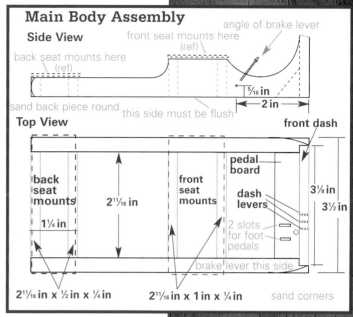

Main Body Assembly

Side View

angle of brake lever

front seat mounts here (ref)

back seat mounts here (ref)

⁵⁄₁₆ in

2 in

sand back piece round   this side must be flush

Top View

front dash

pedal board

back seat mounts

front seat mounts

2¹¹⁄₁₆ in

dash levers

3⅛ in

3½ in

1¼ in

2 slots for foot pedals

brake lever this side

2¹¹⁄₁₆ in x ½ in x ¼ in   2¹¹⁄₁₆ in x 1 in x ¼ in   sand corners

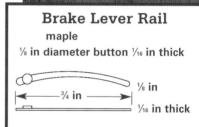

Brake Lever Rail

maple

⅛ in diameter button ¹⁄₁₆ in thick

¾ in

⅛ in

¹⁄₁₆ in thick

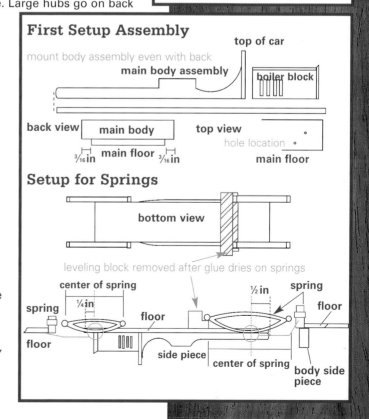

First Setup Assembly

top of car

mount body assembly even with back

main body assembly

boiler block

back view   main body   top view

hole location

³⁄₁₆ in   main floor   ³⁄₁₆ in   main floor

Setup for Springs

bottom view

leveling block removed after glue dries on springs

center of spring   ½ in   spring

¼ in   floor   floor

spring

floor   side piece   center of spring   body side piece

Fenders

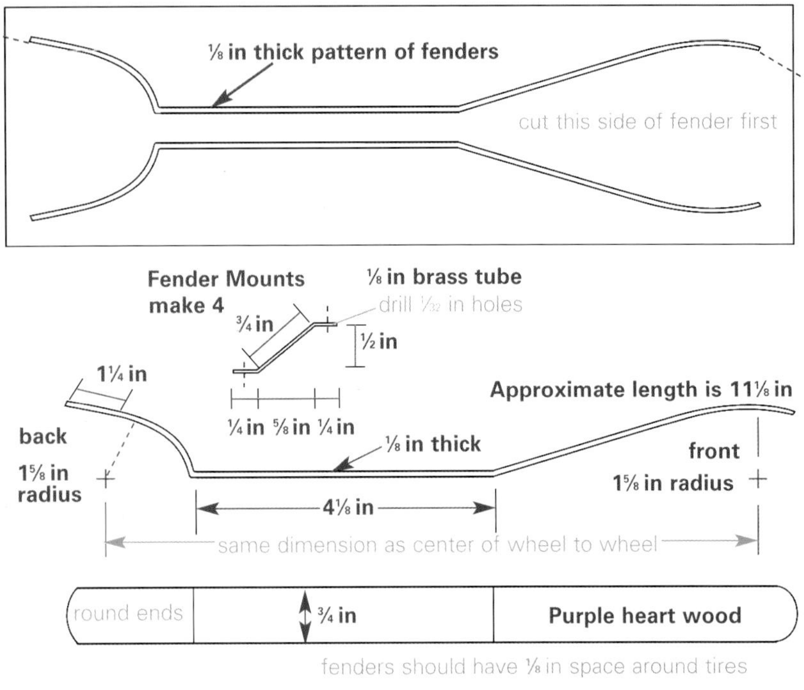
Fender Layout
⅛ in thick pattern of fenders
cut this side of fender first
Fender Mounts
make 4
⅛ in brass tube
drill 1/32 in holes
¾ in
½ in
1¼ in
Approximate length is 11⅛ in
¼ in ⅝ in ¼ in
back
⅛ in thick
front
1⅝ in
radius
1⅝ in radius
4⅛ in
same dimension as center of wheel to wheel
round ends
¾ in
Purple heart wood
fenders should have ⅛ in space around tires

Engine Lever

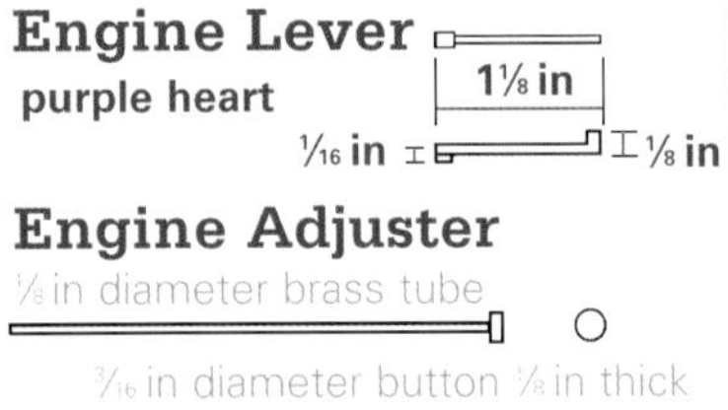
purple heart
1⅛ in
1/16 in
⅛ in
Engine Adjuster
⅛ in diameter brass tube
3/16 in diameter button ⅛ in thick

Passenger Side

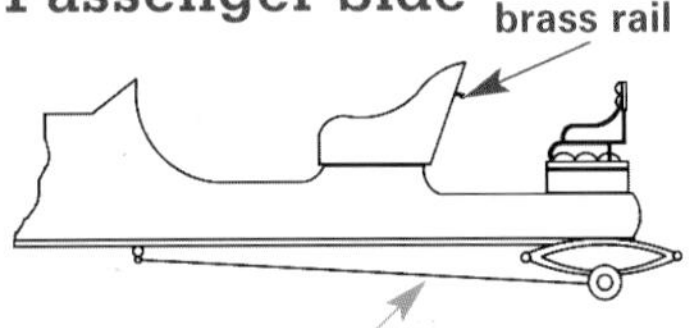
brass rail
brass rod attaches to brake drum
Note toolbox mounts on passenger side fender

Lever Arrangement

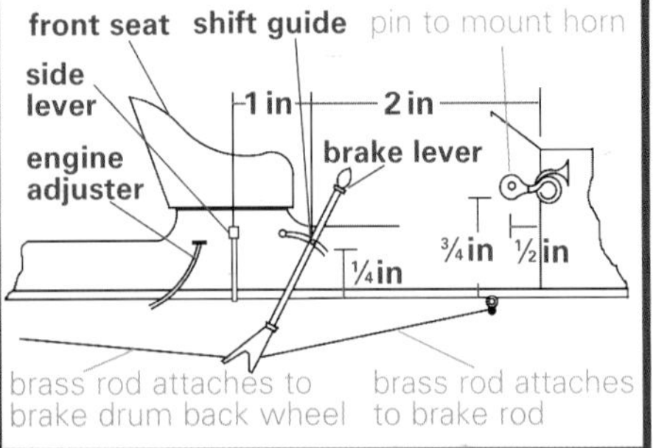
front seat
shift guide
pin to mount horn
side lever
1 in
2 in
engine adjuster
brake lever
¼ in
¾ in
½ in
brass rod attaches to brake drum back wheel
brass rod attaches to brake rod

4 Check that profile fits between tires with proper gap, making sure it is level with center of the wheels from the ground. If not level, cut another profile until satisfied with the fit.

5 Transfer pattern to wood, as shown on fender layout drawing. *Note* Drawing shows which cut to make first so it will be easier to hold when making last cut to remove fender. Make sure to maintain ⅛ in thickness.

6 Once pieces are cut out, round ends of the fenders keeping both fenders the same. Sand smooth and set aside for final assembly.

Final Assembly

1 Drill 2 holes same size as holes in fender mounts into underside of step of fender. Push small pins through fender supports into fender. Supports protrude 90° from inside edge of fenders. Mount on left and right side of fenders.

2 Turn car upside down, align fender between wheels, maintain space between fender and wheels. Fender should protrude to cover wheels.

3 Mark holes on bottom of car for supports and drill holes. Repeat on other side of car for opposite fender. Glue in place with pins and 5-minute epoxy.

4 Mount brake lever on driver side of car into hole. Note angle of lever. Use 1/32 in brass rod to join lever to hole in back brake drum and to brake rod. Use holes drilled in bottom of lever to join drum and brake rod. On passenger side of car using same size brass rod, join brake rod to rear brake drum.

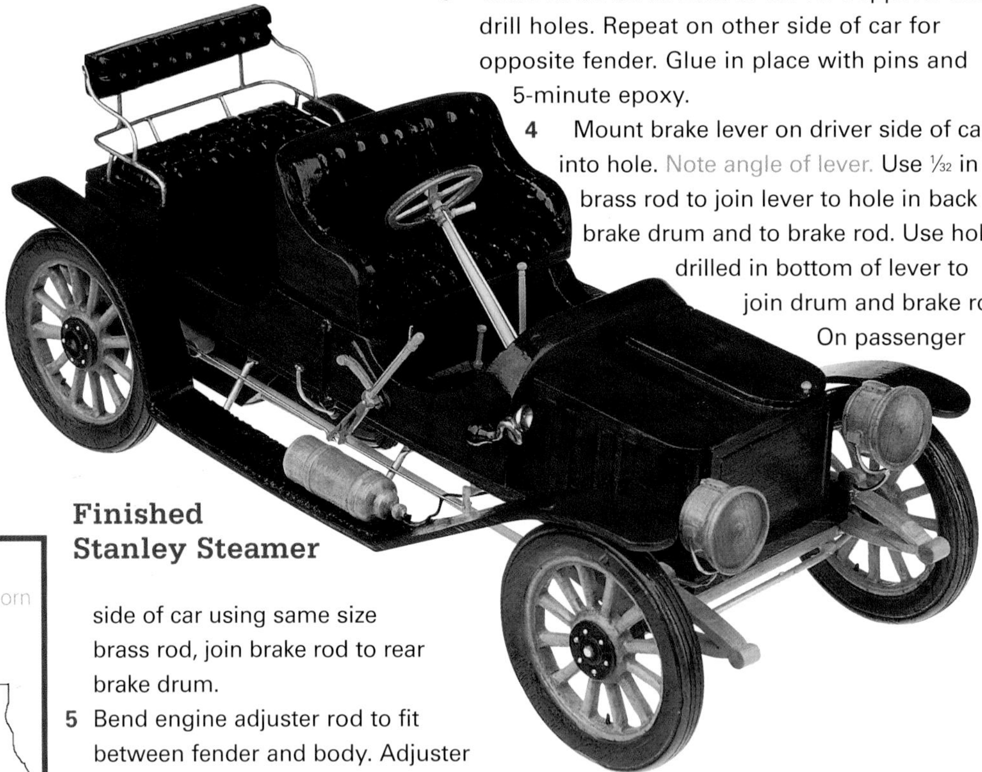

Finished Stanley Steamer

5 Bend engine adjuster rod to fit between fender and body. Adjuster should be long enough to go from engine to underside to front seat on driver side of car. Glue engine lever to car body beside adjuster rod under driver's seat at same time.

6   Cut thin pieces of mahogany to place on floor in front of seats. On piece for front floor drill 2 holes same size as floor shifters. Holes are used to mount floor shifters. Draw a line across the narrow side, measure 1 $\frac{5}{16}$ in from the end. Mark $\frac{1}{4}$ in from the edge on this line, and mark $\frac{7}{8}$ in from last mark on this line. Drill 2 holes to mount shifters, making sure holes are same size as shifter. *Note*   Keep 1 $\frac{5}{16}$ in distance on the driver side of car.

7   Glue mahogany piece in place on floor. The small shifter goes in hole next to seat and the long shifter goes in other hole.

8   Glue front and back seats to car.

9   Mount lights to top of front springs. Glue and slide lights into mounts at the same time.

10   Glue floor and fender mats to car, then add pressure tank and toolbox. Glue pressure tank to driver side of fender with valve towards front of car.

11   Glue small black wire from pressure tank to small hole drilled under car. Toolbox is glued to passenger side fender just back of car entrance, with lock facing outside of car.

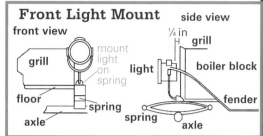

Front Light Mount

front view   side view

grill

$\frac{1}{4}$ in   grill

mount light on spring

light   boiler block

floor

fender

spring

axil   spring

spring   axle

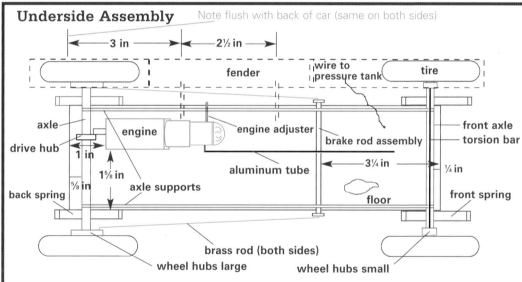

Underside Assembly   Note flush with back of car (same on both sides)

3 in   2½ in

fender   wire to pressure tank   tire

axle

engine   engine adjuster   front axle

drive hub   brake rod assembly   torsion bar

1 in

1⅝ in   aluminum tube   3¼ in   ¼ in

⅝ in

back spring   axle supports   floor   front spring

brass rod (both sides)

wheel hubs large   wheel hubs small

Add axle support by placing notch of support over front axle, cut to length so rods will fit in holes in rear axles. Glue in place.

12   Put 5-minute epoxy in hole and on end of steering shaft. Place steering wheel into hole before glue dries. Center of steering wheel should be $\frac{1}{16}$ in below top edge of front seat and 90° to the dash. Hold in place until glue sets.

13   Set car aside for 2 days until all glues harden. Using dremel with a narrow wire brush, take excess glue off joints using great care and very little pressure.

14   Clear coat entire car with eurethane gloss, including brass pieces. Use very little on lock of toolbox so lock remains loose on toolbox. The car in photo has 5 clear coats.

Shows location of pedals, steering wheel, levers, seat carving

Front springs attach, front axle, torsion bar, lights attach to springs

Shows location of horn, levers, gas tank, spring, front dash

Shows toolbox with lock assembly and hasp

Shows rail fit on back seat, how springs & holes join together, transmission

Shows levers fit in dash, location of steering wheel, floor mats

Under view - shows proper placement of parts, how fender brackets fit

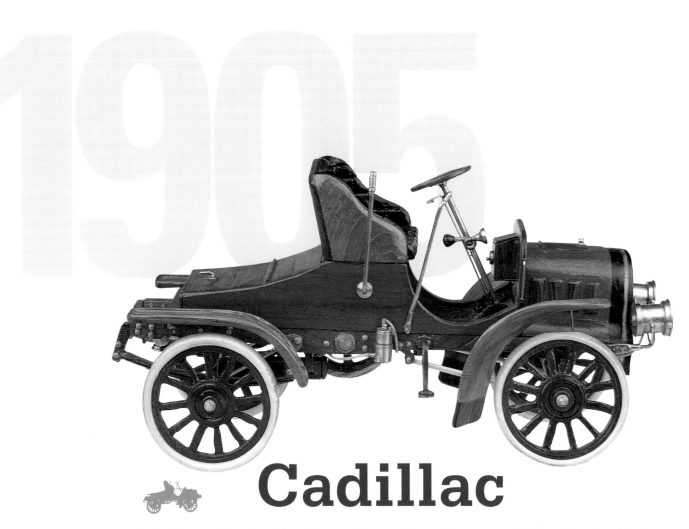

Cadillac

In 1890 Henry M. Leland, American engineer and manufacturer, established Leland and Faulconer Manufacturing Company to build engines for automobile makers. He created his own motorcar, the Model A Cadillac, (designed by Henry Ford), in 1903, which was produced for many years. He operated a meticulous production system that inspired many car manufacturers and his demonstration of and eventually led to mass production.The standardization and interchangeability of parts made the techniques of mass assembly feasible.

A great innovator, Leland sought the assistance of Charles F. Kettering, an electrical engineer, to develop the electric starter which helped the gasoline-powered engine gain acceptance. He is also credited with the V-8 engine. Henry Leland resigned as president of the Cadillac company in 1919 to start the Lincoln Motor Company which passed into the hands of Henry Ford.

The Cadillac model E pictured here was a semi racer type business car that had great power and was capable of high speeds on average roads. It had a single cylinder engine, 9 hp, with a bronze water jacket over the cylinder to cool the engine. It had 2 forward gears and one revese gear in a planetary transmission. The car cost $750.

Car Parts List

Car Part	Material	Size	Pieces
Wheels	mahogany	13 in x 3 in x ¼ in	1
	maple	3 in x 13 in x ⅜ in	1
Body Side Panels	teak	17 in x 2 in x ¼ in	1
Hatch Cover	teak	4½ in x 4 in x ⅛ in	1
Hatch Handle	brass rod	¼ in x ½ in long	1
	brass rod	⅛ in x ⅜ in long	1
	brass rod	1/16 in x ¾ in long	1
Side Rails	teak	12 in x 2 in x ⅜ in	2
	teak	1 in x ¼ in x 1/16 in	2
Front Spring	teak	3½ in x ¾ in x 5/16	1
Front Torsion Bar	maple dowel	⅜ in x ¼ in long	2
	maple dowel	⅛ in x 4 in long	2
Rear Torsion Bar	maple dowel	⅛ in x 2¼ in long	2
Tie Rod	maple	⅛ in x 4½ in long	1
Pedal Board	teak	⅞ in x ½ in x 3⅝ in	1
	African blackwood	¾ in x ¼ in x ⅛ in	1
	African blackwood	¾ in x ⅜ in x 1/16 in	1
	African blackwood	⅜ in x ¼ in x ⅛ in	1
	African blackwood	½ in x ⅛ in x 1/16 in	1
Floor Board	teak	2⅝ in x 2½ in x ¼ in	1
Floor Mats	African blackwood	1¼ in x 1 in x 1/16 in	2
	African blackwood	1¼ in x ¾ in x 1/16 in	1
Under Seat Panel	oak	2¾ in x 1 11/16 in x ¼ in	1
Panels	oak	2¾ in x 1 11/16 in x 1/16 in	1
Panel Knob	brass rod	3/16 in x ¾ in long	1
Entrance Step	teak	1¼ in x 1¼ x ⅜ in	
Seat	teak	3½ in x 2¼ in x ⅛ in	1
	teak	3 in x 2½ in x ¼ in	2
	teak	3¾ in x 2½ in x ¼ in	1
Seat Cushions	African blackwood	3 in x 2½ in x ¼ in	2
	African blackwood	2½ in x 1¾ in x 3/16 in	1
	African blackwood	3½ in x 2¼ in x 3/16 in	1
Chain Pulley and Flywheel	mahogany disk	2¼ in round, ⅜ in thick	1
	maple dowel	⅜ in x 3½ in long	1
	maple dowel	¾ in x, ⅝ in long	1
Rear Fenders	teak	4½ in x 2½ in x ¾ in	1
	maple dowel	⅛ in x 1⅛ in long	4
Front Axle	mahogany	5⅜ in x ½ in x ¼ in	1
Rear Axle	mahogany dowel	¼ in x 5⅜ in long	1
	mahogany dowel	⅝ in x, ½ in long	2
	maple dowel	½ in x ¼ in long	1

Car Part	Material	Size	Pieces
Engine Block	teak	2 in x 3¾ in x 1¾ in	1
	teak	⅝ in x ¼ in x 1/16 in	8
	teak	1¼ in x 1 in x 1/16 in	1
	maple	⅛ in sq, 6 in long	1
	African blackwood	2⅝ in x 3¼ in x ⅛ in	1
	African blackwood	8 in x 3/16 in x ⅛ in	1
	maple	¾ in x 1¾ in x ⅛ in	1
	maple	1 in x ½ in x ⅛ in	1
	brass rod	3/16 in x ½ in long	1
Dash	teak	3¼ in x 2¼ in x ⅛ in	1
	mahogany	1 in x ½ in x ¾ in	1
	mahogany	3/16 in x ⅛ in x 1/16 in	4
	brass rod	1/16 in x 4 in long	1
	brass rod	⅜ in x ⅜ in long	1
	brass rod	⅛ in x ½ in long	1
Fuel Tank	teak	2⅜ in x ½ in x ⅜ in	1
	teak	½ in x ¼ in x 3/16 in	1
	teak	1 in x 5/16 in x ¼ in	1
Cylinder (Optional)	teak dowel	½ in x ⅛ in long	2
	maple dowel	⅜ in x ⅝ in long	1
	teak	½ in x ⅜ in x ¼ in	1
	maple	1¼ in x ⅛ in x ⅛ in	1
Front Fenders	teak	2¾ in sq, ¾ in thick	2
Steering Wheel	as per instructions		
Gas Generator	brass rod	⅝ in x 1 in long	1
	brass rod	⅛ in x, 1½ in long	1
Shift Lever	brass rod	⅛ in x 2⅞ in long	1
	brass rod	3/16 in x, 1 in long	1
	brass rod	⅜ in x, ⅜ in long	1
Brake Lever	brass rod	⅛ in x 4 in long	1
	brass rod	3/16 in x 1 in long	1
Head Lamps	brass rod	¾ in x 1 in long	2
	brass rod	⅛ in x 1¼ in long	2
	brass tube	⅛ in x ¾ in long	2
	brass rod	1/16 in x 3 in long	1
	brass rod	⅛ in x ⅜ in long	4
	plastic disk	11/16 in diameter	1
Taillight	brass rod	⅜ in x 2 in long	1
	brass rod	½ in x, ¾ in long	1
	brass rod	1/16 in x, 1⅝ in long	1
	brass shim stock	½ in long, ⅛ in wide	1

Making Wheels

Note There are some changes in material and dimensions from wheels on p11 but building method is the same. Build wheels and spoke disks from mahogany 13 in x 3 in x ¼ in. Tires are built from maple 3 in x 13 in x ⅜ in. Choose maple that is completely white. Diameters of wheels are larger so use 2¾ in hole saw to build spoke disks, and 2½ in and 3 in hole saws for building tires. *Note* Center hubs of the wheels are 1 in diameter not ¾ in.

Body Side Panels

1 Build body side panels from teak ¼ in thick and large enough to transfer (p5) pattern on this page. Check grain direction as shown on diagram.

2 Make rabbet joint using drill press and drum sander (see diagram). *Note* Router mounted in a table can be used in this step if you are an experienced woodworker. Cut pieces longer than required and cut this joint first. If wood chips on the end when you cut, the chip can be cut off. *Note* Diagram shows left and right for mounting side pieces onto rails. Glue (white carpenter's glue) side pieces together with piece of paper between them and ensure joints face each other to make a left and right. Cut out with scroll saw

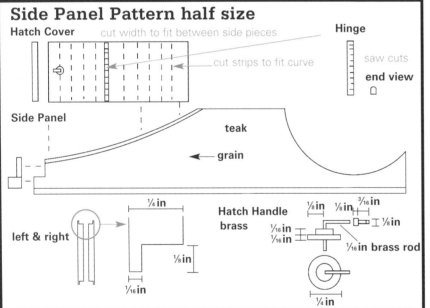

Side Panel Pattern half size

Hatch Cover — cut width to fit between side pieces

Hinge

cut strips to fit curve

saw cuts

end view

Side Panel

teak

← grain

left & right

Hatch Handle brass

¼ in

⅛ in

⅛ in   ⅛ in   ³⁄₁₆ in

¹⁄₁₆ in
¹⁄₁₆ in

⅛ in

¹⁄₁₆ in

¹⁄₁₆ in brass rod

¼ in

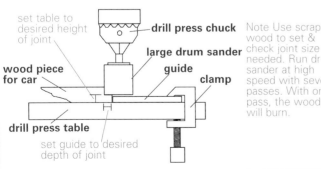

Making Rabbet Joint

set table to desired height of joint

drill press chuck

large drum sander

guide

clamp

wood piece for car

drill press table

set guide to desired depth of joint

Note Use scrap wood to set & check joint size needed. Run drum sander at high speed with several passes. With one pass, the wood will burn.

3 With panels still glued together sand edges square not round with drum sander in drill press. Sand all edges square not round. Hand sand each side until all sanding marks are removed and set aside for final assembly. *Note* If sanding marks are not removed they will appear in the wood when final clear coat is applied.

4 Turn ¼ in brass rod in lathe to make base plate of hatch handle for rear hatch cover. But first drill ¹⁄₁₆ in hole through center of brass piece.

5 Bend ¹⁄₁₆ in brass rod to 90° angle then trim to length to make handle rod.

6 Turn handle from ⅛ in brass rod.

7 Drill ¹⁄₁₆ in hole into handle to mount onto ¹⁄₁₆ in handle rod.

8 Place ¹⁄₁₆ in brass rod through center hole of plate, with handle attached to end.

9 Solder all parts in place. With dremel and wire brush, polish to a bright finish. Set aside for assembly. *Note* Hatch cover is not cut until the body is assembled to give a more accurate dimension and tighter fit.

Making Side Rails

1 Use piece of teak ⅜ in thick with grain running the length of the wood large enough to make rail.

2 Make cardboard pattern using dimensions given on diagram instead of drawing on the wood. When making pattern, begin with straight line to mark top edge of the rail. This line should be longer than the overall length of rail. Mark all distances shown on diagram.

3 Draw lines 90° down the marks on this line. Draw all different widths from top edge of rail on these lines. Join the different widths marked on these lines with straight lines and curves, as shown. Curves joining these lines together are traced around a 10 cent coin.

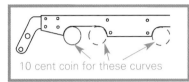

10 cent coin for these curves

4 To keep rails the same, glue (white carpenter's glue) a piece of paper between 2 pieces of teak ⅜ in thick. Trace pattern on teak.

5 Drill ⅜ in diameter hole into rails and cut out section between springs and rail.

6 Cut out remainder of rail and sand smooth keeping all edges sharp not round.

7 Circles on rail show location of ⅛ in diameter round maple buttons to represent rivets on rails. Drill holes with 1/16 in drill bit. Turn small rivets out of bamboo skewer and glue (5-minute epoxy) them into these holes or glue small wood buttons over the holes to represent rivet heads on the chassis rail. Build left and right. *Note* Squares do not go all the way across rail, because it is cut in half with one of the halves removed. When removing half pieces ensure they are removed opposite to each other. This will make a left and right.

8 The part where the spring joins the end of rail is cut smaller than rail in width to give spring mount the appearance of being a separate piece of the rail.

9 Supports protruding from bottom edge are carved into the rail to give appearance of being separate pieces. Use dremel and tiny ball cutter, making a groove around edges into the side of rail. *Note* Ensure proper side of rail is cut, keeping left and right in mind.

10 Use small drum sander in dremel and sand springs on each side slightly narrower than the rails.

11 Cut out two axle support plates, as shown on diagram. Set aside for final assembly.

12 Photo at right shows narrow part of rail where spring is mounted.

Making Front Spring

1 There is only one spring for the front axle of this car. Use 5/16 in thick teak large enough for spring (see diagram). Draw spring on wood and cut out on scroll saw.

2 Use dremel with small saw blade or cut-off wheel and cut shallow grooves around spring, separating each leaf on spring, shown on diagram. *Note* Spring can also be made by gluing (5-minute epoxy) individual bars together which gives a more realistic spring. If building spring from individual pieces they need to be thick enough to give the proper height of spring.

3 Use round toothpicks to simulate all clamp bolts that hold spring together. Sand toothpicks flat on one side. Glue in place with flat side towards spring.

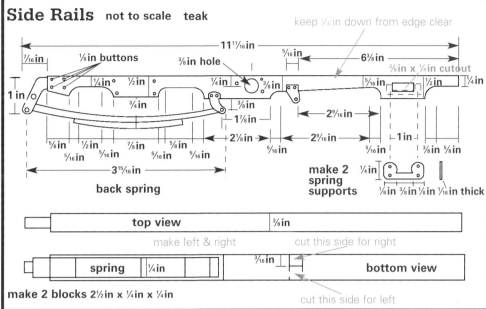

Side Rails not to scale teak

keep 1/16 in down from edge clear

11 11/16 in • 7/16 in • ⅛ in buttons • ⅜ in hole • ¼ in • 5/16 in • 6⅝ in • ⅜ in x ¼ in cutout • ¼ in • ½ in • ½ in • ¾ in • ⅜ in • 1⅞ in • 2 1/8 in • 5/8 in • ½ in • 7/8 in • 5/8 in • 5/16 in • 5/16 in • 5/16 in • 5/16 in • 5/16 in • 2 9/16 in • 2 9/16 in • 1 in • ⅜ in • 5/8 in • 1 in • 3 15/16 in

back spring

make 2 spring supports ¼ in ⅛ in ⅜ in ⅛ in 1/16 in thick

top view ⅜ in

make left & right · cut this side for right

spring ¼ in · 3/16 in · bottom view

make 2 blocks 2½ in x ¼ in x ¼ in · cut this side for left

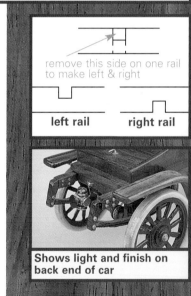

remove this side on one rail to make left & right

left rail **right rail**

Shows light and finish on back end of car

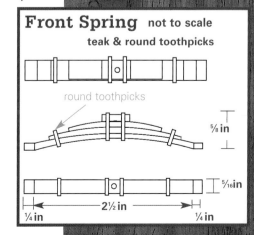

Front Spring not to scale

teak & round toothpicks

round toothpicks

5/8 in

5/16 in

2½ in

¼ in ¼ in

Chain Pulley & Flywheel

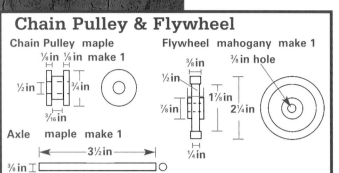

Chain Pulley maple
⅛in ⅛in make 1
½in   ¾in
³⁄₁₆in

Axle   maple   make 1
3½in
⅜in

Flywheel   mahogany   make 1
⅜in   ⅜in hole
½in   1⅞in
⅞in   2¼in
¼in

Assembled Drive Axle

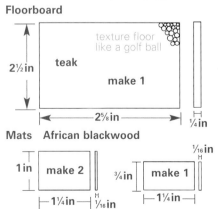

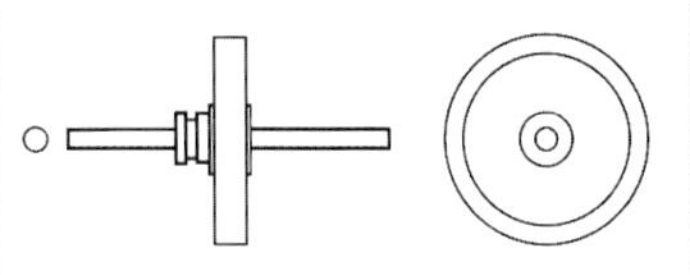

do not glue pulleys to axle until
final assembly

Pedal Board

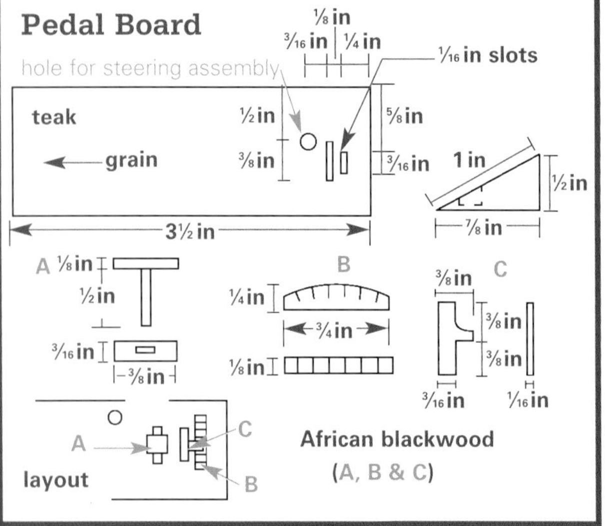

teak
← grain
3½in

⅛in
³⁄₁₆in ¼in
½in   ⅝in
⅜in   ³⁄₁₆in 1 in   ½in
⅐⁄₈in   ¹⁄₁₆ in slots

A ⅛in   B   ⅜in C
½in   ¼in   ¾in   ⅜in ⅜in
³⁄₁₆in   ⅛in   ³⁄₁₆in ¹⁄₁₆in
³⁄₈in

A → C
B
layout
African blackwood
(A, B & C)

Floorboard & Mats

Floorboard

texture floor
like a golf ball
teak
make 1
2½in
2⅝in   ¼in

Mats   African blackwood
1 in   make 2   ¾in   make 1   ¹⁄₁₆in
1¼in   ¹⁄₁₆in   1¼in

Glue toothpicks to front and backsides first, leaving them longer than required. Allow to dry.

4 Glue top and bottom toothpicks in place between front and back ones. Allow to dry. Sand front and back toothpicks even with top and bottom ones.

5 Drill ⅛ in hole located in middle of spring. Hole should be big enough for ⅛ in round dowel to fit loosely. Set aside for final assembly.

Chain Pulley and Flywheel

1 Make axle from ⅜ in maple dowel 3½ in long.
2 Make flywheel from mahogany 2¼ in round and ⅜ in thick.
3 Make ⅜ in diameter hole in center of round disk. Place disk in lathe and machine to proper size and shape, as shown on diagram. *Note This part can also be made from individual pieces glued together. Drill ⅜ in hole in the pieces, then assemble parts on a ⅜ in dowel.*
4 Make chain pulley from ¾ in maple dowel. Place dowel in lathe and machine to shape with ⅜ in hole through center, as shown on diagram. Pulley can also be made with individual pieces glued together. Set aside parts.

Making Pedal Board

1 Make board from teak cut to size and shape as shown on diagram. Build in same manner as Ford car p46. *Note Leave teak piece a little longer to be sanded later to fit between body side panels on assembly.*
2 Cut slots and drill hole the same way as the other cars except location is different. See diagram to cut slots and drill hole.
3 Sand opposite end of pedal board to fit between car body panels.
4 Cut pedal and foot lever from African blackwood, as shown on diagram. Make foot pedal the same as the other cars (p52).
5 Use larger piece to make foot lever and cut to shape with scroll saw.
6 Part marked B on diagram has tiny saw cuts on curved side to look like teeth that lever slides along to lock it in different positions as seen on the real car.
7 Assemble all parts to pedal board and set aside for final assembly.

Floorboard and Mats

1 Make floorboard from teak 2⅝ in x 2½ in x ¼ in. Grain direction doesn't matter.
2 Raise and lower cutter into teak floor leaving small craters behind to look like textured surface of golf ball.
3 Make mats from one piece of African blackwood to be cut 1 in x 1¼ in x ¹⁄₁₆ in and 1¼ in x 1 in x ¹⁄₁₆ in. Texture wood same as floorboard before you cut out pieces as directed on diagram. *Note When cutting thin pieces in band saw stand piece on its edge and then cut through piece. This stops blade from splitting or breaking piece.* Set aside for final assembly.

Under Seat Panel

1   Use red oak a little larger than 2¾ in x 1¹¹⁄₁₆ in x ¼ in required. The 1¹¹⁄₁₆ in dimension has to be exact so panel doesn't go higher than body side panels. Sand flush if necessary. Sand top and bottom of panel if needed. Cut 2¾ in dimension longer so it can be sanded to fit tightly between body panels on final assembly.

2   The 2 panels shown on diagram can either be cut on the face of this panel or cut separately and glued in place. Leave ⅛ in space all around outside edge and ¼ in space up middle between panels. If cutting and gluing the panels, cut panels thicker and glue in place. Allow to dry. Sand to ¹⁄₁₆ in thickness. *Note Sand panels in same direction as wood grain.*

3   Make brass knob same way as knob for engine hatch cover (p49). Drill hole and attach knob to panel. Set aside for final assembly.

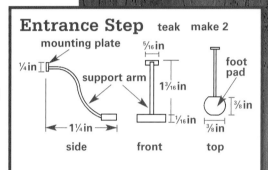

Entrance Step

Use 2 pieces of teak 1⅜ in x 1⅜ in x ½ in. *Note If building from one piece of wood draw all views on wood starting with side view.* Cut part from scrap wood first then cut from teakwood. Curves are not critical as long as dimensions are true and both steps are the same. Cut out 3 separate pieces and glue (5-minute epoxy) them all together for the mounting plate, support arm, and foot pad.

Making the Seat

1   Build from teak the same as the Stanley Steamer (p24). Use dimensions on diagram at right. Make seat cushions from African blackwood and build using same method as Stanley Steamer (p24).

2   Trace side view of seat on cardboard and place on seat side panel for sanding profile. *Note Back seat slopes toward top of seat so wood must be thick enough to sand this slope.*

3   Seat cushions are made same as for the Stanley Steamer (p25) but use a diamond shape pattern.

4   Make center divider from piece of African blackwood, smooth on both sides with top edge sanded round. Glue (5-minute epoxy) to inside center of seat.

5   Seat body should be ⅛ in thick when sanding is complete. Seat cushions are same thickness as those on the Stanley Steamer.

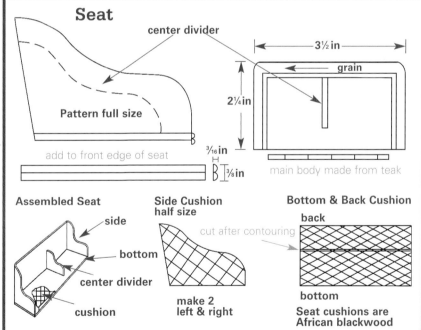

Making Rear Fender

1   Make rear fenders from 2 pieces of teak 4½ in x 2½ in x ¾ in thick. Cut outside shape first. Cut out inside section.

2   Use drum sander and sand the center of fenders leaving a ridge on the edge to form the ⅛ in raised edging on fender.

3   To finish the fender cut small pieces and glue (5-minute epoxy) to form the ridges on

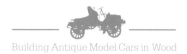

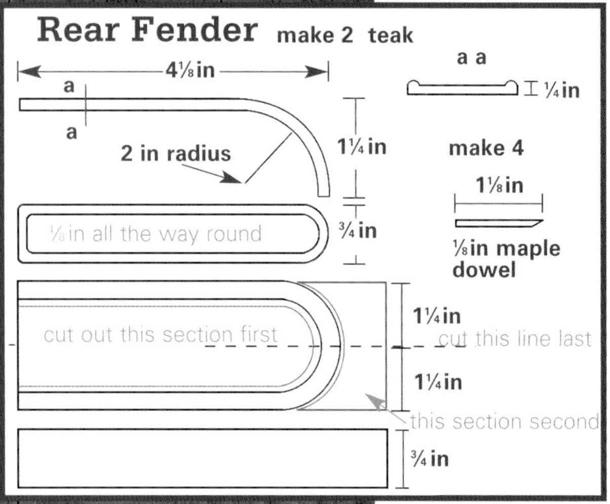
Rear Fender make 2 teak
4 1/8 in
a
a
2 in radius
1 1/4 in
3/4 in
1/8 in all the way round
a a
1/4 in
make 4
1 1/8 in
1/8 in maple dowel
cut out this section first
1 1/4 in
cut this line last
1 1/4 in
this section second
3/4 in

ends of fenders, then sand to shape. *Note* These fenders can also be made in the same manner as fenders for the Ford Model A.

4 To mount fender to car use 4 pieces of 1/8 in maple dowel, 1 1/8 in long. Sand smooth and set aside for final assembly.

Making Front Axle

1 Cut 1/4 in thick mahogany. Drill 1/8 in hole in center of axle. See diagram.
2 Sand round using dremel with drum sander. *Note* Only part of axle really round is the ends of axle where front wheels will be mounted. Use 1/4 in nut as guide for checking roundness of axle by sliding nut onto axle.

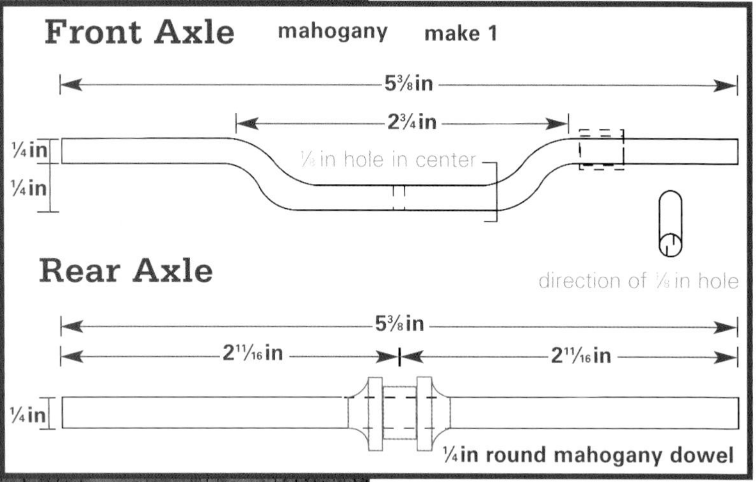
Front Axle mahogany make 1
5 3/8 in
2 3/4 in
1/4 in
1/4 in
1/8 in hole in center
direction of 1/8 in hole
Rear Axle
5 3/8 in
2 11/16 in
2 11/16 in
1/4 in
1/4 in round mahogany dowel

Front Torsion Bar

1 Use 1/8 in maple dowel 8 in long. Cut in half to make 2 pieces 4 in long. Make mounting rings with 5/16 in maple dowel, as shown on diagram.
2 Make rings with 3/8 in maple dowel and drill 1/4 in hole first, deep enough to get 2 pieces 1/4 in long after cutting them to length. Check to see pieces will slide onto front axle all the way up to the curved part. If they don't fit, sand the front axle until they do.
3 Using belt sander, spin dowel on belt by hand, and sand to finished size. This is easier than drilling 5/16 dowel with a 1/4 in drill bit, also 5/16 in dowels are difficult to find. Set parts aside for final assembly.

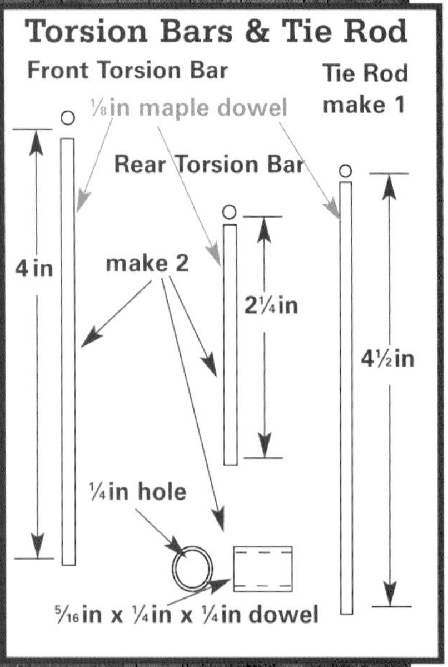
Torsion Bars & Tie Rod
Front Torsion Bar
1/8 in maple dowel
Tie Rod
make 1
Rear Torsion Bar
4 in
make 2
2 1/4 in
4 1/2 in
1/4 in hole
5/16 in x 1/4 in x 1/4 in dowel

Rear Torsion Bar and Tie Rod

Make these parts from 1/8 in maple dowel cut longer than needed to be trimmed on final assembly.

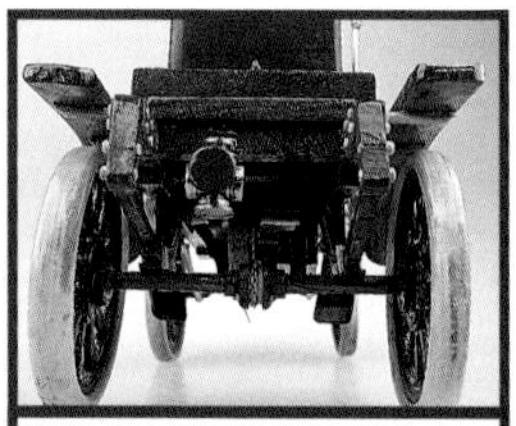
Underside of rear axle & rear light

Making Rear Axle

1 Cut axle from 1/4 in mahogany dowel to length, as shown.
2 Cut maple spacer from 1/2 in dowel 1/4 in long. Drill 1/4 in hole through it.
3 Cut two mahogany parts shown on diagram from 5/8 in diameter dowel. Drill 1/4 in hole through center of dowel. *Note* Build these pieces as one, drill hole and then cut piece into two.
4 Glue axle assembly together, as shown. Place axle assemble into drill press and spin at slowest speed. File parts to shape with small round needle file.
5 Sand axle while still turning in the drill press or do this in small lathe.

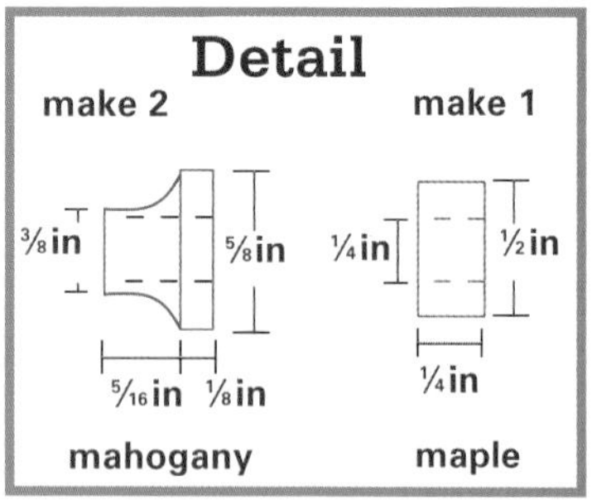
Detail
make 2
make 1
3/8 in
5/8 in
1/4 in
1/2 in
5/16 in
1/8 in
1/4 in
mahogany
maple

1905 Cadillac

Making Engine Block

1. Cut main block from teak ⅛ in larger than diagram dimensions.
2. Cut African blackwood and maple pieces to dimensions given on diagram. Glue (5-minute epoxy) them to block in proper order, as shown.
3. Draw end view onto piece of cardboard to make a pattern, and trace pattern onto end of block.
4. Use band or scroll saw to cut block to shape. Leave line so piece can be sanded to final size that fits the curve of pattern using drill press with drum sander.
5. Make pattern of front grill from cardboard and fit to front of engine block. Adjust pattern to get proper fit. Trace pattern onto African blackwood ⅛ in thick.
6. Cut out starting with inside square, keeping corners sharp. Then cut outside edge off grill leaving line showing. Glue (5-minute epoxy) this to front of block, as shown, making sure curved edges line up. Allow to dry.
7. Sand piece to same contour as engine block using drum sander in drill press, keeping edges sharp.
8. Make grill by first cutting maple ⅛ in sq and long enough to go all the way around inside edge of square cut-out. Make corner cuts 45° angle. Test fit pieces as they are cut out. Glue (sparingly, do not ooze) all pieces in place.
9. Make grill strips from African blackwood strips cut to fit inside maple frame. Cut strips ³⁄₁₆ in thick and wide enough to get 4 or 5 strips inside maple frame. Round off edges the full length as shown on profile view of grill. Glue with 5-minute epoxy. Allow to dry.
10. Use dremel with fine saw blade to cut grooves through strips to look like fine cooling fins. Do not cut into maple frame when doing this.
11. Cut hatch top of engine block from teak. Glue hatch to top of engine block. The piece can be a little thicker and then sanded to proper thickness.
12. Hinge is made from ¹⁄₁₆ in sq teak and glued to backside of hatch which is on dash side of door. Glue hinge on after sanding hatch to proper thickness.
13. Add knob to front edge of hatch and license plate (number is the year I built the car) to bottom edge center of grill, keeping license plate in center of grill.
14. Side vents are placed on the side where they will sit flat and have ⅛ in gap between them. Start ¼ in from dash side of engine block, as shown. Located in same place on both sides of engine block. Set engine block aside for final assembly.

Making the Dash

1. Cut piece of teak 3¼ in x 2¼ in x ⅛ in that has an even grain.
2. Round top corners on belt sander and drill four ¹⁄₁₆ in holes into edge of dash, by hand (less likely to split wood) ¼ in deep into dash using pin vice to hold drill bit.
3. Bend ends of ¹⁄₁₆ in brass rod, as shown. Ends should fit into holes drilled into edge of dash, as shown. *Note Bend one end first and place into one of the holes. Hold* other end with needle nose pliers, align it with hole, and bend rod to fit into next hole. Repeat this procedure on second rail on opposite side of dash.

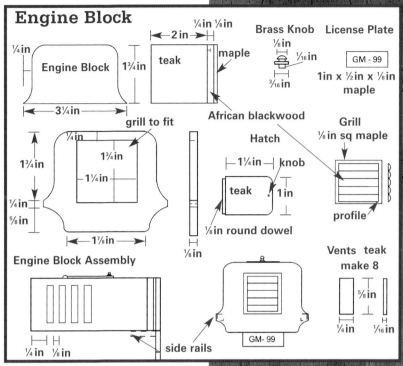

Making Cylinder

1. Build cylinder assembly as shown on diagram.
2. Cylinder body is made from ½ in maple dowel ⅛ in thick with a teak disk ½ in diameter and ⅛ in thick glued (5 minute epoxy) to top also.

Note This assembly is built only as a reminder that the real car had a single cylinder engine. It has nothing to with the real car and is not an item that is seen when on display.

Cylinder

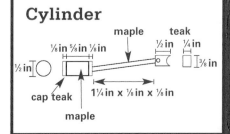

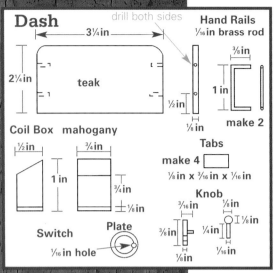

Dash

drill both sides

Hand Rails
1/16 in brass rod

3 1/4 in

2 1/4 in

teak

3/8 in

1 in

1/2 in

1/8 in

make 2

Coil Box mahogany

1/2 in

3/4 in

1 in

3/4 in

1/8 in

Tabs

make 4
1/8 in x 3/16 in x 1/16 in

Knob

Switch

3/16 in

1/8 in

Plate

1/16 in hole

3/8 in

1/4 in

1/8 in

1 1/8 in

1/8 in

1/16 in

4. In band saw cut solid piece of mahogany 1 in x 1/2 in x 3/4 in for coil box. Also cut groove 1/8 in from bottom of coil box all around box.

5. Cut out 4 tabs from piece of mahogany, as shown. Set aside for assembly.

6. Make switch from brass rod 3/8 in diameter, machined to shape, as shown. Machine beginning with the small diameter.

7. Build knob from piece of 1/8 in diameter brass rod using same method as building knobs for the Mercedes Engine block diagram p60.

8. Drill small hole in switch plate, as shown and place knob into hole. Solder in place.

9. See dash layout diagram to begin to assemble parts to dash. Drill hole in coil box to mount switch. Hole is same diameter as small pin machined on switch plate. Smaller tabs are used to resemble mounting tabs for coil box. Set aside for final assembly.

Making Front Fenders

1. Use 2 pieces of teak 2 3/4 in sq x 3/4 in thick with even grain for both fenders.

2. First 2 cuts are straight, as shown.

3. Set band saw table to 45° angle. Make outside cut first starting 5/8 in down from top edge from same side as first cuts made.

4. For inside curve, start saw at top beside cut out piece. The curve will start in from edge far from straight cut, as shown. This is done because sloping cut cannot match the straight cut.

5. Cut far enough away from straight cut so this cut will not cut into straight cut. Remove curved part from block of wood by placing large drum sander in drill press and sanding inside curve until it matches straight cut. Fender should be 3/16 in thick after sanding.

6. Sand outside curve of fender to blend in with straight cut. *Note* When making opposite fender start cutting from bottom of fender towards top. Try cutting a piece of scrap wood first. This will help to get piece right and can be test fitted to car to ensure fit.

Dash Layout

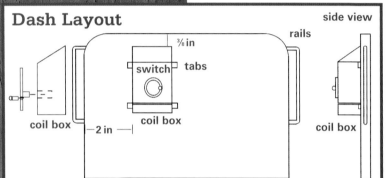

side view

rails

3/8 in

switch

tabs

coil box

coil box

2 in

coil box

coil box

Front Fender fenders have compound curves

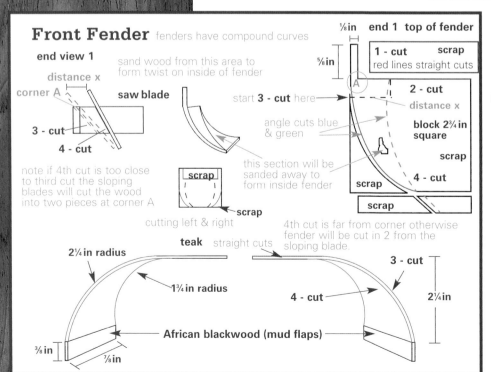

end view 1

distance x

corner A

saw blade

3 - cut

4 - cut

note if 4th cut is too close to third cut the sloping blades will cut the wood into two pieces at corner A

scrap

cutting left & right

scrap

start **3 - cut** here

angle cuts blue & green

this section will be sanded away to form inside fender

1/8 in   **end 1   top of fender**

5/8 in

1 - cut   scrap
red lines straight cuts

A

2 - cut

distance x

block 2 3/4 in square

scrap

4 - cut

scrap

scrap

4th cut is far from corner otherwise fender will be cut in 2 from the sloping blade.

teak   straight cuts

2 1/4 in radius

1 3/4 in radius

3 - cut

4 - cut

2 1/4 in

3/8 in

7/8 in

African blackwood (mud flaps)

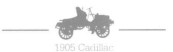

Steering Wheel and Horn

Build steering wheel and horn same way as the Model A Ford (p54) using dimensions shown on diagram at right. Fit remaining parts to this dimension. Steering wheel assembly is built with same dimensions and method as Model A Ford. Horn also built same way as Ford instructions. The assembly of steering column is the same also.

Steering Wheel

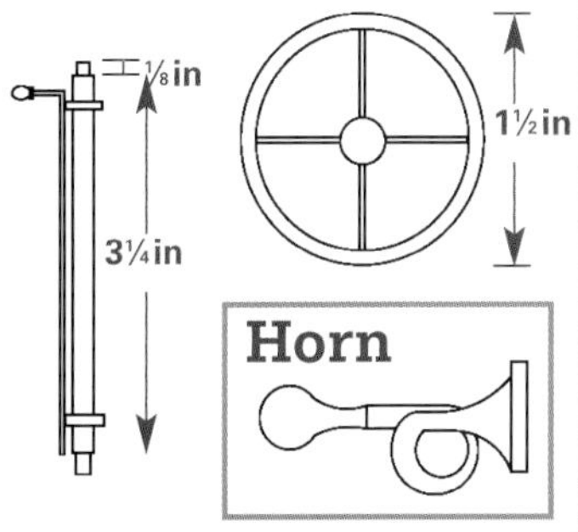
1/8 in
3 1/4 in
1 1/2 in
Horn

Making Gas Generator

1 Make body from 5/8 in diameter brass rod. Begin machining with 1/2 in diameter first. Then turn piece in lathe and machine 3/8 in diameter next.
2 Drill five 1/16 in diameter holes, as shown in diagram. Number 1 will be used to mount generator part to car and number 2 to attach plastic gas line. Three holes 1/8 in deep located in top are used for mounting 3 different knobs.
3 Knobs are machined from 1/8 in diameter brass rod the same as knobs for coil box switch (p38). Make from one piece, separating them as they are made.
4 Place knobs into proper holes lettered on diagram.
5 Place 1/16 in brass rods into the other 2 holes 1/2 in long.
6 Solder all knobs and rods into place. The knob marked b should protrude past all other knobs. Polish with wire wheel in dremel and set aside for final assembly.

Gas Generator

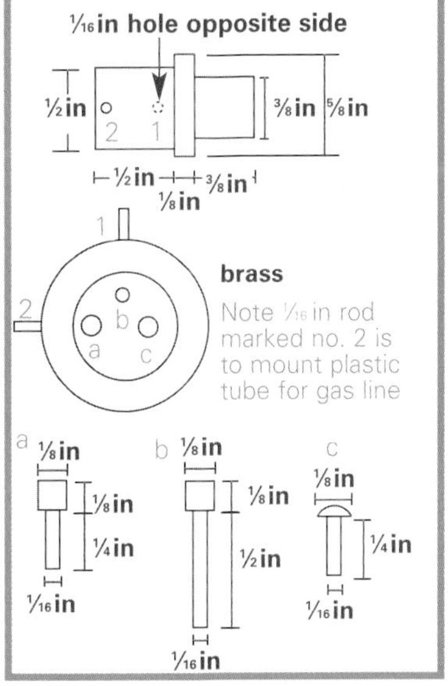
1/16 in hole opposite side
1/2 in
3/8 in
5/8 in
1/2 in
3/8 in
1/8 in
brass
Note 1/16 in rod marked no. 2 is to mount plastic tube for gas line
a 1/8 in
1/8 in
1/4 in
1/16 in
b 1/8 in
1/8 in
1/2 in
1/16 in
c 1/8 in
1/4 in
1/16 in

Making Shift Lever

1 Machine 1/8 in diameter brass rod on one end, as shown. Handle is mounted here.
2 Machine handle from 3/16 in diameter rod using same method as building knob for switch on coil box (p38). Dimensions shown on shift lever diagram. Make 2. The second one is for the brake lever.
3 Solder to brass rod and make bend at end of rod with pliers.
4 Machine small guide plate, shown on diagram
5 Flatten handle by same method used on levers of the Mercedes. Do not flatten rod. Set aside for final assembly.

Shift Lever

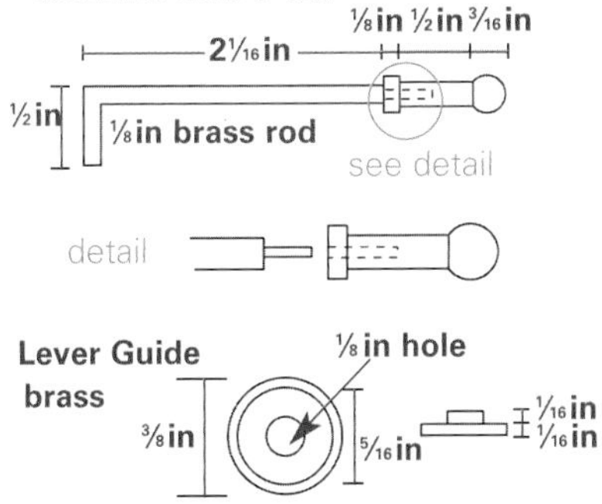
1/8 in 1/2 in 3/16 in
2 1/16 in
1/2 in
1/8 in brass rod
see detail
detail
Lever Guide brass
1/8 in hole
3/8 in
5/16 in
1/16 in
1/16 in

Brake Lever

same detail as above

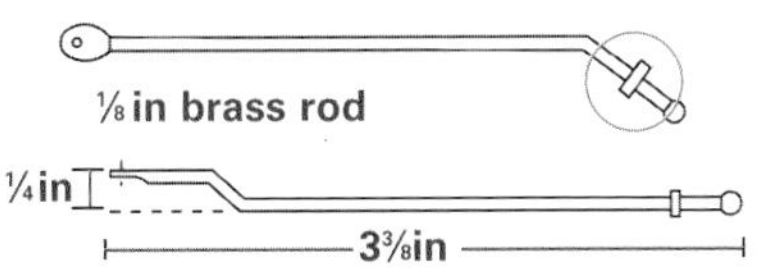
1/8 in brass rod
1/4 in
3 3/8 in

Making Brake Lever

1 Machine brass rod as for shift lever. Also for the handle. The difference is length of rod and number of bends required. *Note* Flatten on end with a hammer and drill hole to fit a tack pin.
2 Solder handle to lever and flatten handle the same as for shift lever. Overall length is not critical and can vary ± 1/8 in. Set aside for final assembly.

Fuel Tank

1 Use piece of teak cut to shape, as shown. Curve on one of the mounts should match diameter of rear axle.
2 Drill hole into piece of teak that matches axle diameter, then cut part way around this hole. Build remaining parts as shown on diagram.
3 Place mount with curve on end of tank opposite grooved end.
4 Mount on side can be glued 1/2 in from end.

Note Glue mount on proper side of tank, as shown on end view.

Fuel Tank make 1 teak

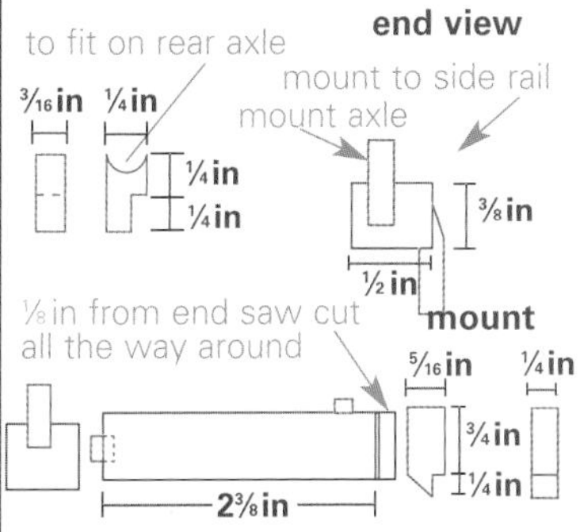
to fit on rear axle
end view
mount to side rail
mount axle
3/16 in
1/4 in
1/4 in
1/4 in
3/8 in
1/2 in
1/8 in from end saw cut all the way around
mount
5/16 in
1/4 in
3/4 in
1/4 in
2 3/8 in

Building Antique Model Cars in Wood

Radiator & lamps

Making Lamps

1. Build main lamp body from piece of ⅞ in brass rod and machine to resemble diagram. *Note* Body can also be made from individual pieces, machining back plate and front ring, then attaching them to a ⅝ in diameter brass tube.
2. Mark seven No. 68 holes on front ring with a pencil and drill by hand deep enough to make a mark in the face of ring to represent screws on the real lamp.
3. On body make four 1/16 in holes and one ⅛ in hole, as shown. The ⅛ in hole is for main mounting rod made from ⅛ in brass rod bent to 90° angle, as shown.
4. Flatten ⅛ in brass tube on one end and drill 2 holes into the flat end large enough for tack pins. Slide this tube onto mounting rod on the long side. *Note* See assembly diagram for directions to mount tubes to ⅛ in brass rod.
5. Knobs are machined from ⅛ in diameter brass rod. Make 5, one for taillight. Make taillight lens, p53.
6. Form 1/16 in brass rod to shape, as shown on parts diagram, to fit between mounting rod and main lamp body. Check diagram.
7. Build taillight in same manner as the Model A Ford (p53). Machine parts as shown on diagram starting with the ⅜ in brass rod.
8. Make ¼ in hole through center and cut 2 small grooves on each end.
9. Drill 1/16 in hole in same direction as ¼ in hole on one end. Used to hold knob. Make lens, p52.
10. Drill 1/16 in diameter hole through the brass, through drilled ¼ in hole. This 1/16 in hole will be used to mount lens assembly and mounting rod to light.
11. Make mounting plate by drilling required holes into piece of brass shim stock. Then cut to size. Center hole should be 1/16 in diameter and 2 outside holes are large enough for tack pins.
12. Slide mounting plate onto mounting rod leaving rod protruding through mounting plate ¼ in. See diagram.
13. Solder all parts together, polish with dremel and wire brush and glue lens in place. Set aside for final assembly.

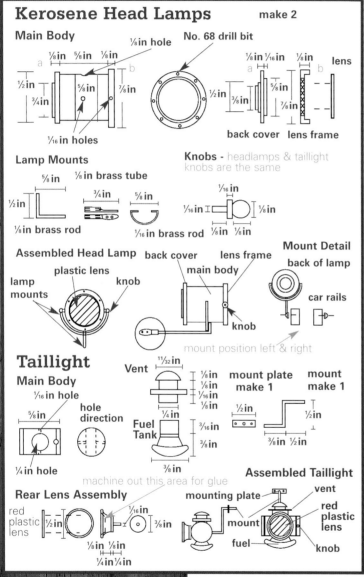

Kerosene Head Lamps make 2

Main Body

⅛in hole No. 68 drill bit lens

⅛in ⅝in ⅛in a b
a b
½in ⅛in 1/16in ⅛in
¾in ⅞in ½in ⅜in ⅝in
⅞in
1/16 in holes back cover lens frame

Lamp Mounts Knobs - headlamps & taillight knobs are the same

⅝ in ⅛ in brass tube 1/16 in
½in ¾ in ⅝ in 1/16 in I ⅛ in
⅛in brass rod 1/16 in brass rod ⅛in ⅛in

Assembled Head Lamp back cover lens frame Mount Detail back of lamp

lamp mounts plastic lens main body knob car rails

knob mount position left & right

Taillight Vent 11/32 in mount plate make 1 mount make 1

Main Body
1/16 in hole ⅛in ⅛in 1/16in ⅛in
⅝ in hole direction ¼ in ½in ½in
Fuel Tank 3/16 in ⅜in ½in
¼ in hole ⅜ in ⅜ in

machine out this area for glue Assembled Taillight

Rear Lens Assembly mounting plate vent
red plastic lens ½in 1/16 in ⅜in mount red plastic lens
⅛in ⅛in fuel knob
¼in ¼in

Chassis Assembly

1. Slide flywheel onto drive axle. Make sure pulley with groove is on same side as shown. *Do not glue flywheel to axle.* It will move along axle so drive chain can line up with rear wheel axle.
2. Slide front spring into square holes located at front end of rails. Ensure small blocks on side rail are on proper side of rail, as shown and slide drive axle into drilled ⅜ in side rail holes.
3. Place cross member on back of rails between rails.
4. Ensure chassis is 3¼ in wide. Then take apart and glue (5-minute epoxy) all parts. Put back together.

Rear underside of rear axle & rear light

5 Check width. Before glue dries turn chassis over and glue engine block in place, ensure front of rails are against back of grill.

6 Add cover plates over square holes where front spring was placed. Fill hole with glue behind cover plate. Set aside and dry overnight.

Undercarriage Assembly

1 Glue (5-minute epoxy) rear axle in place. Make sure it protrudes same distance on both sides of rails and is proper distance from back of car measured from end of rail where spring mounts start to protrude out from rail. Allow to dry.

2 Line up flywheel with rear axle by aligning 2 pulleys with grooves in a straight line. Mark location of flywheel on axle with a pencil, slide axle out of the way, add glue, and slide back into place. Allow to dry.

3 Add cross member to hold cylinder head in place. Place other end of assembly against drive axle. Now place cross member at end of cylinder head against member. Mark on rail where cross member lines up. Add glue to parts, and replace back into chassis.

4 Glue fuel tank to undercarriage which rests on rear axle. Other mount should go against inside of chassis rail, as shown.

5 Add rear wheels to rear axle leaving axle protruding $1/16$ in from wheel hub. Place $1/8$ in dowel in rear hole on front spring leaving it protruding $1/2$ in from bottom of spring.

6 Hold front axle and slide torsion bar rings into place. Place front wheels onto axle. Place axle over $1/8$ in dowel protruding out of spring and place $1/8$ in dowel into drilled hole in front axle.

7 Check fit of axle onto chassis. Add glue to parts and replace. Before glue dries turn car over and let car level itself on wheels. Leave in this position until glue dries.

8 Turn assembly back over and add tie rod and trim to fit between front wheels against hubs on both wheels.

9 Add torsion bars which go from small blocks to rings on front axle. Trim bars to fit and lightly sand one end round so they will rest on the rings.

10 Rear torsion bars go from axle where the rear spring meets the axle. Glue other end to inside of chassis rail. Distance between these 2 points is not critical.

11 Turn back over and glue floorboard in place against dash and flush with top edge of rails. Should just fit between flywheel and dash. If not, make a small notch to clear flywheel and glue in place with 5-minute epoxy

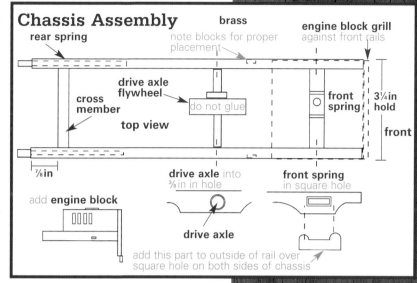

Chassis Assembly

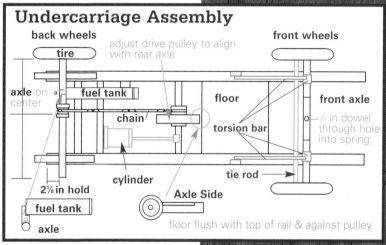

Undercarriage Assembly

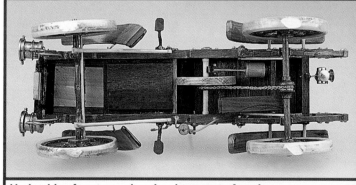

Underside of parts on chassis, placement of engine

Main Body Assembly

1. Fit body side panels onto rails and place side rails into rabbet joint of side panel. Front end of side panel goes against dash.

2. At other end of side panel, glue cross members to finish back. Add under seat panel between body side panels. Dry.

3. Trim pedal board to make a tight fit. Glue. *Note* Trim side that is opposite to pedals and steering wheel to keep them the correct distance from edge.

4. Rear hatch cover top should be flush with edge of body panels when placed in rabbet joints. Add seat assembly, as shown, keeping it even with both sides of car.

5. Mark 2 holes on front rail and drill holes with drill and pin vice same size as holes in light mounts. Glue tack pins through mounts of lights into drilled holes. Repeat for opposite light.

6. To add taillight, drill $\frac{1}{16}$ in hole through cross member of chassis $1\frac{1}{4}$ in from rail on passenger side of car. Place taillight mount in hole up to mounting plate. Make 2 holes with same drill through cross member.

7. Place 2 tack pins through holes in mounting plate and glue to cross member.

8. Add gas generator 3 in back from dash on driver's side. Drill $\frac{1}{16}$ in hole into car side rail and glue generator-mounting rod into this hole. Dry.

9. Place orange plastic hose for gas line (use piece of electrical wire with wire removed) over other $\frac{1}{16}$ in rod and glue other end of hose to underside of car.

10. Add shift lever and brake lever (on driver's side). See diagram and drill holes to mount these levers to car. The lever closest to bottom of seat is the shift lever.

11. Glue entrance steps (see diagram) to chassis side rails, under edge of body panels.

12. Drill 2 holes (see diagram) and place mounts into holes. Glue rear fenders to mounts.

13. Place front fenders behind wheel and mark locations of holes, as shown. Mount fenders to car with $\frac{1}{16}$ in brass rod. Drill $\frac{1}{16}$ in hole in edge of fender, then bend rods so that when mounted to car it will leave $\frac{1}{4}$ in gap between fender and tire. Take your time. Don't bend rods while in the fender. Keep removing rods from fender until right shape is formed. Drill holes into car to match placement of fender, then glue fenders in place. Add steering wheel and align (see Model A Ford, p55, 56).

14. Place floor mats as shown, Clean off excess glue. Apply 3 coats of gloss finish.

Steering & horn, dash & floor board for brake pedals

Levers, generator, side step, front fender

Main Body Assembly

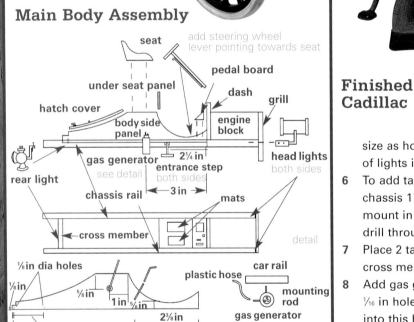

seat

add steering wheel lever pointing towards seat

pedal board

under seat panel

dash

grill

hatch cover

body side panel

engine block

head lights
both sides

gas generator
see detail

$2\frac{1}{4}$ in

entrance step
both sides

rear light

chassis rail

3 in

mats

cross member

detail

$\frac{1}{8}$ in dia holes

$\frac{1}{8}$ in

$\frac{5}{8}$ in

1 in $\frac{5}{8}$ in

$\frac{3}{16}$ in $1\frac{3}{8}$ in

$2\frac{3}{8}$ in

car rail

plastic hose

mounting rod

gas generator

Finished Cadillac

Steering wheel & horn, dash & floor board for brake pedals

1903

Ford Model A

Henry Ford was a technological genius and a folk hero, and he was the creative force behind the automobile industry that changed the economic and social character of the United States. In his first years he was associated with different companies and built several racing cars but by 1903 he was ready to market an automobile through his Ford Motor Company in Detroit which was incorporated with $28,000 cash put up by ordinary citizens. The Model A Ford Runabout, sometimes called the Sidewinder because of the side crank, was launched in July 1903 and was an instant money-maker. The first car was sold to a Chicago dentist for $850 and Henry Ford earned enough from sales to pay 10 percent of the dividends at the end of the year. This simple, light, right-hand-drive automobile was highly efficient. It had a 2-cylinder opposed engine that could develop 8 hp at 10,000 rpm and a planetary transmission with two forward speeds. The car ran on a 72-inch wheel base with wooden wheels. The more expensive deluxe model had a removable tonneau which sat two passengers in the back above the engine. The other model without the back seat, pictured here, cost $750. The car rode high off the ground because it had to travel over old rutted wagon trails which it shared with horse and buggy drivers.

In 1904 Ford made the Model F, Models C, D, E in 1905, and Model N in 1906 which was the forerunner to the Model T which appeared in 1908. In 1927 the Model A was modified and reintroduced but it was outsold by other companies and was discontinued in 1931.

Car Pieces

This car can be built with or without the engine. The option not to show the engine makes it easier to construct, takes less time, and certainly does not detract from the overall appearance of the car. I have included engine instructions for those who wish to make it.

Car Parts List

Car Part	Material	Size	Pieces
Wheels	bloodwood	13 in x 3 in x ¼ in	1
	African blackwood	12 in x 3 in x ⅜ in	1
	black electrical wire	¹⁄₁₆ in dia 2 in long	1
Hubs	African blackwood	⅝ in round ¹⁄₁₆ in thick	8
Body Side Pieces	bloodwood	10 in x 2¼ in x ¼ in	1
Front Dash Block	bloodwood	2¹¹⁄₁₆ in x 1¼ in x 1¾ in	1
Entrance Trim	African blackwood	2¾ in x 2⅞ in x ³⁄₁₆ in	2
Chassis	oak	¼ in square 8¾ in long	2
	oak	¼ in x ⅛ in 14 in long	1
Floor Board	mahogany	2¾ in x 2⅞ in x ³⁄₁₆ in	1
Front Dash	bloodwood	¾ in x 1⅛ in x ¹⁄₃₂ in	2
	bloodwood triangle	1¼ in x ¼ in x 3 in	1
	brass tube	³⁄₃₂ in x 2½ in long	1
	brass rod	¹⁄₁₆ in x ½ in long	2
Under Seat Panel	bloodwood	2⅞ in x 1¾ in x ¼ in	1
	bloodwood	2¼ in x ¾ in x ¹⁄₃₂ in	1
	bloodwood	2¼ in x ½ in x ¹⁄₃₂ in	1
	bloodwood dowel	⅛ in x ¼ in long	2
	African blackwood	dowel ⅛ in x ⅛ in long	2
Rear Panel Trim	African blackwood	⅛ in square 14 in long	1
Engine Hatch	bloodwood	4 in x 3 in x ¼ in	1
	brass hinge	small	2
Pedals	African blackwood	2 in x 3 in x ⅛ in	1
Entrance Step	African blackwood	2 in x 1 in x ¼ in	1
	African blackwood	½ in x ½ in x ⅛ in	1
Radiator	African blackwood	½ in x ½ in x 2 in	1
	brass shim stock	½ in x ½ in	2
	brass pins	½ in long	8
Front Springs	bloodwood	3 in x 1¼ in x ½ in	1
	African blackwood	dowel ⅛ in x ¼ in long	4
Rear Springs	bloodwood	3½ in x 1½ in x ½ in	1
	African blackwood	dowel ⅛ in x ¼ in long	2
	African blackwood	dowel ⅛ in x ½ in long	4
Seat	bloodwood	3¾ in x 2 in x 1¾ in	1
	mahogany	3¾ in x 2 in x ⅛ in	1
	African blackwood	¼ in x ³⁄₁₆ in x ⅛ in	12
	African blackwood	1½ in x 1¼ in x ⅛ in	2
	brass rod	¹⁄₁₆ in x 6 in long	1
Front Fenders	African blackwood	4¼ in x 1⅜ in x 2¼ in	1
	African blackwood	³⁄₁₆ in x ³⁄₁₆ in x ½ in	4
Back Fenders	brass rod	¹⁄₁₆ in x ¾ in long	4
	African blackwood	4 in x 2¼ in x ¾ in	2
	brass rod	¹⁄₁₆ in x 2 in long	1

Car Part	Material	Size	Pieces
Front Axle	bloodwood dowel	¼ in x 6½ in long	1
	bloodwood	½ in x ½ in x 4 in	1
	African blackwood	dowel ⅛ in x ⅛ in long	4
Rear Axle	bloodwood dowel	¼ in x 6½ in long	1
	bloodwood dowel	½ in x ¼ in long	2
	bloodwood dowel	⅝ in x ¼ in long	2
	African blackwood	½ in x ¼ in long	1
Mounting Block	bloodwood	2 in x 3 in x ⁵⁄₁₆ in	1
Tie Rod	bloodwood dowel	¹⁄₁₆ in x 9 in long	1
Engine Optional	mahogany	sizes from drawing	
	walnut / maple		
	African blackwood		
Steering Wheel	brass I.D. tube	⅛ in x 4⅛ in long	1
	brass tube	³⁄₁₆ in long to fit over above tube	2
	brass rod	³⁄₁₆ in x 3⅜ in long	1
	brass rod	⁵⁄₁₆ in x ½ in long	1
	brass rod	⅛ in x ¼ in long	1
	brass rod	¹⁄₁₆ in x ⅝ in long	4
	walnut dowel	1½ in x 2 in long	1
Head Lamp	brass rod	¾ in x ¾ in long	1
	brass rod	½ in x ¼ in long	1
	brass tube	⅜ in	1
	brass rod	¹⁄₁₆ in x 4 in long	1
	plastic clear	⅝ in round disk	1
Side Lamp	brass rod	¾ in x ⅞ in long	2
	brass rod	½ in x ½ in long	2
	brass rod	½ in x ³⁄₁₆ in long	2
	brass tube	¼ in x ¾ in long	2
	brass rod	¹⁄₁₆ in x 8 in long	1
	plastic clear	⅝ in diameter	2
Taillight	brass rod	½ in x ½ in long	1
	brass rod	⅜ in x ⅜ in long	1
	brass rod	⅜ in x 1 in long	1
	brass rod	⁵⁄₁₆ in x ³⁄₁₆ in long	1
	brass rod	¹⁄₁₆ in x 2 in long	1
	plastic clear	⅜ in diameter	1
Break Lever	brass tube	³⁄₃₂ in x 1⅜ in long	1
Crank	brass rod	⅛ in x 1¾ in long	1
	brass eyelets	⅛ in diameter inside	2
Front Dash Rail	brass rod	¹⁄₁₆ in x 10 in long	1
Horn	brass rod	⅛ in x 5 in long	1
	brass rod	⅜ in x ¼ in long	1
	African blackwood	dowel ⅜ in x ½ in long	1

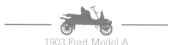

Making Wheels

Make the wheel assembly as given on p11, using dimensions at right.

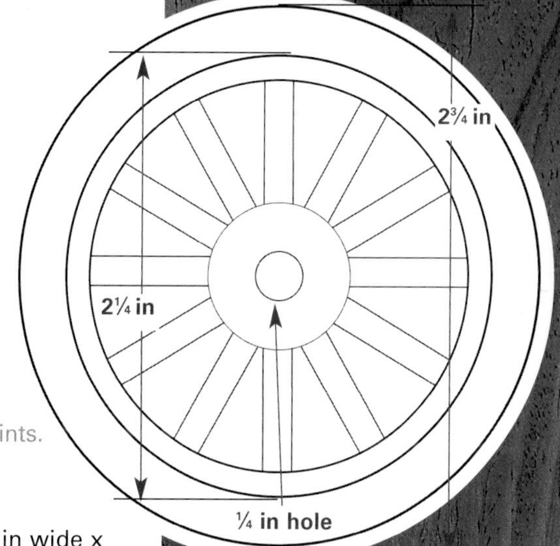
$2\frac{3}{4}$ in
$2\frac{1}{4}$ in
$\frac{1}{4}$ in hole

Making Body Sides

1. Use 2 pieces of bloodwood 10 in x $2\frac{1}{4}$ in x $\frac{1}{4}$ in thick with lengthwise grain.
2. Glue pieces together (white carpenter's glue) with heavy sheet of paper between so they can be separated after cutting.
3. Transfer (p5) pattern to wood and cut out with band or scroll saw.
4. Separate pieces and mark R and L on inside. Make rabbet joint (p32) $\frac{1}{4}$ in deep and $\frac{1}{8}$ in wide along edges, as shown.
5. Mark another rabbet joint $\frac{1}{8}$ in deep and $\frac{1}{8}$ in wide (see pattern). Cut. *Note* Experienced woodworkers can use a router to make the bloodwood rabbet joints.
6. Save cut-out entrance piece A to make the pattern for trim on entrance. *Note* Pattern shows location of floor and panel under seat mount on p46.
7. Glue bloodwood pieces together to make front dash block $2\frac{11}{16}$ in long x $1\frac{1}{4}$ in wide x $1\frac{3}{4}$ in high. Check grain direction.

Main Body Side Panel Pattern half size

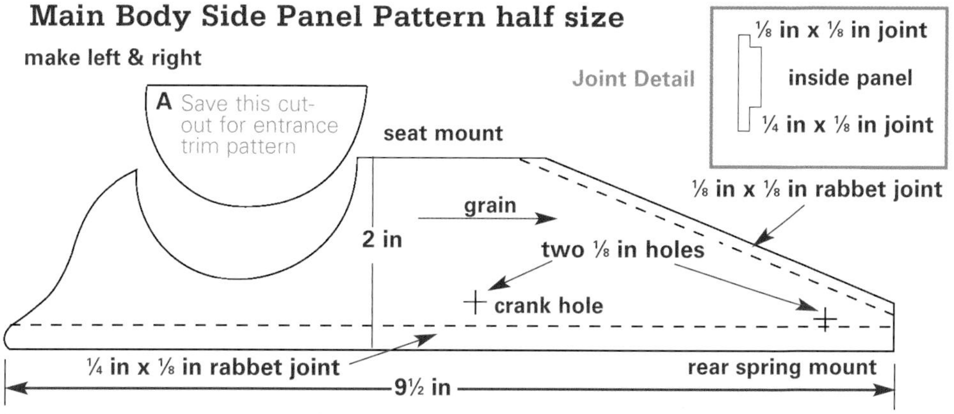
make left & right
A Save this cut-out for entrance trim pattern
seat mount
Joint Detail
$\frac{1}{8}$ in x $\frac{1}{8}$ in joint
inside panel
$\frac{1}{4}$ in x $\frac{1}{8}$ in joint
$\frac{1}{8}$ in x $\frac{1}{8}$ in rabbet joint
grain
2 in
two $\frac{1}{8}$ in holes
crank hole
$\frac{1}{4}$ in x $\frac{1}{8}$ in rabbet joint
rear spring mount
$9\frac{1}{2}$ in

Making the Chassis

1. Use 2 pieces $\frac{1}{4}$ in sq oak $8\frac{3}{4}$ in long for outside stringers. Use oak $\frac{1}{4}$ in x $\frac{1}{8}$ in x 14 in long to be cut for cross members.
2. Make a drawing to size and place $8\frac{3}{4}$ in pieces in place on drawing to mark notches.
3. Cut out notches with hand or scroll saw so cross pieces will fit tightly. On final assembly this part must be square and flat to keep wheels level. *Note* To ensure this, pin pieces to a ceiling tile with wax paper between wood and tile. Use 24-hour epoxy.

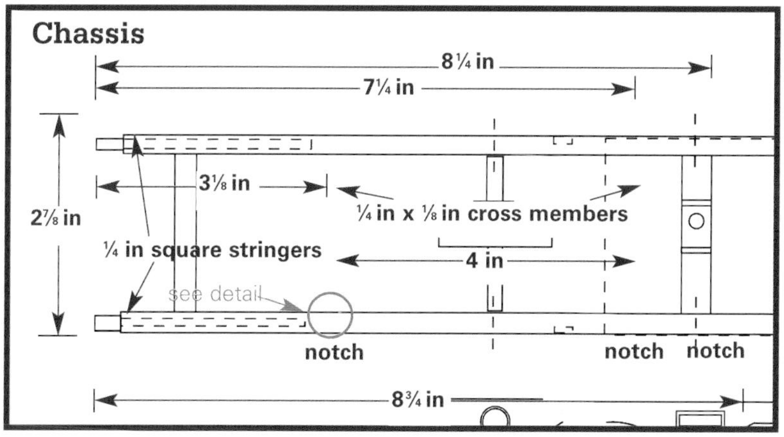
Chassis
$8\frac{1}{4}$ in
$7\frac{1}{4}$ in
$3\frac{1}{8}$ in
$\frac{1}{4}$ in x $\frac{1}{8}$ in cross members
$2\frac{7}{8}$ in
$\frac{1}{4}$ in square stringers
4 in
see detail
notch
notch
notch
$8\frac{3}{4}$ in

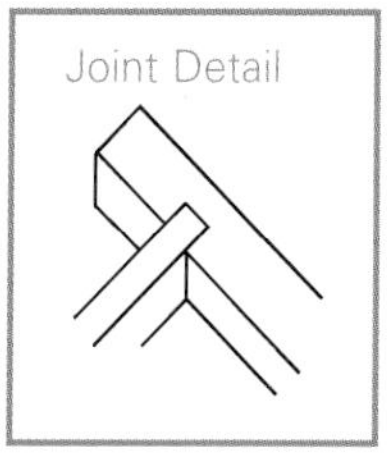
Joint Detail

Making Entrance Trim

1. Using entrance piece A trace curve onto piece of blackwood $\frac{3}{16}$ in thick. *Note* Cover first with masking tape to make traced line visible.
2. Cut along outside of line. Sand to line. Test fit into side piece. Repeat for other side.
3. Cut some of wood from inside of curves for both pieces. Glue (24-hour epoxy) to body sides (as shown).
4. When dry, clamp sides together evenly on all edges. Use dremel tool with small drum sander and sand until a $\frac{1}{8}$ in strip remains around edge, as shown. This is the trim.

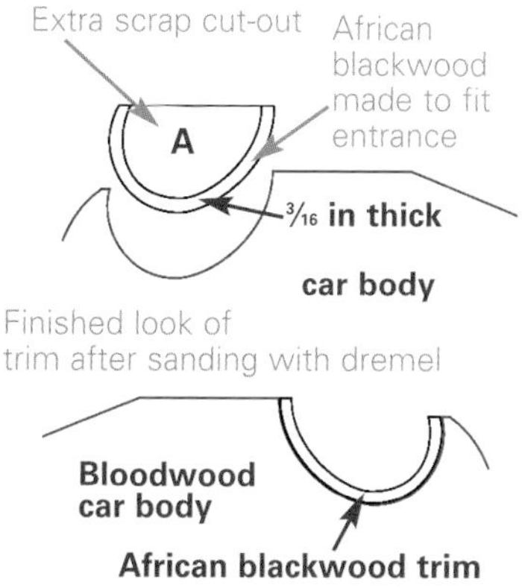
Extra scrap cut-out
African blackwood made to fit entrance
A
$\frac{3}{16}$ in thick
car body
Finished look of trim after sanding with dremel
Bloodwood car body
African blackwood trim

Car Body Assembly

¹⁄₈ in x ¹⁄₈ in rabbet joint

¹⁄₄ in x ¹⁄₈ in rabbet joint

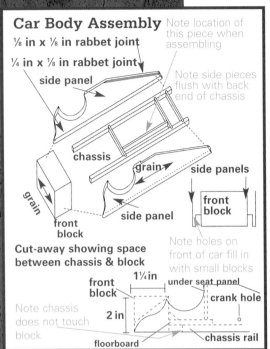

side panel

chassis

grain

side panels

grain

front block

side panel

front block

Note location of this piece when assembling

Note side pieces flush with back end of chassis

front block

Note holes on front of car fill in with small blocks

Cut-away showing space between chassis & block

front block

1¼ in

under seat panel

crank hole

Note chassis does not touch block

2 in

floorboard

chassis rail

Car FloorBoard

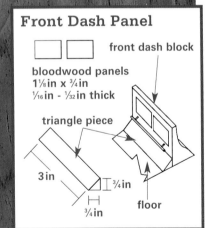

Corner A

¾ in

1⅛ in

¼ in

Corner A

¹⁄₁₆ in

³⁄₈ in

textured

Optional - do not texture square. Use to display an access panel under pedals

mahogany piece
2¾ in x 2⅞ in x ³⁄₁₆ in

Front Dash Panel

front dash block

bloodwood panels
1⅛ in x ¾ in
¹⁄₁₆ in - ¹⁄₃₂ in thick

triangle piece

3 in

¾ in

floor

¾ in

Car Body Assembly

1 Place chassis on work table and fit side pieces and front dash block in rabbet joint along bottom side of car.

2 Glue in place (24-hour epoxy) and clamp (one large clamp across width of car, smaller to clamp chassis along bottom of car towards back). *Note* Put masking tape in clamps to prevent clamp marks on wood.

3 Spread glue on ends of front dash block. Sides on chassis should be flush with back end of chassis and clamp to chassis. Front dash block, jutting past front of car. *Note* Front block sticks out past sides of car. Check joints for proper alignment. Dry completely. *Note* Do not glue any other parts at this time.

4 Trim front dash block, being careful not to cut into side pieces.

5 Place large drum sander into drill press and sand front block to the profile of side pieces. *Note* Keep front block square to drum sander to keep it even with both sides of car body. Run drill press at medium speed and use new 220 - 240 grit sanding drum. Use light pressure so wood won't burn.

Making Car FloorBoard

1 Use a piece of ³⁄₁₆ in thick mahogany that fits between sides of car body and even with front dash and ¼ in past seat mount. Piece should rest on chassis stringers that project from sides of car body.

2 Using dremel tool with ¹⁄₁₆ in cutter, cut 2 small slots for pedals, as shown. This car has right hand drive.

3 Use dremel tool with small ball cutter to dimple surface of floor to give a textured look and glue in place. *Note* Optional - Leave pedal area untextured

Making Front Dash Panel

1 Cut 2 pieces bloodwood ¾ in x 1⅛ in, as thin as possible. Center the 2 pieces of bloodwood on front dash block, mark location, glue.

2 Cut another piece of bloodwood ¾ in x ¾ in, long enough to fit between body side panels resting on floor against front dash block. Cut piece in half to get triangle. Glue as shown with 5-minute epoxy.

Making Brass Rail

1 Use ³⁄₃₂ in outside diameter brass tube 2½ in long. With pin vice and hand drill make 2 holes ¹⁄₁₆ in diameter ¼ in from each end of tube. Align holes and drill through one side of tube only.

2 Into these holes solder 2 pieces of brass rod ¹⁄₁₆ in diameter by ½ in long (used to mount rail to front dash).

Brass Rail

¹⁄₁₆ in holes drilled ¼ in from each end

¼ in

³⁄₃₂ in brass tube
2½ in long

two ³⁄₃₂ in x ½ in brass rods

3 Place rail above triangle piece. Drill holes for mounting pins ¼ in deep in front dash to hold rail in place. Polish rail with brass wire wheel in dremel at medium speed. Clean rail with rubbing alcohol and wipe with clean cloth. *Note* If you touch mounting pins with fingers, glue will not stick to brass. Glue with 5-minute epoxy.

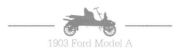

Making Under Seat Panel

1 Use piece of bloodwood ¼ in thick to fit between side pieces and high enough to go from floor to seat mount, as shown at right.
2 Glue the 2 panels to this piece to suggest access doors to engine.
3 Build panels by gluing 2 thick pieces onto the ¼ in piece evenly spaced on all edges with ¼ in between them. Sand to 1/32 in thick on belt or disk sander. Grain must be same direction on all 3 pieces.
4 Cut piece of bloodwood the size of a round toothpick into 2 pieces ¼ in long and glue to bottom edge of top panel to appear as hinges.
5 With drill bit same size as bloodwood toothpick, drill hole in middle of top panel ⅛ in from edge and deep enough to hold ¼ in piece, leaving half it to stick out for the door knob. *Optional* Machine this knob from brass on a small metal lathe. Clean brass with rubbing alcohol before gluing.

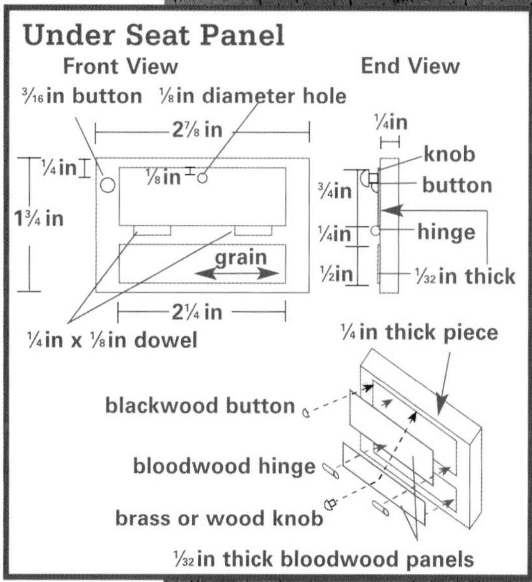
Under Seat Panel
Front View
End View
3/16in button
⅛in diameter hole
2⅞ in
¼in
⅛in
1¾ in
grain
2¼ in
¼in x ⅛in dowel
¼in
knob
button
¾in
¼in
hinge
½in
1/32in thick
¼in thick piece
blackwood button
bloodwood hinge
brass or wood knob
1/32in thick bloodwood panels

Making Radiator Cutout

1 On band saw table place the stop ½ in behind blade measuring from cut side of blade. Cut should be 2¼ in long and ½ in deep across front of car, even from both sides. Make two ½ in cuts, remove stop, and cut across front of car, removing 2¼ in long piece. Radiator will fit into this cutout.

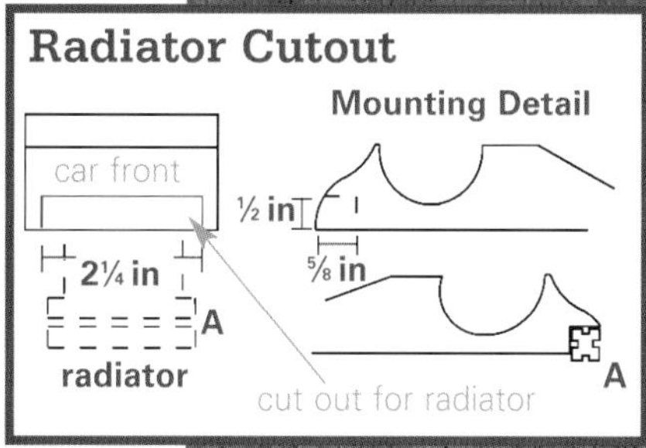
Radiator Cutout
Mounting Detail
car front
½ in
2¼ in
⅝ in
A
radiator
cut out for radiator
A

Making the Engine (Optional)

Note All measurements must be exact so engine will fit into car.

Engine block has four ⅛ in diameter holes drilled in bottom for valve rods. Do not drill holes through block. Diagram shows bottom view of engine block with arrangement of 4 holes in relation to each other and cylinder offsets. Build parts as shown. Engine block - mahogany, bearing block - maple, flywheel - mahogany, lubrication tank - maple, cylinder head - African blackwood, planetary transmission - maple, drain plug - African blackwood, muffler - maple and walnut, drive pulley - African blackwood, valve push rods - bamboo (use barbecue skewer turned on lathe)

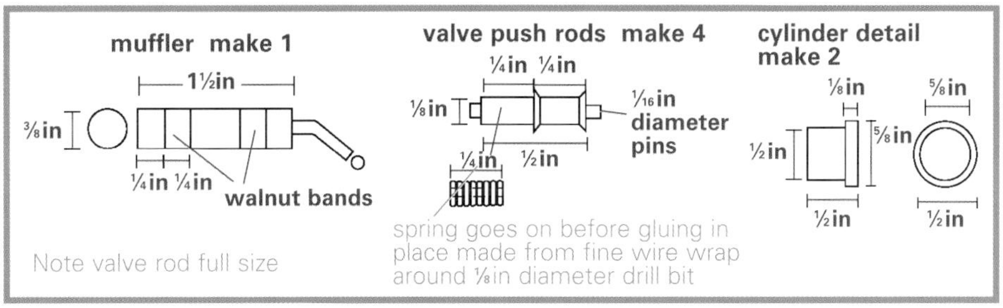
muffler make 1
1½in
⅜in
¼in ¼in
walnut bands
Note valve rod full size
valve push rods make 4
¼in ¼in
⅛in
1/16in diameter pins
¼in
½in
spring goes on before gluing in place made from fine wire wrap around ⅛in diameter drill bit
cylinder detail make 2
⅛in
⅝in
½in
⅝in
½in
½in

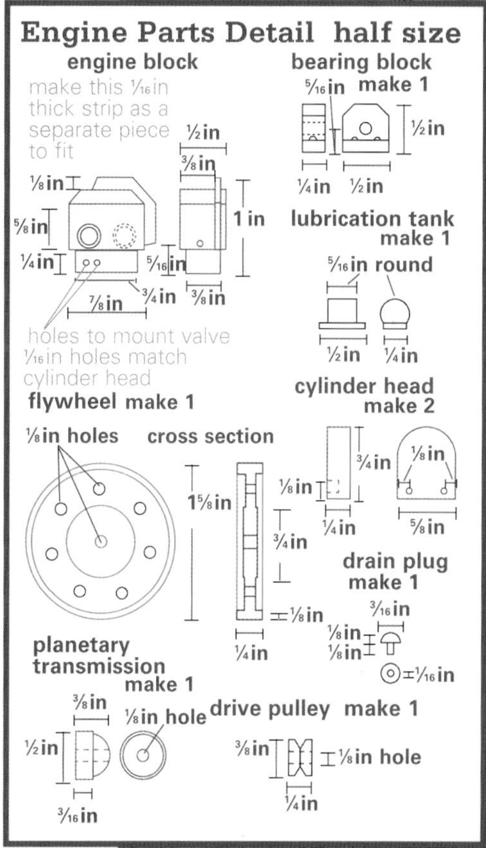
Engine Parts Detail half size
engine block
make this 1/16in thick strip as a separate piece to fit
½in
⅜in
⅛in
⅝in
¼in
1 in
5/16in
⅞in
¾in
⅜in
holes to mount valve 1/16in holes match cylinder head
bearing block
5/16in make 1
½in
¼in ½in
lubrication tank make 1
5/16in round
½in ¼in
cylinder head make 2
¾in
⅛in
⅛in
¼in
⅝in
flywheel make 1
⅛in holes
cross section
1⅝in
¾in
⅛in
¼in
drain plug make 1
3/16in
⅛in
⅛in
1/16in
planetary transmission make 1
⅜in
½in
⅛in hole
3/16in
drive pulley make 1
⅜in
⅛in hole
¼in

Making the Muffler

1 From walnut dowel ⅜ in diameter cut off 2 disks ⅛ in thick. From maple dowel ⅜ in diameter cut 2 pieces ⅜ in long and 1 piece ½ in long.
2 Glue walnut between maple pieces to form muffler, as shown above.
3 Add tailpipe to muffler by drilling ⅛ in diameter hole in one end and placing ⅛ in dowel into holes.

General Engine Arrangement

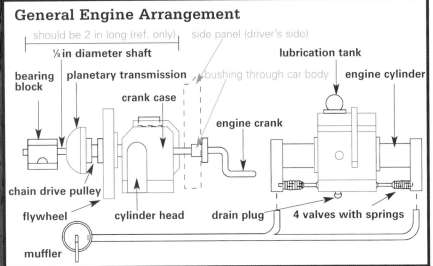

should be 2 in long (ref. only)
side panel (driver's side)

⅛ in diameter shaft

bearing block

planetary transmission

crank case

lubrication tank

bushing through car body

engine cylinder

engine crank

chain drive pulley

flywheel

cylinder head

drain plug

4 valves with springs

muffler

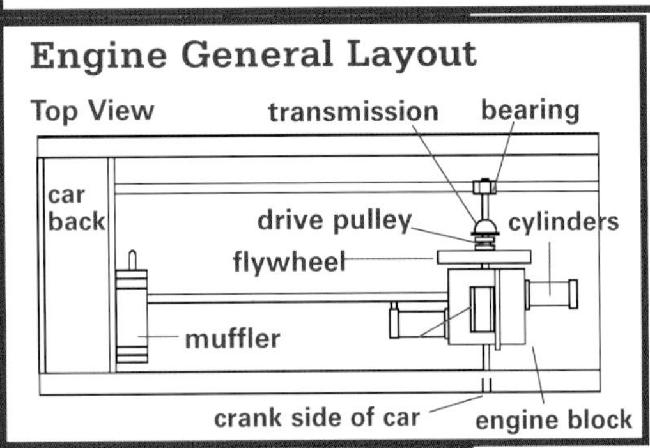

Engine General Layout

Top View   transmission   bearing

car back

drive pulley   cylinders

flywheel

muffler

crank side of car   engine block

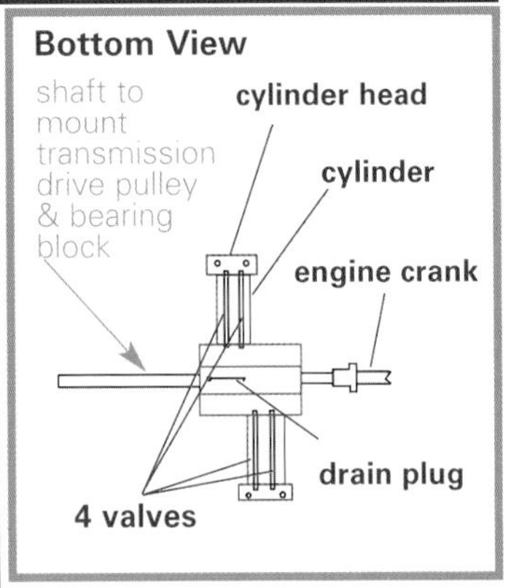

Bottom View

shaft to mount transmission drive pulley & bearing block

cylinder head

cylinder

engine crank

drain plug

4 valves

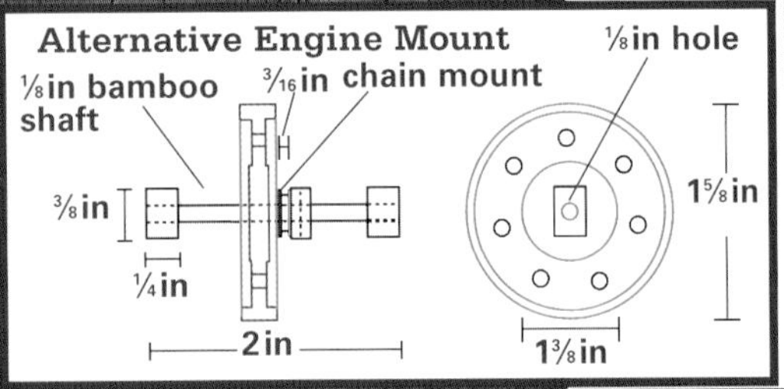

Alternative Engine Mount

⅛ in bamboo shaft   ³⁄₁₆ in chain mount   ⅛ in hole

⅜ in

¼ in

2 in

1⅝ in

1⅜ in

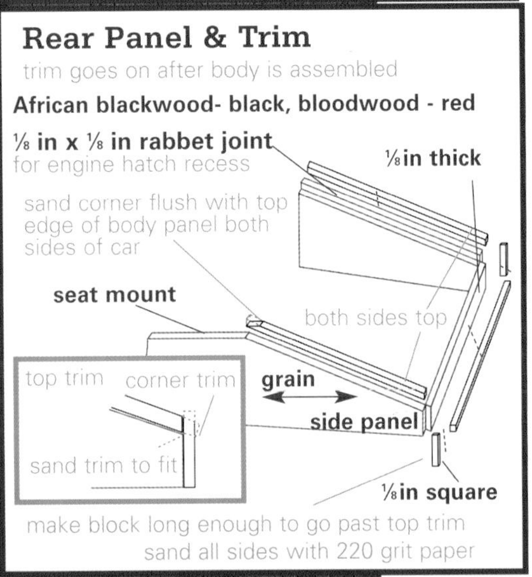

Rear Panel & Trim

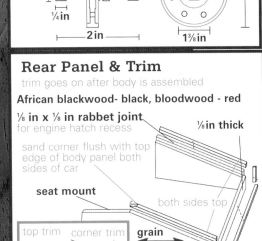

trim goes on after body is assembled

African blackwood- black, bloodwood - red

⅛ in x ⅛ in rabbet joint for engine hatch recess

⅛ in thick

sand corner flush with top edge of body panel both sides of car

seat mount

both sides top

top trim   corner trim   **grain**

side panel

sand trim to fit

⅛ in square

make block long enough to go past top trim sand all sides with 220 grit paper

Assembling Engine

1 Glue cylinder to cylinder heads. Place coiled wire over push rods and place into holes in engine block. Test fit cylinders with push rods between block and cylinder head. Check that valves are not too long (this would prevent cylinder from touching engine block). Glue in place with 5-minute epoxy. Push bamboo barbecue skewer (1½ in long ⅛ in diameter) into engine block on flywheel side far enough to hold in place and glue.

2 Slide all other parts onto this rod in order as shown. Do not glue at this time.

3 Locate bearing block. When satisfied with fit of engine under seat mount, mark bearing block, remove engine, trim ⅛ in rod, leaving it protruding just past the bearing block located on top of cross piece of cross member.

4 Remove parts, glue in proper order as you put them back. Align engine with crank handle hole in side of car.

5 Install muffler and exhaust tube. Exhaust tube is made from ⅛ in diameter dowel. Make bends in tube by making multiple cuts in dowel (do not cut right through dowel). Hold bent tube in place by filling cuts with carpenter's glue. Allow to dry.

Making Alternative Chain Mount

Note This assembly required if not building the engine to give appearance of an engine with flywheel protruding from bottom.

1 Use 2 maple blocks ⅜ in x ⅜ in x ¼ in thick. Drill 1⅛ in hole in blocks to mount shaft made from bamboo barbecue skewer.

2 Make drive pulley and flywheel, as shown on engine parts detail. Place in engine compartment and align with crank handle hole at side of car.

3 Do not glue pulleys in place until rear axle has been glued to car. Adjust pulleys to keep the chain straight.

Making Rear Panel and Trim

1 Glue African blackwood trim to side panels. Fit bloodwood end panel to back of car leaving open joint ⅛ in x ⅛ in. Glue in place with 24-hour epoxy. Dry.

2 Sand sides lightly with 220-grit sandpaper on a wood block. Do not round edges.

Making Engine Compartment Hatch

Note 3-piece hatch is hinged if engine is involved, otherwise make without hinge.

1 Use enough ¼ in thick bloodwood to cover engine compartment with grain

running across width. Lower panel should fit against back panel of car, flush with sides and top. Glue.

2   Hatch opens on 2 small hinges installed between hatch and upper panel. Fit tight fitting upper panel to hatch panel and hinges. Mark car body at hinge joint. Test to open and close easily.

3   Drill hole with $\frac{1}{16}$ in drill bit. Make hatch knob from $\frac{1}{8}$ in diameter brass rod. Turn in lathe leaving $\frac{1}{16}$ in stem to fit in hatch hole.

4   Place panels back on car body and check fit. Glue upper panel in place. Do not glue on upper hatch. Allow to dry.

5   Use belt sander to sand in direction of grain of upper panel flush with seat mounting. Hand sand (in direction of grain) top of completed panels flush with trim pieces. Install knob in hatch cover.

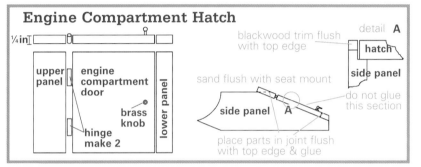

Building the Radiator

1   Using a dremel tool or band saw cut 3 small grooves in 3 sides of piece of African blackwood $\frac{1}{2}$ in square at end and 2 in long.

2   On brass shim stock (thin gauge), draw two $\frac{1}{2}$ in squares. Make 4 points $\frac{1}{8}$ in from the edge at each corner, as shown. With hand drill or dremel, drill holes in brass to fit 4 brass string art picture nails. Then cut out the 2 squares and file edges smooth. *Note* Cutting out squares after drilling holes is easier.

3   Place stock against African blackwood block. Mark and drill 4 holes to fit nails. Repeat for opposite end. Radiator assembly diagram shows details.

Making the Seat

1   Laminate pieces of bloodwood (grain running lengthwise) together to make a block $3\frac{3}{4}$ in x 2 in x $1\frac{3}{4}$ in high. Use 24-hour epoxy glue and clamp until dry. Cut out center section of bloodwood block to form shape seen on diagram.

2   Use mahogany $3\frac{3}{4}$ in x 2 in x $\frac{1}{8}$ in thick for bottom of seat. See diagram and cut slot into wood.

3   Using belt sander, sand back of seat on a slight angle. Round inside corners with dremel tool or drum sander in drill press. Do not sand through back.

4   Glue piece to bottom of seat with 5-minute epoxy. Check position of slot on seat. Cover the side pieces of seat with masking tape on outside of seat panels.

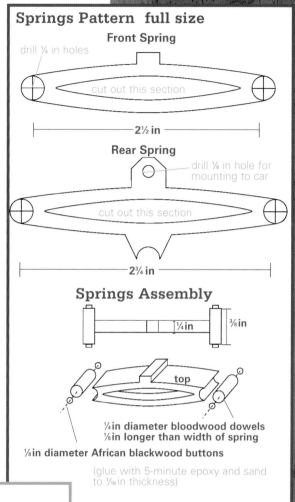

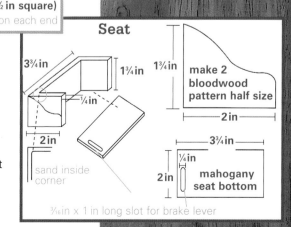

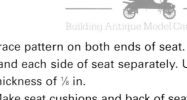
Seat Assembly

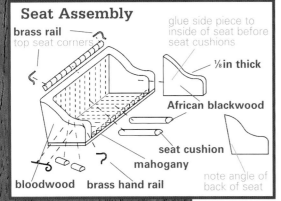

brass rail
top seat corners
glue side piece to inside of seat before seat cushions
1/8 in thick
African blackwood
seat cushion
mahogany
note angle of back of seat
bloodwood   brass hand rail

Front Axle

African blackwood - black
bloodwood - red

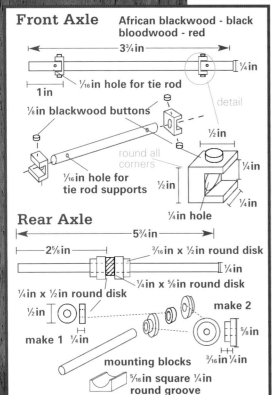

3¾ in
¼ in
1/16 in hole for tie rod
1 in
1/8 in blackwood buttons
detail
½ in
round all corners
1/16 in hole for tie rod supports
¼ in
½ in
¼ in
¼ in hole

Rear Axle

5¾ in
2⅝ in
3/16 in x ½ in round disk
¼ in
¼ in x 5/8 in round disk
¼ in x ½ in round disk
½ in
make 2
make 1   ¼ in
5/8 in
mounting blocks
3/16 in ¼ in
5/16 in square ¼ in round groove

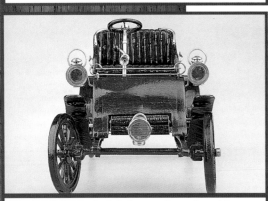

Shows front axle joining springs, head lamp, rod location, alignment of lights & steering wheel, top dash brass rail

5   Trace pattern on both ends of seat. With a drum sander in drill press sand each side of seat separately. Using same tool sand seat to finished thickness of 1/8 in.

6   Make seat cushions and back of seat from strips of African blackwood ¼ in wide x 3/16 in thick. Cut enough strips to cover seat back and seat area.

7   Sides of seat are flat on inside. Make pattern of side from cereal box and cut out piece from 1/8 in thick African blackwood. Glue in place with 5-minute epoxy.

8   Sand strips of African blackwood to shape, as shown. Sand strips a bit smaller in width around back corners for better fit. Glue little pieces the width of each strip along top edge staying in line for a uniform seat cushion.

9   Using dremel with a sharp cutter, contour cushions where they touch each other. Put grinding stone in dremel and go over cushions at slowest speed to give leather look.

10   Use brass rod 1/8 in diameter, to make top corner finishing rail. To get a more realistic look hammer pieces flat on the ends before forming them. Drill holes small enough to fit in pins, then shape pieces to fit, then place on seat and drill the holes. Mount the brass in the seats with pins to look like rivets.

11   Make brass rail on side, as shown, from 1/16 in brass rod. To make brass mounting pins (L and R) use 2 pieces of brass the same diameter and solder them to the formed piece. Solder pins on using third hand to hold them. Leave pins long and trim later with side cutters.

12   Using pin vice and drill bit the same size as brass mounting pins, drill holes into side of seat. Do not drill all the way through side.
Note After soldering, clean brass in rubbing alcohol before gluing with 5-minute epoxy.

Making Front Axle

1   Use bloodwood ¼ in square at end and 6½ in long. Place in small lathe and turn to ¼ in round dowel. Cut to 5⅞ in.

2   Use bloodwood ½ in square at end and 4 in long. Cut out notches at each end, as shown. Set pieces on end and place in drill press vice. Drill both ends with ¼ in diameter drill bit.

3   Use belt sander and lightly sand corners. Check that axle fits into ¼ in hole.

4   Use band saw to cut blocks off ½ in from each end. Slide pieces onto axle.

5   Glue in place with 5-minute epoxy. Before glue dries place axle on piece of wood with blocks level to each other to line up.

6   Using 1/16 in drill bit, drill by hand, keeping axle on piece of wood so both holes will line up, as shown. Use a piece of African blackwood and make four 1/8 in round buttons to glue on blocks to resemble pins.

Making Rear Axle

1   Repeat steps 1 and 2 of front axle instructions and trim to 5¾ in.

2   Use hole saw with inside dimension of 5/8 in to cut 2 disks from ¼ in thick bloodwood and use ½ in hole saw to cut 2 more disks from same piece of bloodwood. Use piece of ¼ in thick African blackwood and hole saw ½ in diameter to cut 1 disk. These disks are for differential for rear wheel drive. Slide disks over end of axle.

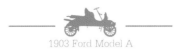

3 Round all edges on disks using 1/4 in dremel and spinning them on belt or drum sander. Note Slide disks back on axle in proper order (see diagram). Do not glue in place until final assembly.

Making Mounting Blocks

1 Use bloodwood 5/16 in thick and large enough to hold and with drill press drill two 1/4 in holes (one hole 3/8 in from end and the other 1/2 in from center of first hole).
2 Make 4 cuts beside holes leaving 1/16 in thick piece of wood beside holes and cut. Make next cut through center of holes across previous cuts, causing two locks to fall off, leaving 2 blocks still attached to bloodwood.
3 Make next cut 1/8 in behind holes to make last two half blocks fall off.

Making Tie Rod

1 From bloodwood cut a piece 1/16 in square and 7 in long. Hand sand to make dowel.
2 Cut off 2 pieces 3/4 in long. Place these into 1/16 in holes of front axles. Sand the ends to fit the holes. Glue in place with 5-minute epoxy and allow to dry.
3 Lay other dowel piece across glued pieces to measure correct length and cut. Glue piece in place with 5-minute epoxy. Tie rod is complete.

Making Front Fenders

1 Use African blackwood 4 1/4 in x 1 3/8 in by 2 1/4 in. Cover one side with masking tape and mark center with punch. Draw 1 7/8 in radius circle and 1 15/16 in radius circle inside it.
2 Using scroll or band saw, cut outside circle first. Cut second circle leaving lines showing. Sand wood to thickness of 1/16 in. Piece will be cut in half to make 2 fenders. Trace (p5) fender pattern on cereal box and cut out.
3 Lay pattern on curve of wood cut for fenders to determine where to cut fenders in half. Put masking tape on outside of 2 pieces and trace fender pattern to it.
4 Use drum sander in drill press and sand to pattern lines to get correct shape. Both fenders are the same. Make 4 pieces African blackwood 3/16 in square at end and 1/2 in long. Glue (5-minute epoxy) to underside of each fender in 2 places, as shown. Dry. With 1/16 in drill bit, make mounting holes (drill only half the length of these mounts).

Making Rear Fenders

1 Use 2 blocks African blackwood 4 in x 2 1/4 in x 3/4 in thick. Trace pattern as for front fender.Cut pieces on outside line only with a band or scroll saw.
2 Using dremel and small drum sander, sand center of fender on outside, stopping 1/4 in from each end of fender to leave a small ridge.
3 Finish ends of fenders with drum sander in dremel and sand wood leaving a ridge across ends joining side ridges. Accent ridges with medium ball cutter in dremel to make small groove along inside edge of ridges.
4 Cut out inside line of pieces, leaving pieces 1/4 in thick, even though diagram shows 3/16 in. With drum sander in drill press sand inside curve of fender to 3/16 in thickness.

Rear Fender Pattern half size

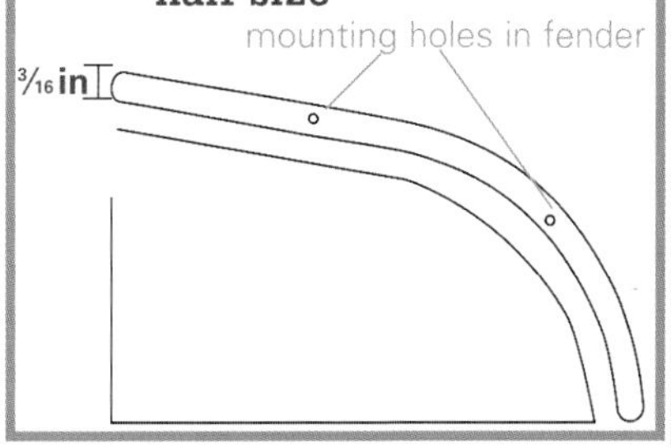
mounting holes in fender
3/16 in

Mounting Block

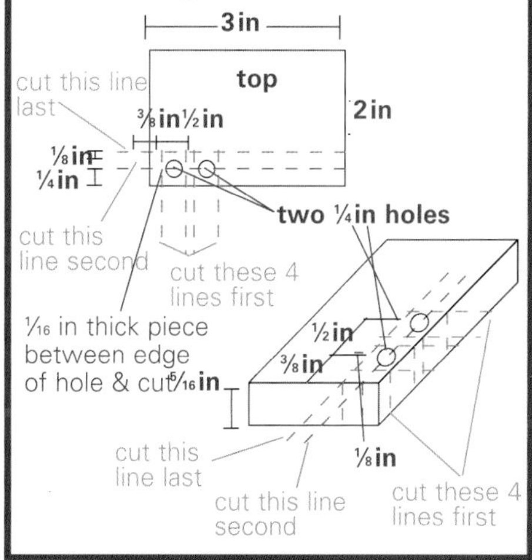
3 in
top
2 in
cut this line last
3/8 in 1/2 in
1/8 in
1/4 in
two 1/4 in holes
cut this line second
cut these 4 lines first
1/16 in thick piece between edge of hole & cut
1/2 in
3/8 in
5/16 in
1/8 in
cut this line last
cut this line second
cut these 4 lines first

Tie Rod Assembly

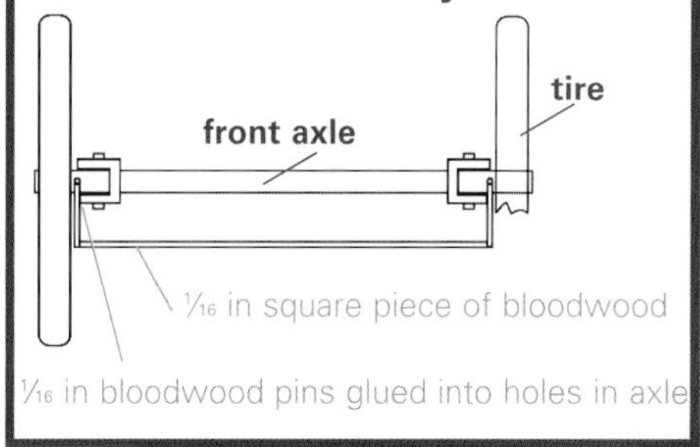
tire
front axle
1/16 in square piece of bloodwood
1/16 in bloodwood pins glued into holes in axle

Front Fenders African blackwood

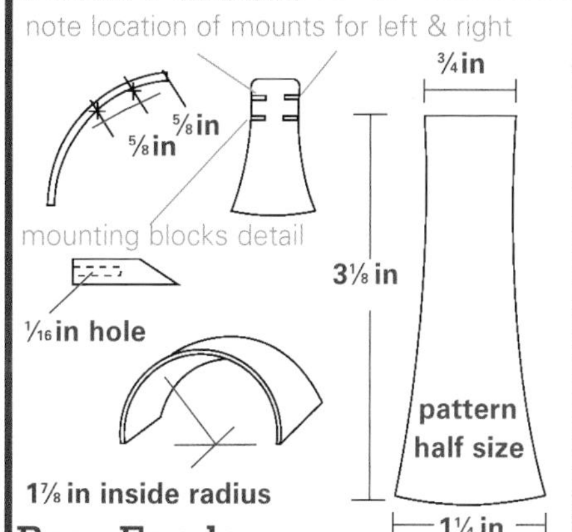
note location of mounts for left & right
3/4 in
5/8 in
5/8 in
mounting blocks detail
3 1/8 in
1/16 in hole
pattern half size
1 7/8 in inside radius
1 1/4 in

Rear Fenders
African blackwood

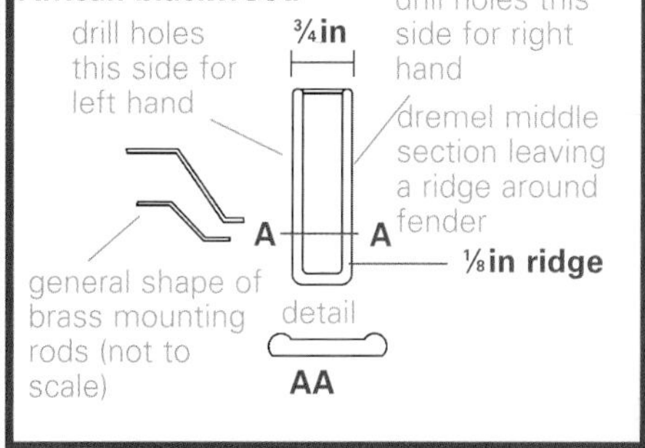
drill holes this side for left hand
3/4 in
drill holes this side for right hand
dremel middle section leaving a ridge around fender
A
A
1/8 in ridge
general shape of brass mounting rods (not to scale)
detail
AA

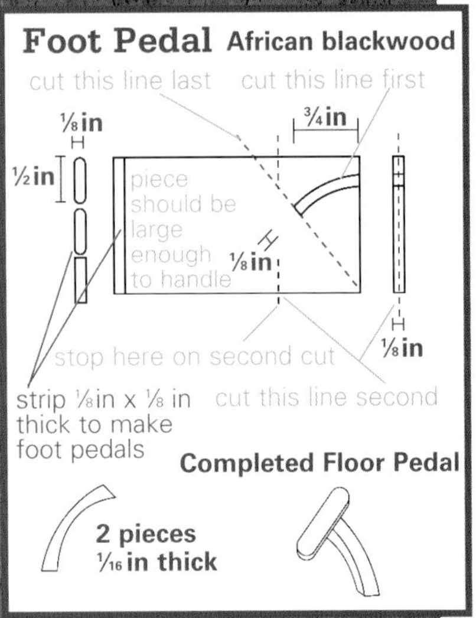
Foot Pedal African blackwood
cut this line last
cut this line first
1/8 in
3/4 in
1/2 in
piece should be large enough to handle
1/8 in
stop here on second cut
1/8 in
strip 1/8 in x 1/8 in thick to make foot pedals
cut this line second
Completed Floor Pedal
2 pieces 1/16 in thick

5 With pin vice and drill bit same size as brass rod (1/32 in diameter) drill holes 3/8 in deep in side of fender (L and R, as shown). *Note* Brass rods will be bent to shape in final assembly. Holes to mount fenders will be drilled in car body at final assembly.

Making Foot Pedals

1 Use African blackwood 1/8 in thick, large enough to handle. Cover one side with masking tape. Draw pedal bar curves on tape. Cut curved lines with band or scroll saw.
2 Cut down width past curved cuts, leaving 2 pieces 1/16 in thick and still attached to main piece. Place support piece underneath to stop pieces from falling through blade clearance hole. Make final cut releasing the 2 pieces from main piece. Using remaining 1/8 in piece, cut 1/16 in thick strip, long enough for 2 foot pedals, each 1/2 in long.
3 Sand and cut to shape, as shown.

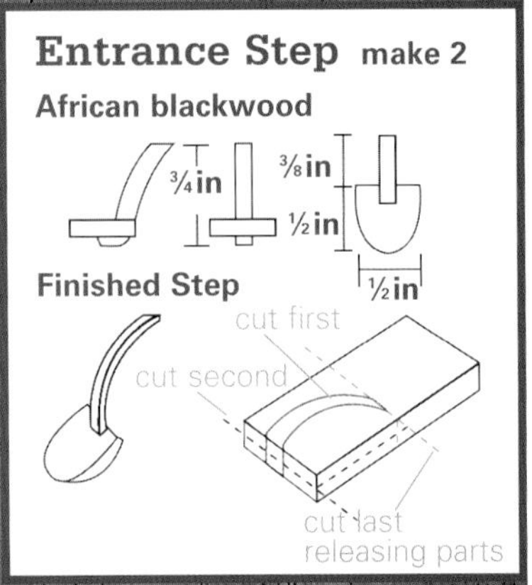
Entrance Step make 2
African blackwood
3/4 in
3/8 in
1/2 in
1/2 in
Finished Step
cut first
cut second
cut last
releasing parts

Making Entrance Step

1 Use African blackwood 2 in x 1 in x 1/4 in thick. Cover one side with masking tape. Draw curved lines, on tape. Follow cutting order on diagram to cut out support arms.
2 Use remainder of wood to cut out foot rests, as shown. Sand to shape.
3 Cut a notch in flat side of foot rests on the center the same size as support arms, used to join support arms to footrest. Glue pieces together with 5-minute epoxy. Dry. *Note* Support arms may have to be trimmed when installed. Step should not be lower than front fenders.

Making Head Lamp

1 Use 3/4 in diameter brass rod 3 in long. Drill 3/8 in hole 1/2 in from one end, as shown. Drill only half way through. Place piece in metal lathe with hole sticking out. Begin cutting lens mount face of brass rod by making 1/16 in deep recess 11/16 in diameter to hold lens in place.
2 Use boring tool to make 1/2 in diameter cut 1/8 in deep to make a recess for gluing plastic lens in place.

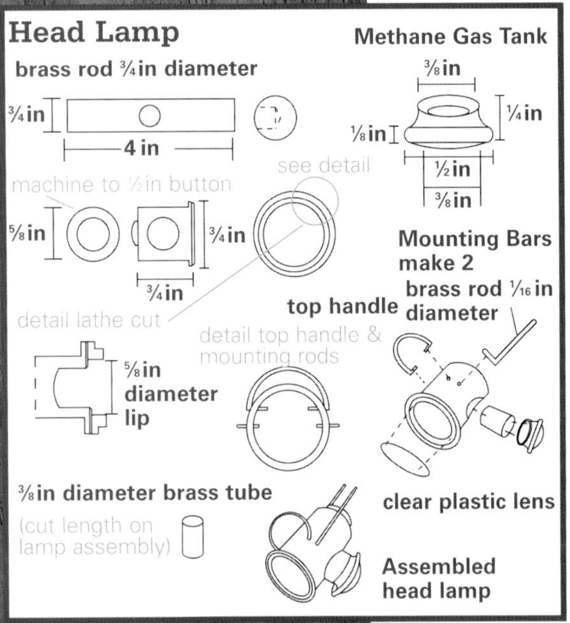
Head Lamp
brass rod 3/4 in diameter
3/4 in
4 in
Methane Gas Tank
3/8 in
1/4 in
1/8 in
1/2 in
3/8 in
see detail
machine to 1/2 in button
5/8 in
3/4 in
3/4 in
Mounting Bars make 2
brass rod 1/16 in diameter
top handle
detail lathe cut
detail top handle & mounting rods
5/8 in diameter lip
3/8 in diameter brass tube
(cut length on lamp assembly)
clear plastic lens
Assembled head lamp

3 Cut body to shape by turning down brass to 5/8 in diameter leaving a lip on the front to form lens mount. With parting tool cut 1/8 in deep groove at 3/4 in mark to form button at end of lamp.
4 Use needle file to round edges and fine steel wool to polish brass. Use parting tool to cut beside the 1/8 in groove to cut off lamp leaving enough material to form a button on back of lamp.
5 Place a piece of 3/8 in diameter brass rod in hole of lamp body and cut off leaving 3/16 in protruding. Use 1/2 in diameter brass rod 1 in long and drill 3/8 in hole 1/8 in deep in one end. Machine to shape, forming fuel pot.
6 Use 1/2 in diameter wood dowel and wrap brass rod around it to form U shape. From same brass rod cut 2 pieces 2 in long and bend 1/8 in from one end to form L shape (to be trimmed later at assembly).
7 Drill four 1/16 in holes (2 for handle, 2 for mounting rods), as shown.
8 With third hand hold body piece with 3/8 in rod and fuel pot in place and solder together. Place U shape handle on top of lamp and bend end 1/8 in to fit in mounting holes for lamp. Put handle and mounting rods in place and solder. When cool, clean with rubbing alcohol. Use dremel with a brass or nylon brush and polish lamp. Clean again with rubbing alcohol.
9 Use 5/8 in diameter hollow punch to punch out disk from piece of clear plastic (use clear plastic from a purchased item sealed in a plastic vacuum formed package).

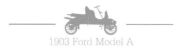

10 Put 5-minute epoxy in recess of lamp. Put glue on plastic lens and place in lamp. Dry. Make one lamp.

Making Side Lamps

1 Use ¾ in diameter brass rod 3 in long. Drill ¼ in hole ⅝ in from both ends. Drill through brass rod. Place piece in metal lathe with hole sticking out and cut a recess 1/16 in deep and 11/16 in diameter to hold lens in place.
2 Use boring tool to make ⅜ in diameter cut ⅛ in deep to form a recess for gluing plastic lens in place. Turn down brass to ½ in diameter leaving lip on front to form lens mount, as shown.
3 Use parting tool to cut groove ⅛ in deep at ¾ in mark to form button at end of lamp. Use needle file to round brass edges. Polish brass.with fine steel wool.
4 Use parting tool to cut off body by cutting beside ⅛ in groove leaving material to form button on back of lamp. Repeat procedure at opposite end of brass rod.
5 Place ¼ in brass rod in hole of lamp body leaving ⅛ in protruding.
6 Use ½ in diameter brass rod 1 in long and drill ¼ in hole ⅛ in deep at end. Machine fuel pot and top vent to shape. Use 1/16 in diameter brass rod wrapped around ½ in diameter wood dowel to form U shape for top handle. From same brass rod cut 2 pieces 2 in long and bend ⅛ in from one end forming Z shape (to be trimmed at assembly).
7 Drill three 1/16 in holes (2 for handle, 1 for mounting rods, L and R required).
8 Use third hand to hold body piece with ¼ in rod and fuel pot in place and solder them together. Place U shape handle on top of lamp, bend end ⅛ in to fit mounting holes for handle. Place handle and mounting rod in place and solder.
9 When cool, place in rubbing alcohol to clean. Use dremel with brass or nylon brush to polish lamp. Clean again with rubbing alcohol.
10 Use ⅝ in diameter hollow punch to make lens p52. *Note* Mix glue slowly to eliminate air bubbles.

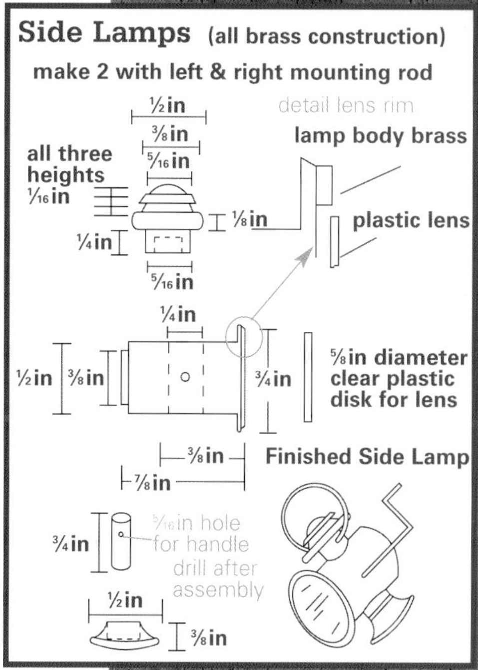
Side Lamps (all brass construction)
make 2 with left & right mounting rod
all three heights 1/16 in
detail lens rim
lamp body brass
plastic lens
⅝in diameter clear plastic disk for lens
Finished Side Lamp
1/16 in hole for handle drill after assembly

Making Taillight

Follow same building process as side lights (no handle). Use red vinyl from tool wrench package for lens. Cut out with ⅜ in diameter hollow punch. Glue with 5-minute epoxy.

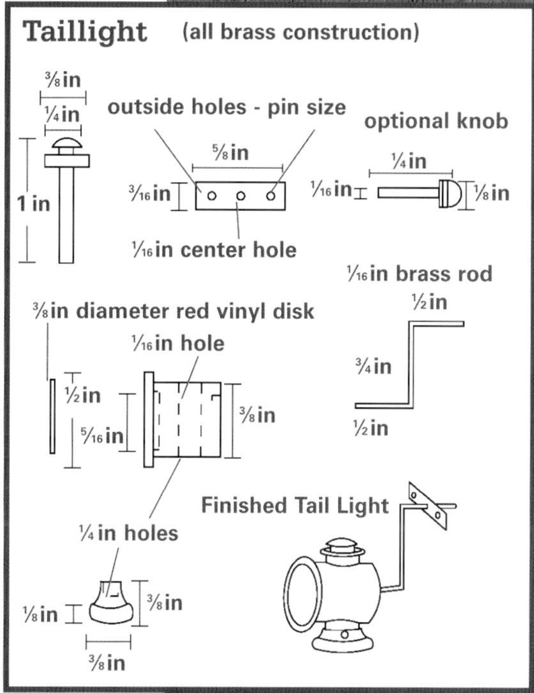
Taillight (all brass construction)
outside holes - pin size
optional knob
1/16 in center hole
1/16 in brass rod
⅜in diameter red vinyl disk
1/16 in hole
¼ in holes
Finished Tail Light

Making Brake Lever

1 Use brass tube 3/32 in diameter 1⅜ in long and flatten with hammer (not completely or edges will crack).
2 Use small round file or dremel with grinding stone to cut notch ½ in from one end. Grind notches on rod for lever handle. With drill bit same size as tack pin, drill hole ¼ in from other end to mount lever to car.

Making the Crank

1 Bend ⅛ in diameter brass rod, as shown. One side is longer (to be trimmed later).
2 Use eyelets to make handle and brushing for crank when passing through car body into engine.
3 Push crank into eyelet and trim brass rod so bend will not hit the car side.

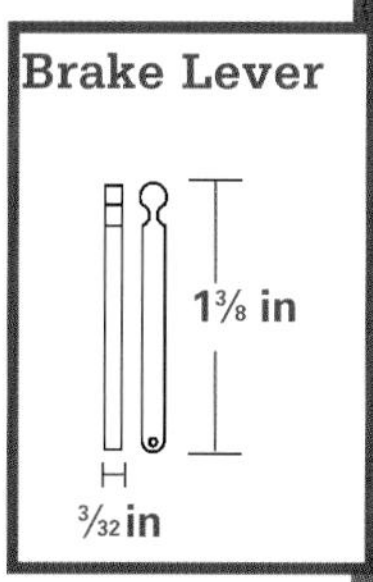
Brake Lever
1⅜ in
3/32 in

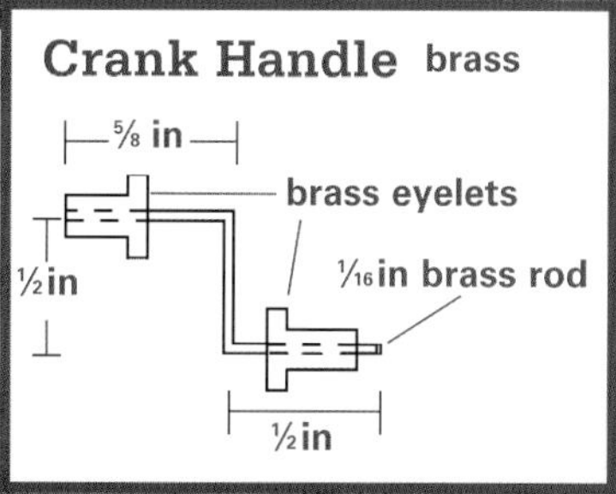
Crank Handle brass
⅝ in
brass eyelets
½ in
1/16 in brass rod
½ in

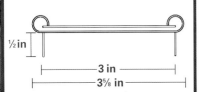

Front Dash Rail

½ in

3 in
3⅝ in

Making Front Dash Rail

1   Shape ¹⁄₁₆ in rod, by wrapping around drill bit.

2   In ⅛ in rod drill 2 holes ⅛ in from each end using ¹⁄₁₆ in diameter drill bit.

3   Cut ⅛ in rod in half (2 pieces ¾ in long) with ¹⁄₁₆ in hole in each piece. Use third hand to assemble. Slide ⅛ in rod pieces on bottom rail (used to mount rail).

4   Use solder gun or microtorch to solder parts together. Align mounting pins. Clean finished rail with alcohol and polish with fine steel wool. Set aside.

Making Steering Wheel

1   Use brass tube ⅛ in diameter and second tube which should slide over first tube. From larger tube cut 2 pieces ³⁄₁₆ in long.

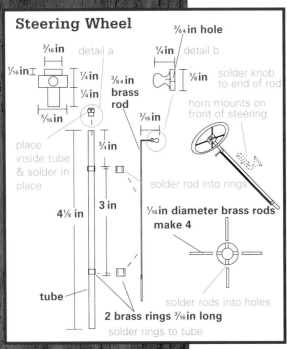

Steering Wheel

³⁄₆₄ in hole

³⁄₁₆ in   detail a

¹⁄₁₆ in

¼ in
¼ in

⁵⁄₁₆ in

¼ in   detail b

³⁄₆₄ in brass rod

⅛ in   solder knob to end of rod

place inside tube & solder in place

¾ in

horn mounts on front of steering

4⅛ in

tube

3 in

³⁄₁₆ in

solder rod into rings

¹⁄₁₆ in diameter brass rods make 4

solder rods into holes

2 brass rings ³⁄₁₆ in long

solder rings to tube

2   On ⁵⁄₁₆ in diameter rod mark and drill four ¹⁄₁₆ in diameter holes in one end. Place in metal lathe with holes sticking out and machine to shape, as shown.

3   In ⅛ in diameter rod drill ³⁄₆₄ in hole at one end ⅛ in deep. Use needle file to shape knob. Do not cut into hole.

4   Bend ³⁄₆₄ in brass rod, as shown. *Note*   Steering wheel can be made from wood by placing a wood dowel in lathe and cut inside lip first. Cut out center leaving lip. Remove wheel on final cut. Use parting tool to cut small groove ⅛ in from end of dowel. Use needle file to round edge of groove and remove wheel from round dowel. Slide 2 brass rings onto tube and place steering wheel center into steering wheel column tube. Using microtorch, solder parts in place, as shown.

5   Place four ¹⁄₁₆ in diameter rods into holes of wheel column center. Using a third hand, line up rods and solder in place. Place ³⁄₆₄ in rod and knob on steering wheel column and solder in place.

6   Place steering wheel column with 4 rods upside down over steering wheel on table. Keep steering wheel column in center of steering wheel and mark 4 rods to fit in groove on steering wheel. Trim rods to fit into groove. Turn assembly over. Glue (5-minute epoxy) steering wheel to shaft on 4 rods.

Note   An alternative method is to use rubber O ring as shown for Locomobile steering wheel, (p76). Put four ¹⁄₁₆ in rods in place and trim to diameter of rubber ring, flatten outside tips of rods. Make 4 slits in rubber ring to match the four ¹⁄₁₆ in rods. Slide rubber ring onto flattened rods and adjust until rubber ring is round. Glue with 5-minute epoxy.

Making the Horn

1   Place piece of brass rod ⅜ in diameter in metal lathe and cut inside of bell on end of rod.

2   Remove edge of bell with a file. Rough cut outside shape and finish with small round file. Polish inside and outside with steel wool. Remove bell from rod keeping cut straight. Use 2 pairs of fine needle nose pliers on ⅛ in diameter brass rod and form horn tube around ends of pliers.

3   Make horn bulb from African blackwood turned in lathe. Drill hole at one end. Shape outside of bulb with file. Do not cut into drilled hole. Use third hand to hold bell and tube and solder in place. Solder horn to steering wheel, then glue bulb to horn.

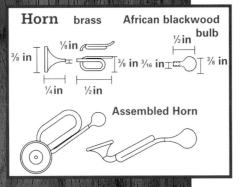

Horn   brass   African blackwood bulb

⅜ in   ⅛ in   ½ in

¼ in   ½ in   ⅜ in   ³⁄₁₆ in   ⅜ in

Assembled Horn

1903 Ford Model A

Assembly Stage One

1. Drill holes same size as mounting rods for side lamps on car body below top edge of front dash.

2. Place front dash rail on top of dash and mark holes for mounts. Install floor pedals into slots in floorboard. Drill hole for steering wheel in floor, located on edge of triangle piece, lined up with middle of 2 pedals.

3. Mark and drill holes for head lamps inside the groove in front of radiator and same size as mounting rods.

4. Mount radiator into cutout at front of car with 2 holes facing front. Glue in place. Do not glue head lamp now. Turn car over and glue springs in place, with 24-hour epoxy.

5. Turn car over while still wet and place on level board resting on springs. Springs are ½ in back from front of car when turned over. Dry

6. Glue wheels to front and rear axles, leaving axles sticking out ¼ in past wheels. Slide brass rings onto axle and check fit. Remove and clean brass rings. Glue in place with 5-minute epoxy. Allow to dry. Turn car over. Glue front and rear axles in place over springs. Mix extra glue and smear over springs to add extra strength. When gluing front axle make sure tie rod is on inside between front and rear axles.

7. Add mounting blocks to axles on opposite side of spring, gluing them to axles (use 5-minute epoxy because it dries clear).

8. Slide drive chain around drive pulley and differential. Tie 2 ends of chain together with fine wire or black fishing line, not too tight. Pull chain around until joint is out of sight, behind engine under seat mount. Glue joint on chain with 5-minute epoxy. Glue differential to axle.

9. Add four ¹⁄₁₆ in bloodwood rods between mounting blocks and differential for support, as seen on a real car.

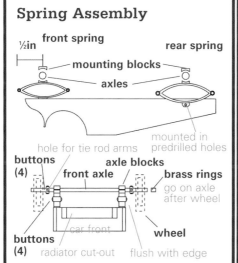

Spring Assembly

½in front spring
rear spring
mounting blocks
axles
hole for tie rod arms
mounted in predrilled holes
buttons (4)
front axle
axle blocks
brass rings go on axle after wheel
car front
wheel
buttons (4)
radiator cut-out
flush with edge

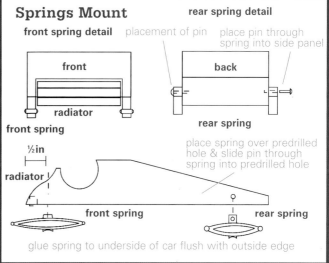

Springs Mount

rear spring detail
front spring detail
placement of pin
place pin through spring into side panel
front
back
radiator
rear spring
front spring
½in
radiator
place spring over predrilled hole & slide pin through spring into predrilled hole
front spring
rear spring
glue spring to underside of car flush with outside edge

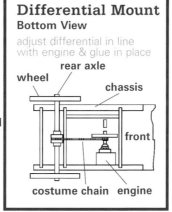

Differential Mount
Bottom View
adjust differential in line with engine & glue in place
rear axle
wheel
chassis
front
costume chain   engine

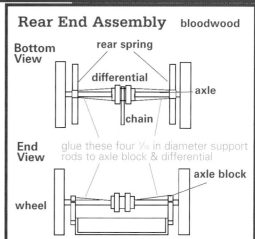

Rear End Assembly bloodwood
Bottom View
rear spring
differential
axle
chain
End View
glue these four ¹⁄₁₆ in diameter support rods to axle block & differential
axle block
wheel

Shows front springs attached to body & axles, front fender attaches to car body, head lamp mounted through radiator

Side step, under seat panel, entrance trim

Final Assembly

Wheel Trim
make 4
¼ in brass tube ¼ in long

ring glued to outside of axle after wheel is placed on axle

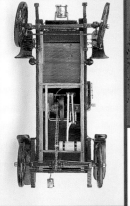

Shows underside parts placement

Shows rear springs attached to car, axle assembly with chain, alignment of axles, back fender, bottom placement of chassis, engine cover, taillight, how engine fits into car

1   Place car on wheels. Place front fenders with rods inserted in mounting holes over wheels, leaving ⅜ in gap between fender and wheel. Locate and mark holes for mounting pins and drill same size holes. Place fender in holes. Align second fender. Glue both fenders to car. Install rear fenders same way, bending mounting rods to fit car body.

2   Glue head lamp and side lamps in place. Glue front rail in place.

Finished Ford

3   Glue seat on seat mount area with 24-hour epoxy. Slit in seat projects past car body to let brake lever slide through to be attached to outside of car body panel. Allow to dry. Brake lever protrudes ¼ in past bottom of seat. Drill same size hole as brake lever in car body. Glue with 5-minute epoxy. Place mounting pin at same time. Add taillight. Drill hole same size as mounting rod, 1 in from passenger side of car and ⅛ in from bottom edge. Glue with 5-minute epoxy. At the same time glue crank in hole on driver side panel and make a button to cover hole on opposite side of car.

4   Glue side steps on center of car entrance behind front fenders. Install steering wheel with 24-hour epoxy. Measure 2½ in from center of wheel to back of seat. Hold wheel in position with masking tape until dry.

5   Use 5-minute epoxy and fill in any visible space on car. Dry thoroughly. Apply 3 coats of gloss finish.

Side lamp & end of top dash brass rail & entrance trim

Side lamp attached, front fender attaches to car

Dash, brass foot rail, location of pedals, shape of front fender

1903

Mercedes

In 1872 Gottlieb Daimler, a German mechanical engineer, and Wilhelm Maybach worked in the firm of Nikolaus A. Otto, the man who invented the four-stroke internal-combustion engine. Both men left the next year because they thought Otto wasn't aware of the engine's potential for the automobile. They started their own engine building shop and in 1885 patented the first successful high-speed internal-combustion engine that ran at 900 rpm and developed a carburetor that Maybach designed that could use gasoline as fuel. Their many design efforts culminated in a four-wheel automobile in 1889 that was steered by tiller. The car had a framework of light tubing instead of the usual wood, rear-mounted engine, belt-driven wheels, and four speeds. The Daimler Motor Company was founded in 1898 and they built the first Mercedes car in 1899.

The name Mercedes was suggested by a major Daimler investor, Emil Jellinek, who named the line after his eldest daughter because he thought the German Daimler name would not sell in France. Maybach was the chief designer of the Mercedes automobiles. For the earliest Mercedes cars Maybach improved on existing designs for a 24-horsepower engine by providing mechanical inlet valves that could be throttled by the driver. He probably also developed Daimler's son Paul's conception of the light pressed-steel chassis with the honeycomb radiator.

The 1903 Mercedes car that appears in this book incorporated these developments and had a 35-horsepower engine and a top speed of 80 mph. The engine was mechanically operated and the final drive was chain. It had two brake pedals and an array of gauges and a multi-site feed lubricator on the dash. The car was raced by the great Camille Jenatzy. It ran quieter, was more flexible, and handled better than any other car of the time.

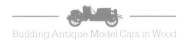

Car Pieces

Car Parts List

Car Part	Material	Size	Pieces
Wheels	walnut	14 in x 3½ in x ⅜ in	1
	poplar	9 in x 2½ in x ¼ in	1
Main Floor	poplar	6¼ in x 2⅞ in x ⅛ in	1
Seat Block	poplar	2½ in x 1½ in x ⅞ in	1
	poplar	1⅞ in x ⅞ in x ⅛ in	2
Engine Block	poplar	3 in x 2⅛ in x 1⅞ in	1
	African blackwood	1⅞ in x 2¼ in x ¼ in	1
	poplar	2¼ in x ⅛ in x ⅛ in	3
	brass	¼ in x 12 in	1
	brass rod	¼ in dia, as purchased	1
	brass rod	⅛ in dia, as purchased	1
Pedal Board	poplar	⅜ in sq x 2⅞ in	1
Engine Splash Guard	poplar	5 in x 1⅞ in x 1 in	1
Rear Axle	maple dowel	¼ in x 5 in long	1
	maple	½ in sq x ¼ in thick	1
Drive Axle	maple dowel	¼ in x 4⅛ in long	1
Drive Pulley	mahogany dowel	1 in x 1 in	1
Chain Pulley	African blackwood	dowel 1 in x 1 in long	2
Gas Tank	poplar	2 in x 1¾ in x 1 in long	1
	maple dowel	¼ in x ⅜ in long	1
	African blackwood	dowel ¾ in x ½ in long	1
Steering Wheel	brass rod	¼ in x 3 in long	1
	brass ring	⅝ diameter, 1/16 in thick	1
	brass shim stock	1 in sq	1
	brass shim stock	⅛ in wide strip, ⅜ in long	1
	brass rod	⅛ in x ½ in long	1
	mahogany dowel	1⅛ in round x ⅛ in thick	1

Car Part	Material	Size	Pieces
Chain Guards	tin plate	1 in x ⅞ in	1
Steering Box	African blackwood	5/16 in sq x 1 in	1
Steering Joints	African blackwood	⅜ in sq x ½ in	1
Tie Rod	African blackwood	1/16 in sq x 4⅝ in	1
Steering Arm	African blackwood	2½ in x ⅜ in x ⅛ in	1
Grease Fittings	African blackwood	dowel ⅛ in x 3 in	1
Engine Crank	maple dowel	3/16 in x 1½ in long	1
	mahogany	3/16 in x ⅝ in x ⅛ in thick	1
	African blackwood	dowel ⅛ in x ¾ in	1
Front Axle	poplar	5 in x 1½ in x ¼ in	1
	mahogany	1⅜ in x 7/16 in x ⅛ in	2
Seats	poplar	1½ in x 1⅝ in x ⅛ in	2
	poplar	1⅝ in x 1½ in x 1⅛ in	2
Side Rails	poplar	13 in x 1½ in x ⅜ in	2
Dash	mahogany	2⅞ in x 1¾ in x ⅛ in	1
Gauges & Fittings	brass	as per instructions	
Horn	brass rod	⅜ in x 1 in long	1
	brass rod	⅛ in x 4 in long	1
	African blackwood	dowel ⅜ in x 1 in long	1
Rear Trunk	scrap material	2½ in x 1½ in x ¾ in	1
	scrap material	2½ in x 1½ in x ⅜ in	1
	black leather	6 in sq	1
	aluminum	¼ in x 1 in long	2
Tack Pins	aluminum	¼ in x 2 in long (as needed)	
Head Lamps	brass rod	¾ in x 3 in long	1
	brass rod	1/16 in x 8 in long	1
	plastic disks	⅝ in round	2
Side Lamps	brass rod	½ in x 5 in long	1
	brass rod	1/16 in dia, as purchased	1
Side Tanks	brass rod	⅜ in x 1⅛ in long	2
	brass rod	¼ in x 1 in long	1
	tin	⅛ in strip x 2 in long	2
Brake Levers	brass tube	⅛ in OD, 1⅞ in long	2
	brass rod	3/16 in x ¾ in long	2

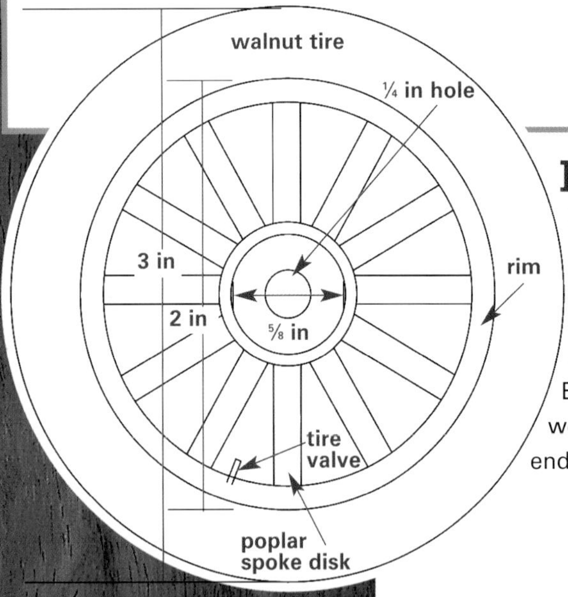
walnut tire
¼ in hole
rim
3 in
2 in
⅝ in
tire valve
poplar spoke disk

Making Wheels

Build wheels same as p11 using 14 in x 3½ in x ⅜ in walnut for tires and 9 in x 2½ in x ¼ in poplar for spokes. This wood is very soft and can easily break. Cut out carefully.

Making Main Floor

Build floor from poplar 6¼ in x 2⅞ in x ⅛ in. Use wood with very little color change in the grain from end to end.

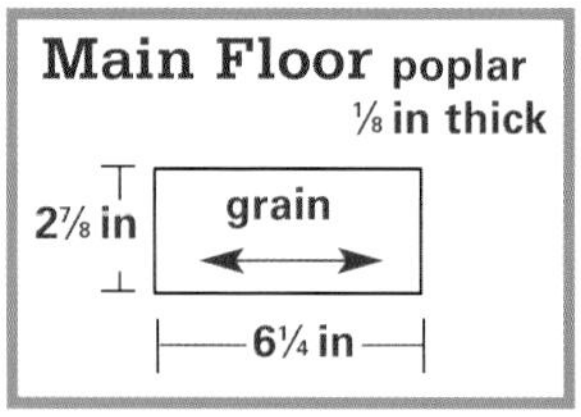
Main Floor poplar
⅛ in thick
2⅞ in
grain
6¼ in

1903 Mercedes

Making Side Rails

1. Transfer (p5) pattern to ⅜ in thick poplar. Trace out individual pieces and join A's together, lining up by drawing 14 in line and placing top of rails on line.
2. First cut out section between spring and rail, as shown. Cut out rear spring hook with drill bit to fit in hole of loop, and drill out loop. Cut remainder of section on scroll saw.
3. Using a dremel with various cutters, cut or sand rails to shape, as shown. Spring part of rail is ¼ in wide, leaving rail ⅜ in wide. Back part of rail with hook is slightly smaller than rail to give appearance of a separate piece. Top view of rail tapers towards front of rail. Front of rail shows a round pin ⅜ in long. Spring is ¼ in wide, and top of rail is ¼ in wide.
4. Cut a groove on both sides in each layer of springs of side rail to separate springs to look like individual bars. Use a cut-off wheel in dremel to give thinnest cut.
5. Make dots (rivets) on rails from small poplar buttons or round toothpicks. Sand smooth and set aside.

Making Front Axle

1. Make from maple ¼ in thick. Cut out on a scroll saw.
2. Cut out center of axle with dremel with flat face cutter, leaving small edge on outside edges to give an I-beam appearance. *Note* Do not cut too deep. Smooth out with small grindstone.
3. License plate is made from mahogany 1⅜ in x ⁷⁄₁₆ in x ⅛ in thick. Numbers and letters are those of real car. Make from ⅜ in vinyl stick-on, purchased in office supply stores.

Making Wheel Hubs, Drive Pulleys, Axle

1. Cut ¼ in maple dowel 4⅛ in long for drive axle. Make drive pulley from 1 in mahogany dowel 1 in long. Place dowel in lathe. Center drill with ¼ in diameter drill bit. Machine pulley to dimensions shown.
2. Using drill press drill six ⅛ in holes into African blackwood dowel 1 in diameter and 1 in long. Holes are ⅛ in from edge of disk. Make 2 chain drive pulleys. Place dowel in lathe and use parting tool to machine, as shown.
3. Make wheel hubs from African blackwood dowel ⅝ in with ¼ in hole in center and long enough to cut and machine 8 pieces.

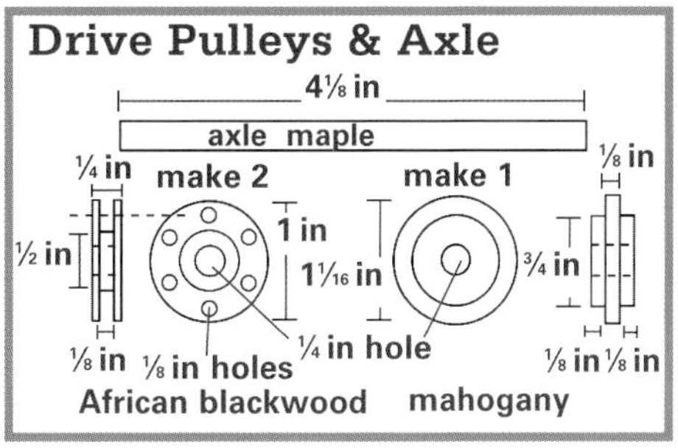

Drive Pulleys & Axle

Wheel Hubs

Making Engine Block

1. Use poplar piece 3 in x 2⅛ in x 1⅞ in. Make small step on bottom of block with a band saw. Cut block to length and shape as shown.
2. Mark 2 holes and drill with ¹⁄₁₆ in diameter drill bit on both sides of block. Use African blackwood ¼ in thick to cover front of block. Glue with 24-hour epoxy. Bottom is flush with 2⅛ in dimension. Dry. Sand edges flush with engine block.
3. Use ¼ in wide brass strip and bend tightly around African blackwood to form

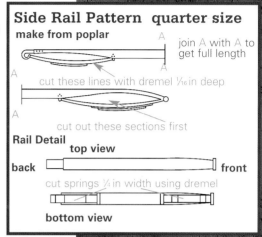

Side Rail Pattern quarter size
make from poplar
join A with A to get full length
cut these lines with dremel ¹⁄₁₆ in deep
cut out these sections first
Rail Detail
top view
back front
cut springs ¼ in width using dremel
bottom view

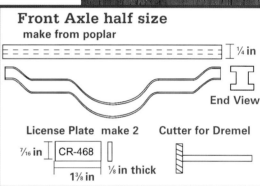

Front Axle half size
make from poplar
¼ in
End View
License Plate make 2
CR-468
⁷⁄₁₆ in
1⅜ in
⅛ in thick
Cutter for Dremel

Making Rear Axle

1. Use ¼ in diameter maple dowel 5 in long. Machine ends to give axles "caps".
2. Make axle mounts from maple ½ in square and sanded to shape. Drill ¼ in center hole first, then bend to shape. See diagram for directions and order cuts are made (4 pieces).
3. Make 2 African blackwood pulleys using same method as making drive pulleys.

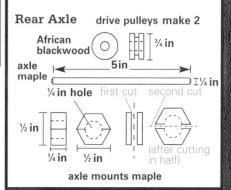

Rear Axle drive pulleys make 2
axle mounts maple

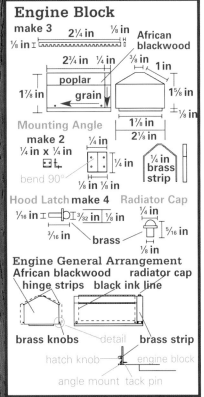

Engine Block

make 3

poplar
grain

Mounting Angle
make 2
¼ in x ¼ in
bend 90°

¼ in
brass
strip

Hood Latch make 4   Radiator Cap
brass

Engine General Arrangement
African blackwood   radiator cap
hinge strips   black ink line

brass knobs   detail   brass strip
hatch knob   engine block
angle mount   tack pin

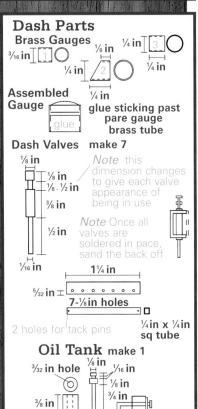

Dash Parts

Brass Gauges

Assembled Gauge
glue   glue sticking past
pare gauge
brass tube

Dash Valves   make 7

Note this dimension changes to give each valve appearance of being in use

Note Once all valves are soldered in pace, sand the back off

7-⅛ in holes
2 holes for tack pins
¼ in x ¼in sq tube

Oil Tank make 1

³⁄₃₂ in hole

clear plastic

---

radiator sides. Rough one side of strip with coarse sandpaper. *Note* Keep sanded side up for gluing with 24-hour epoxy. Clamp until dry. Drill ⅛ in diameter hole in top of radiator through brass strip for mounting radiator cap. Drill 4 holes same size as tack pins in brass strip to make the mounting angles.

4   Machine radiator cap in lathe from ¼ in diameter brass rod, cutting ⅛ in diameter first. Shape top of cap with needle files and round top edge. Remove with parting tool. Use same process to make 4 hatch knobs for engine block detail. Glue into 4 holes previously drilled.

5   Cut poplar strip 2¼ in x 2 in x ⅛ in thick for hinges on engine block. Mark strip into even number of divisions ⅛ in apart along 2¼ in length. Use band saw and cut ¹⁄₁₆ in notches on these marks. Trim strip to proper width, as shown. *Note* Glue pieces to engine block between brass and end of block, even on both sides. Locate on edge of each angle cut and on top in center of block.

6   With black ball point pen draw a line to show a door on both sides.

Making the Dash

1   Use ⅛ in thick mahogany and cut out firewall (see diagram).

2   Build all brass parts on dash. Make faces of 3 small gauges from paper purchased at a hobby store that supplies radio control models. Numbers shown on diagram beside gauges show proper location for mounting.

3   For dash valves use ¼ in sq brass tube 1¼ in long and divide tube into 7 equal parts. Center punch marks. Do not flatten tube. Use ⅛-diameter drill bit in drill press and drill through tube.

4   Use pin vice and drill by hand 2 small holes through face of square tube, as shown. Holes are used to place tack pins through valve assembly when part is mounted on dash.

5   To build valves, turn a ⅛ in diameter brass rod in lathe. Turn ¹⁄₁₆ in x ½ in long stem first. The ½ in and ⅜ in measurements must be exact. Dimensions for top of valves vary so they will be at different heights when installed. Place valves in drilled ⅛ in holes in sq tube with stems even across bottom. The ⅛ in diameter of valve is flush with top of square tube. Solder in place.

6   Remove back of sq tube by sanding it off close to valves without sanding valves. Polish with a wire brush in dremel at medium speed. Set aside.

Making Floor Valves

1 Turn different sizes of brass rods in lathe. Drill three ¹⁄₁₆ in holes into ¾ in long valve. See diagram for end view of part that shows alignment of rods.

2 Bend rod #1, to a 90° angle before soldering in place. Trim to ¼ in length on both sides of bend. Center hole mounts valve to floor of car. See number beside

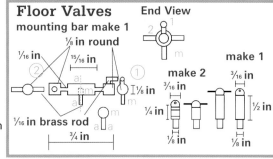

Floor Valves   End View
mounting bar make 1
⅛ in round
¹⁄₁₆ in   ¹⁵⁄₁₆ in   make 2   make 1
¹⁄₁₆ in brass rod
¾ in

each hole for proper alignment of rods. Rod # 2 should stick out ¹⁄₁₆ in on each side. Mounting rod should stick out ⅜ in from edge of valve. Solder rods in place on valve.

Making Oil Tank and Hand Rail

1 Use ¼ in round clear acrylic plastic with ³⁄₃₂ in diameter hole drilled through center.

2 Machine brass parts to shape beginning with smallest diameter and working

towards larger. Fit parts into plastic. Glue in place with 5-minute epoxy. Brass rod inside plastic gives appearance of oil in tank.

3   Make handrail from $\frac{1}{16}$ in diameter brass rod longer than required. Form handrail by wrapping rod around $\frac{3}{8}$ in diameter drill bit to 90° angle. Trim rod to dimensions shown on diagram. Flatten ends (with a hammer) just enough to drill holes large enough to fit a tack pin to mount to dash.

Mounting Parts to Dash

1   Locate valve assembly in center of dash. Valve stem should be $\frac{1}{4}$ in up from bottom edge of firewall. Drill 2 holes into firewall using holes in valve assembly as guides. Put 5-minute epoxy behind valve assembly, and using tack pins, place part onto dash in previously drilled holes. Allow to dry. Trim tack pins flush with back of firewall. Glue oil tank to end of valve assembly, as shown.

2   Lay dash flat on table. Attach gauges to dash by locating brass tubes on dash and half filling with 5-minute epoxy. Dry. Place paper gauges into brass tubes, and cover paper gauges with more 5-minute epoxy. Let glue bulge out past end to give appearance of a glass cover.

3   Mount handrail to dash and drill small holes through handle into dash using handle as a guide. Place pins through holes, gluing at same time. Dry. Trim pins flush with back of firewall. Set aside.

Making Seat Block

1   Use poplar piece $2\frac{1}{2}$ in x $1\frac{1}{2}$ in x $\frac{7}{8}$ in and 2 pieces $1\frac{7}{8}$ in x $\frac{7}{8}$ in x $\frac{1}{8}$ in. Cut main seat block from one piece. Sand smooth by hand with fine sandpaper. Draw lines as shown on seat block with black ballpoint pen. Line across top is $\frac{1}{4}$ in from top of block. Make a cardboard pattern of curved design and trace around it.

2   Make cardboard pattern of 2 seat sidepieces and trace onto $\frac{1}{8}$ in thick wood. Cut outside line leaving line showing. Clamp 2 pieces together and sand to final shape on belt sander. Use drum sander in drill press for curved ends.

3   Join sidepieces to seat block as shown. Keep bottom and top even with seat block. Sidepieces should stick out the same dimension from bottom of seat block on each end. Use 24-hour epoxy. Dry.

Making Engine Crank Assembly

1   Machine crankshaft from $\frac{3}{16}$ in maple dowel, 2 in long in lathe to sizes shown on diagram, starting with $\frac{1}{16}$ in diameter.

2   Shape crank handle from African blackwood 1 in long and $\frac{1}{8}$ in diameter in lathe starting with $\frac{1}{16}$ in diameter and cut piece to length, as shown. Place piece back in lathe with $\frac{1}{16}$ in sticking inside lathe and machine other end to required shape, using thread cutting tool to machine small groove on end.

3   Make crank arm from mahogany $\frac{3}{16}$ in wide and 2 in long (piece is longer

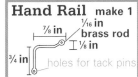

Hand Rail   make 1

Dash Layout   mahogany

Seat Block   poplar

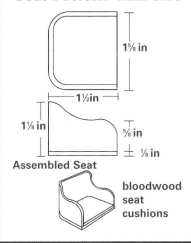

Making Seats

1   Transfer (p5) pattern to poplar. Use seat building method given for Ford Model A (p49). Make seat cushions from bloodwood and cut to shape to fit into the seat.

Seat Pattern   half size

Assembled Seat

bloodwood seat cushions

Making Engine Splash Guard

1   Use 5 in x $1\frac{7}{8}$ in (must be exact) x 1 in poplar. Draw end profile on wood and sand to shape.

2   Drill holes in poplar, deep enough ($\frac{1}{2}$ in) to remain when piece is cut to length. *Note* Front of piece has small flat edge $\frac{1}{8}$ in wide below $\frac{1}{8}$ in diameter hole. To get proper angle cut, trim piece to $4\frac{3}{4}$ in length and mark $\frac{1}{8}$ in lip on front of piece where $\frac{1}{8}$ in hole was drilled. Mark $\frac{1}{2}$ in distance on top of piece from same end as $\frac{1}{8}$ in lip was marked. Place piece on table saw and line up blade with $\frac{1}{2}$ in mark on top of piece and line used to mark $\frac{1}{8}$ in lip on bottom. Set table to this angle by tilting saw table and tighten in place. Keep cut straight. Sand smooth. Set aside.

Engine Splash Guard   poplar

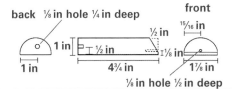

than required for handling). Drill two 1/16 in holes 1/2 in apart. With a pencil draw shape onto piece of wood freehand around the 2 holes. Shape with dremel with sanding drum. Sand 2 inside curves between holes first, working around end, leaving it still attached to piece of wood. Cut piece to length in band saw. Finish shaping opposite end to finish the part.

4 To assemble, place crank arm over crankshaft and place crank handle into crank arm, as shown. Glue with 5-minute epoxy and set aside.

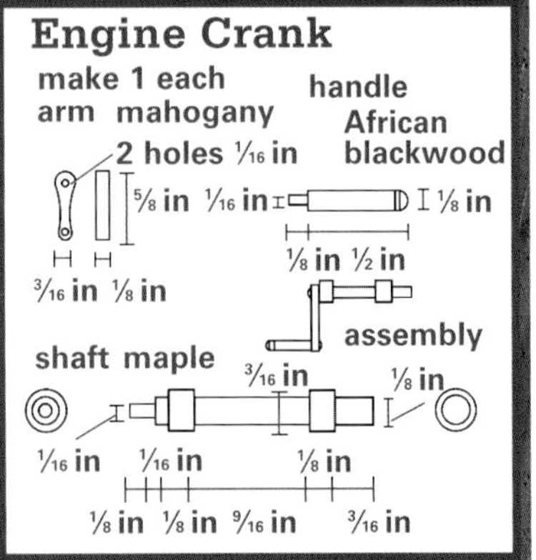
Engine Crank
make 1 each
arm mahogany
handle
African
blackwood
2 holes 1/16 in
5/8 in
1/16 in
1/8 in
1/8 in 1/2 in
3/16 in 1/8 in
assembly
shaft maple
3/16 in
1/8 in
1/16 in
1/16 in
1/8 in
1/8 in 1/8 in 9/16 in
3/16 in

Making Rear Trunk

1 Use any piece of wood or scrap 2 1/2 in x 1 1/2 in x 3/4 in thick for trunk, and another piece 2 1/2 in x 1 1/2 in x 3/8 in thick for lid.

2 Cover pieces with black leather (I used a black leather purse from a thrift store) 1 in wide and long enough to go around block. Join in the middle of back. Glue using 24-hour epoxy. Dry.

3 For lid, cut piece of leather 4 in x 3 in and glue lid in middle of piece. Dry. Cut edges of leather so corners can be folded over. Place 24-hour epoxy over top of block and underside of lid. Squeeze leather between lid and block and clamp tight to look like a lid. Dry.

4 Build lock and latch the same as on Stanley Steamer, p26. Build hinge from aluminum 1/4 in wide x 1 in long. Fold piece in half along length. Squeeze together in needle nose pliers on bent side. Peel aluminum apart pushing it back towards pliers leaving a hump in the aluminum.

5 Drill 4 holes, as shown, same size as tack pins. Trim aluminum off each side leaving holes to form hinge. Line up middle of hinge with joint between box and lid and drill small holes large enough for tack pins. Place tack pins across top and down front and back of trunk. Place pins 1/8 in from edges of trunk and space them evenly, as shown.

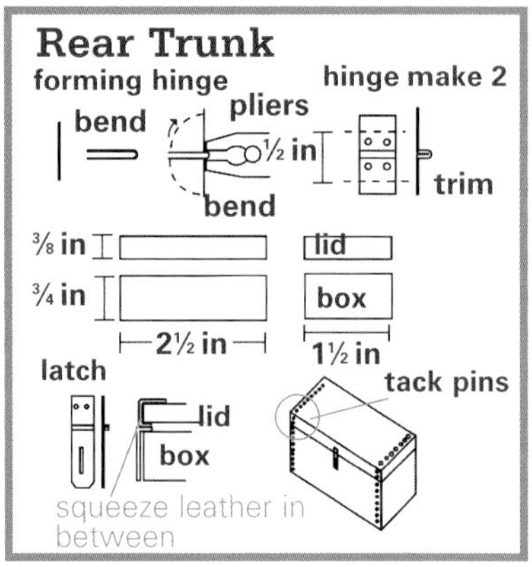
Rear Trunk
forming hinge
hinge make 2
bend
pliers
1/2 in
trim
bend
3/8 in
lid
3/4 in
box
2 1/2 in
1 1/2 in
latch
tack pins
lid
box
squeeze leather in between

Making Gas Tank

1 Use solid maple sanded to shape. *Note* Keep 1 3/4 in dimension exact so gas tank will fit between chassis rails. Drill 1/4 in hole into gas tank (make sure hole is drilled on proper side of tank. Gas tank cap is on the left side of car.

2 Gas cap is made from 3/8 in African blackwood dowel turned to shape on lathe. Cut 1/4 in maple dowel 3/8 long and glue into hole in gas tank, then glue cap to end of dowel. Set aside.

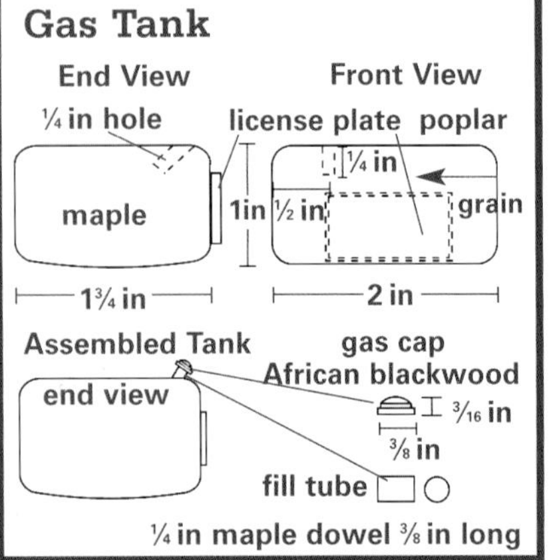
Gas Tank
End View
Front View
1/4 in hole
license plate
poplar
1/4 in
maple
1in
1/2 in
grain
1 3/4 in
2 in
Assembled Tank
gas cap
African blackwood
end view
3/16 in
3/8 in
fill tube
1/4 in maple dowel 3/8 in long

Making Pedal Board

1 Cut poplar into triangular shape 3/8 in x 3/8 in x 2 7/8 in (grain across sloping side of board).

2 Drill hole for steering wheel and cut 3 slots for pedals. *Note* Holes are different sizes drilled on sloping side of board. Cut slots with dremel using 1/16 in diameter cutter. Slots can go through board but don't cut into edges.

3 Make pedals from African blackwood using same method as Model A Ford (p52). Sand pedal board smooth. Install pedals so center pedal is higher towards top of board than two outside pedals.

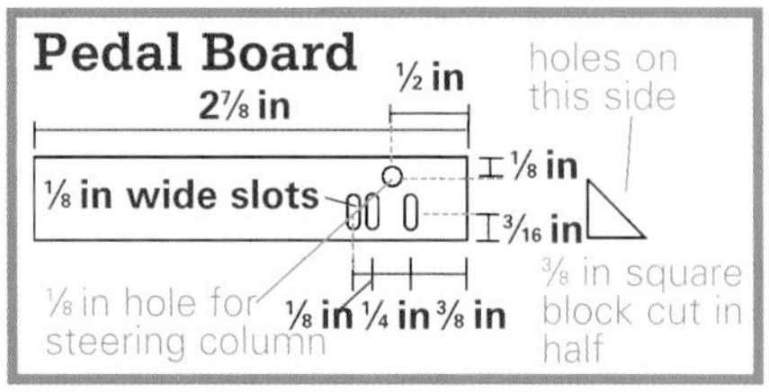
Pedal Board
2 7/8 in
1/2 in
holes on this side
1/8 in
1/8 in wide slots
3/16 in
3/8 in square block cut in half
1/8 in hole for steering column
1/8 in 1/4 in 3/8 in

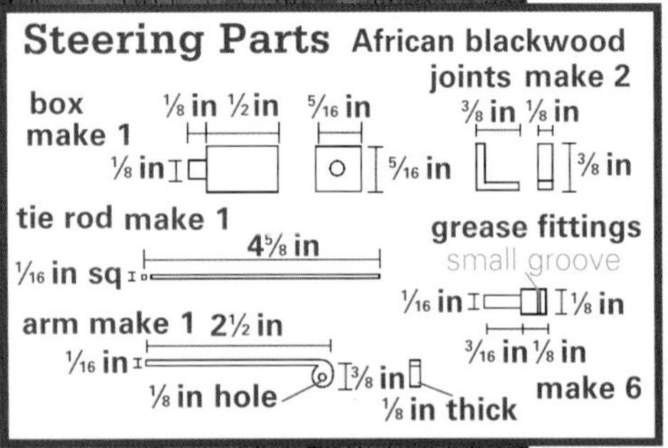
Steering Parts
African blackwood
joints make 2
box
make 1
1/8 in 1/2 in
5/16 in
3/8 in 1/8 in
1/8 in
5/16 in
3/8 in
tie rod make 1
4 5/8 in
grease fittings
1/16 in sq
small groove
1/16 in
1/8 in
arm make 1 2 1/2 in
3/16 in 1/8 in
1/16 in
3/8 in
make 6
1/8 in hole
1/8 in thick

Making Steering Wheel Parts

1 Use African blackwood for steering box. Method A Turn 5/16 in square block 3/4 in long in lathe and cut 1/8 in diameter pin, as shown. Method B Use 5/16 in square block, 1/2 in long and drill 1/8 in hole in center of block and glue 1/8 in pin in the hole. Pin should stick out 1/8 in.

2 Make tie rod from 1/16 in square piece of wood 4 5/8 in long (piece is longer than required for later trimming). Sand by sliding piece between sandpaper held in your fingers. *Note* Pull (not push) piece through sandpaper

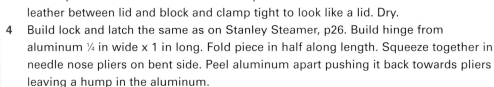

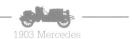

3 Steering joints are made with 3/8 in sq piece of wood 1 in long. Cut to shape, as shown. Slice off 1/8 in pieces with band or scroll saw. *Note* When slicing cover hole in saw so pieces will not fall through hole beside blade.

4 Make steering arm from wood 3 in long x 1/2 in wide x 1/8 in thick. Place masking tape over piece and draw pattern, as shown. Drill 1/8 in hole first, then cut to shape on scroll saw. Sand smooth. Make grease fittings from 1/8 in round piece of wood 4 in long in lathe. Shape by cutting 1/16 in diameter first. Place a thread cutting tool in holder and machine small groove, as shown. Place parting tool in holder, and cut piece off to length 6 times, pulling piece of wood out each time you turn the parts. Set aside.

Making Steering Wheel

1 Make main body from 1/4 in brass tube. Make top and bottom steering column from 1/4 in brass rod turned on lathe to fit into brass tube. *Note* The 1/16 in diameter on top piece is needed for steering wheel assembly.

2 Cut 5/8 in diameter throttle rim on lathe from 5/8 in brass tube to 1/16 in long using a thread-cutting tool. Throttle bar is made from 1/8 in diameter brass tube flattened with a hammer, then drilled and cut to size with side cutters. Round ends of bar on belt sander.

3 Use snips to cut cross piece from brass shim stock and file edges smooth. Make steering wheel from 1 1/8 in mahogany dowel. Use method described in Model A Ford (p54).

4 Throttle knob is made from 1/8 in diameter brass rod turned in lathe beginning with small diameter. File rest of knob to shape.

Steering Wheel Assembly

1 Fit all machined brass parts of steering wheel column onto 1/4 In brass tube. Solder.

2 Place center support over 1/16 diameter nipple on end of shaft and slide throttle bar over cross piece on the nipple. With small ball peen hammer, lightly tap nipple and rivet pieces together.

3 Slightly bend throttle bar up so throttle ring can be slid under it. Place throttle knob into hole at end of throttle bar and solder ring and knob in place. Using dremel with wire brush at slow speed, polish steering column. Glue steering wheel to column over center support. Use 5-minute epoxy. Set aside.

Making Brake Levers

1 Make 2 brake levers from brass tube with 1/8 in outside diameter x 1 7/8 in long.

2 Machine small handles from 3 1/16 in diameter brass rod to shape shown on diagram. One end of handle must slide into end of brass tube 1/4 in. Solder handle to rod.

3 Place rod and handle on piece of metal and flatten handle and rod with hammer to oval shape. At end of rod without handle, flatten tube 1/4 in from end. Drill small hole to fit a tack pin. Repeat for other lever. Using same tube as levers, cut piece 1/8 in long for a spacer between levers. Slide pin through hole of one lever, slide spacer onto pin, and slide other lever onto pin, holding spacer between levers. Solder together.

Making Chain Guards

1 Use tin cut from flattened tin can. Cut tin larger than diagram, draw pattern on tin, and cut out pattern (2 needed). File edges smooth. Mark dots on tin 1/8 in from edge and 1/8 in apart, evenly spaced. *Note* Make L & R.

2 Lay tin on hard plastic or hockey puck and punch marks with an automatic center punch to make rivets. Repeat for second piece. Drill 2 small holes in 1/8 in strip to fit tack pins. Using dremel with wire brush at high speed, polish tin to antique look. Form piece, as shown. Set aside.

Chain Guards tin plate make 2

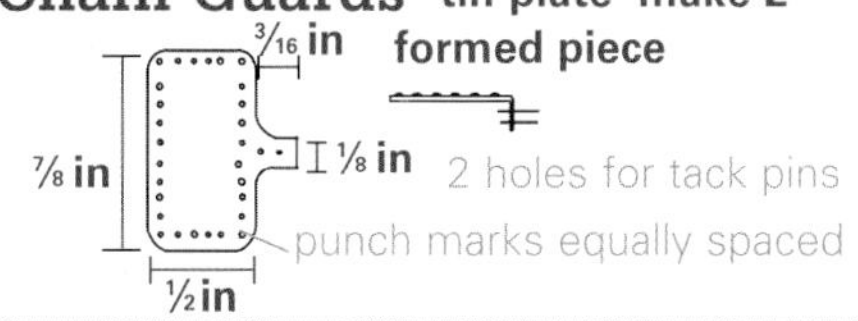
3/16 in
formed piece
7/8 in
1/8 in
2 holes for tack pins
punch marks equally spaced
1/2 in

Steering Wheel all brass except steering wheel

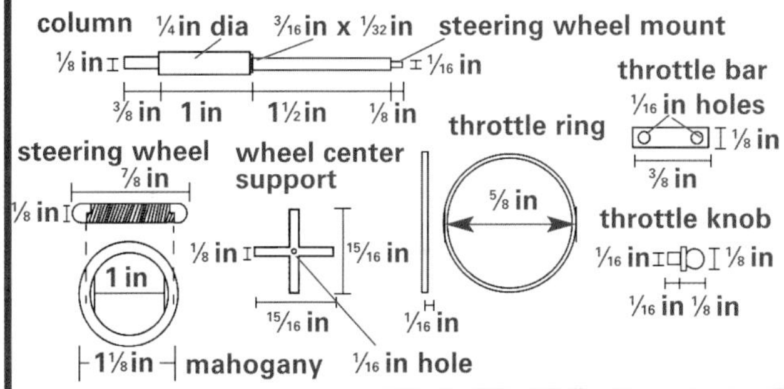
column
1/4 in dia
3/16 in x 1/32 in
steering wheel mount
1/8 in
1/16 in
3/8 in 1 in 1 1/2 in 1/8 in
throttle bar
1/16 in holes
1/8 in
3/8 in
throttle ring
steering wheel
7/8 in
1/8 in
1 in
1 1/8 in
mahogany
wheel center support
1/8 in
15/16 in
15/16 in
1/16 in
1/16 in hole
5/8 in
throttle knob
1/16 in
1/8 in
1/16 in 1/8 in

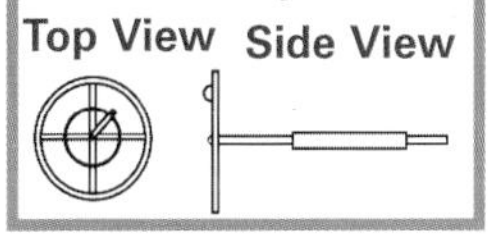
Assembly
Top View
Side View

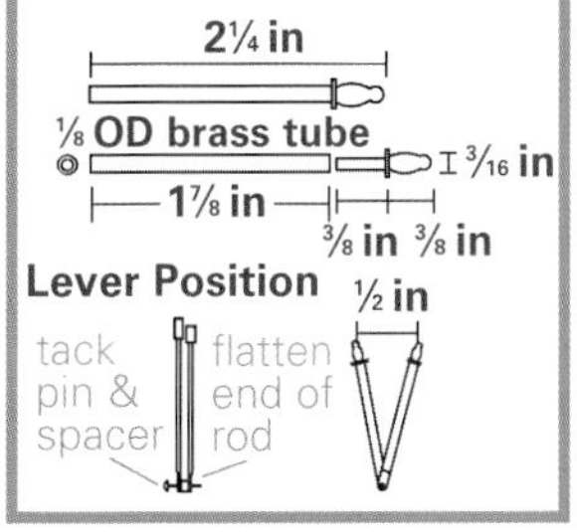
Brake Levers
2 1/4 in
1/8 OD brass tube
3/16 in
1 7/8 in
3/8 in 3/8 in
Lever Position
1/2 in
tack pin & spacer
flatten end of rod

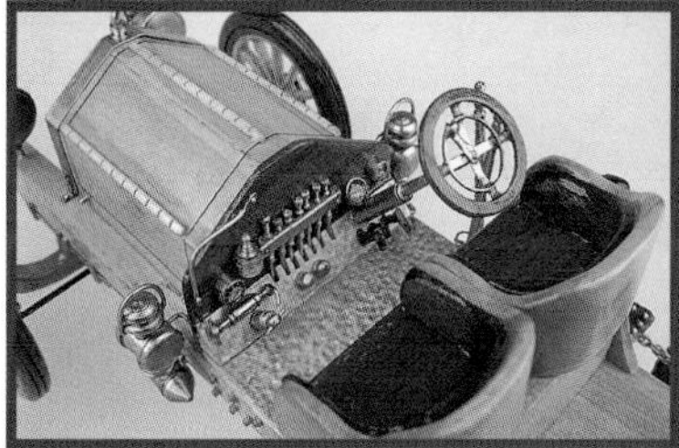

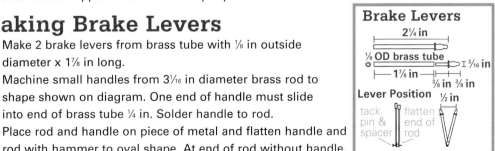

Location of parts on dash, throttle ring on steering wheel

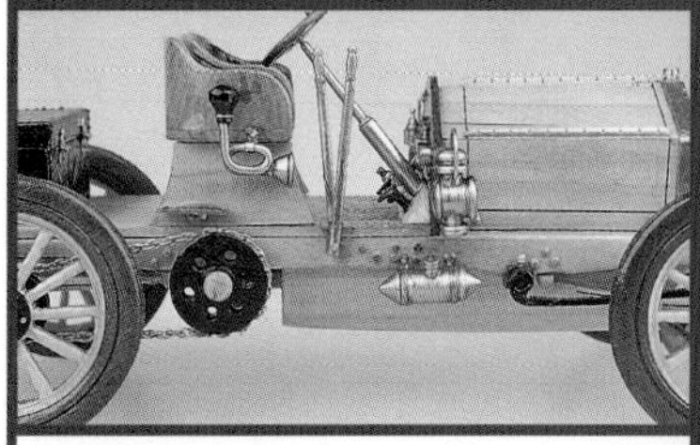

Location of drive pulley, brake levers, horn

Making Side Tanks

1   In lathe chuck hold solid brass rod $\frac{3}{8}$ in diameter and long enough to machine parts. Make 2 tanks. Place machined tank in drill press and drill hole in center the size of a small pin to attach fill cap. Make fill caps same way as radiator cap machined from $\frac{3}{16}$ in diameter brass rod.

2   Cut tin strips $\frac{1}{8}$ in wide from tin can. Wrap tin strips around $\frac{3}{8}$ in drill bit and bend ends with pliers, as shown. Drill hole in each strip same size as tack pin to mount tank to car. Place fill caps and tin strips onto tank and solder together. Holes in the straps should be towards back of tank, just past center point.

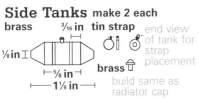

Side Tanks make 2 each
brass $\frac{3}{16}$ in tin strap   end view of tank for strap placement
$\frac{1}{8}$ in $\frac{5}{8}$ in   brass   build same as radiator cap
$1\frac{1}{8}$ in

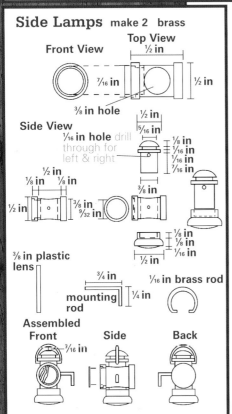

Side Lamps make 2 brass

Front View

Top View $\frac{1}{2}$ in
$\frac{7}{16}$ in $\frac{1}{2}$ in
$\frac{3}{8}$ in hole

Side View $\frac{1}{2}$ in $\frac{5}{16}$ in
$\frac{1}{16}$ in hole drill through for left & right $\frac{1}{8}$ in $\frac{1}{16}$ in $\frac{1}{16}$ in $\frac{7}{16}$ in
$\frac{1}{2}$ in $\frac{1}{8}$ in $\frac{1}{8}$ in
$\frac{1}{2}$ in $\frac{3}{8}$ in $\frac{9}{32}$ in $\frac{3}{8}$ in
$\frac{1}{8}$ in $\frac{1}{8}$ in $\frac{1}{16}$ in
$\frac{3}{8}$ in plastic lens $\frac{1}{2}$ in
$\frac{3}{4}$ in $\frac{1}{16}$ in brass rod
mounting rod $\frac{1}{4}$ in

Assembled
Front   **Side**   **Back**
$\frac{3}{16}$ in

Making Head Lamps

1   Make bodies same as Model A Ford p52, but mount differently. Make lens, p52.

2   Ring (see diagram) is made from $\frac{1}{16}$ in brass rod formed around $\frac{3}{8}$ in drill bit. Once released, brass rod should spring to $\frac{1}{2}$ in diameter. Cut to shape.

3   Use same brass rod and form around $\frac{1}{2}$ in drill bit, and bend, as shown. Cut $\frac{1}{16}$ in diameter brass rod $\frac{1}{2}$ in long and solder to piece just formed for lamp mount. Drill holes inside lamp body same size as mount and slide mount into holes. Drill another 2 holes in top of lamp, and slide top ring into holes leaving a $\frac{3}{16}$ in gap between ring and lamp. Align mount and the ring and solder in place. Repeat for second lamp.

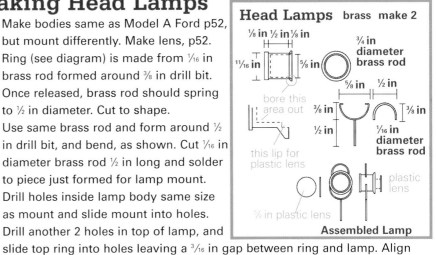

Head Lamps brass make 2
$\frac{1}{8}$ in $\frac{1}{2}$ in $\frac{1}{8}$ in
$\frac{3}{4}$ in diameter brass rod
$\frac{11}{16}$ in $\frac{5}{8}$ in
bore this area out $\frac{5}{8}$ in $\frac{1}{2}$ in
this lip for plastic lens $\frac{3}{8}$ in $\frac{3}{8}$ in
$\frac{1}{2}$ in $\frac{1}{16}$ in diameter brass rod
$\frac{1}{2}$ in plastic lens   plastic lens
Assembled Lamp

Making Side Lamps

1   Make lamp body from $\frac{1}{2}$ in brass rod 1 in long. Place in drill press and drill $\frac{3}{8}$ in hole. Machine rod in lathe to shape. Machine lip for lens and remove material inside rod up to the $\frac{3}{8}$ in hole. Cut off light body with parting tool.

2   Place body in drill press and drill $\frac{1}{16}$ in hole in one side. *Note* Drill L and R lamp body.

3   Build vent and burner from $\frac{1}{2}$ in brass rod and machine to dimensions shown ($\frac{3}{8}$ in diameter must be exact). Drill $\frac{1}{16}$ in hole in drill press through the piece.

4   Machine oil pot from $\frac{1}{2}$ in brass rod in lathe. Drill $\frac{3}{8}$ in hole $\frac{1}{8}$ in deep, then machine remaining part around this hole. Use a parting tool to separate part from rod.

5   Make $\frac{1}{16}$ in brass ring same way as for head lamp. Assemble lamp, as shown. Mounting bar is $\frac{1}{16}$ in diameter and 1 in long (trimmed later) with 90° bend before placing into mounting hole.

6   Align all parts and solder together. Make 2 side lamps. Polish with dremel and set aside.

Making Horn

1   Build horn same way as for Stanley Steamer (p21) noting different sizes required. Build bell first, then form $\frac{1}{8}$ in diameter brass rods to shape. Solder $\frac{1}{8}$ in rod to bell.

2   Use $\frac{1}{8}$ in wide tin strip to mount horn to car. Drill hole through tin to fit a tack pin. Make horn bulb from $\frac{3}{8}$ in dowel of African blackwood turned in lathe, shaped with files.

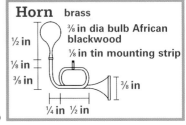

Horn brass
$\frac{1}{2}$ in $\frac{3}{8}$ in dia bulb African blackwood
$\frac{1}{8}$ in tin mounting strip
$\frac{1}{8}$ in
$\frac{3}{8}$ in $\frac{3}{8}$ in
$\frac{1}{4}$ in $\frac{1}{2}$ in

First Stage Assembly

1   Glue side rails to floor with back of floor even with notched end. Check distance between rails. Glue dash to engine block with edges sticking out equally. Dry. Place assembly on top of car rails and glue with bottom of dash flush against floor's front edge, glue engine and dash in place. Dry.

2   Turn car over and glue engine splash guard flush with front bottom edge of radiator with sloping side towards front of car. On straight end of splash guard,

place ¼ in dowel in hole letting it stick out ¾ in from back of splash guard resting on drive axle.

3   Place front axle on car. Both sides stick out same distance from sides of car measuring from springs. Glue. Use small end of flat toothpicks and make spring clamps and axle bolts.Cut and glue toothpicks in place.

4   Slide drive pulley onto axle. Cut pulley so axle will sit on side rails. Glue. Dry. Glue drive pulleys onto ends of drive axle letting axle stick out slightly past pulleys. Glue rear axle to rear springs. Axle must be centered to car, as done on front axle.

5   Slide pulleys onto axle making sure they line up with drive axle pulleys and mark with a pencil. Slide pulleys off axle, place glue on marks and slide pulleys back. Dry. *Note Pulleys must line up or chains will not be straight.*

6   Wrap chains around pulleys and tie together with fine wire, placed where it will not be seen, under back wheel hub. On ends of front rails, add small African blackwood buttons to each side of spring pivots.

7   Glue gas tank between rear springs, sticking out ½ in from end of floorboard.

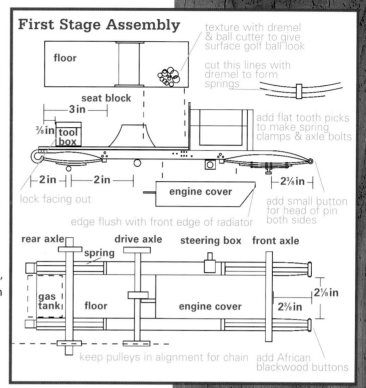

First Stage Assembly

floor

texture with dremel & ball cutter to give surface golf ball look

cut this lines with dremel to form springs

seat block

3 in

³⁄₈ in tool box

add flat tooth picks to make spring clamps & axle bolts

2 in   2 in

lock facing out

engine cover

2³⁄₈ in

add small button for head of pin both sides

edge flush with front edge of radiator

rear axle   drive axle   steering box   front axle

spring

gas tank   floor

engine cover

2³⁄₈ in

2⅛ in

keep pulleys in alignment for chain   add African blackwood buttons

Final Assembly

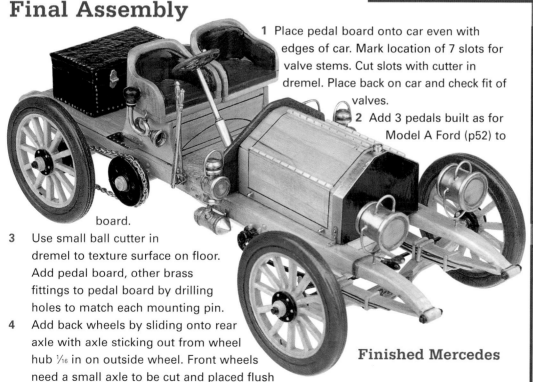

1   Place pedal board onto car even with edges of car. Mark location of 7 slots for valve stems. Cut slots with cutter in dremel. Place back on car and check fit of valves.

2   Add 3 pedals built as for Model A Ford (p52) to board.

3   Use small ball cutter in dremel to texture surface on floor. Add pedal board, other brass fittings to pedal board by drilling holes to match each mounting pin.

4   Add back wheels by sliding onto rear axle with axle sticking out from wheel hub ¹⁄₁₆ in on outside wheel. Front wheels need a small axle to be cut and placed flush with inside wheel, sticking out ¹⁄₁₆ in on outside of wheel. To position front wheels, place scrap wood under front axle until car is high enough to place the ends of axle in center of wheel. This keeps car level. Glue. Dry wheels overnight.

Finished Mercedes

5   Glue support arms to inside hubs of car with arms pointing towards back of car and

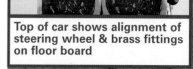

Front wheels, crank, pins on springs, lights mount to car, tie rod & steering arm - how front rail curved

Top of car shows alignment of steering wheel & brass fittings on floor board

Front rail curving with spring pins on, bolt to hold crank in place, lights mounted to car

How floor boards are roughed & pedal placement, view of lamps

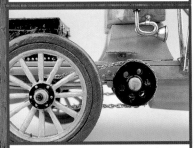

Side of rear wheel, how chain goes around rear axle to drive pulley

Top - over engine, contouring of axle & wheels, pedal board

Curving rear part of rail, gas tank with cap, rear trunk

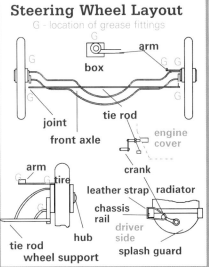

Steering Wheel Layout
G - location of grease fittings
arm, box, G G G, tie rod, joint, front axle, arm, tire, crank, leather strap, radiator, chassis rail, engine cover, driver side, hub, tie rod, wheel support, splash guard

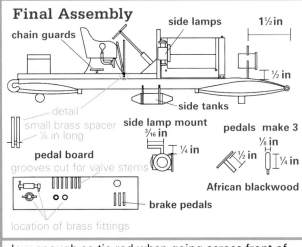

Final Assembly
chain guards, side lamps, 1½ in, ½ in, detail, small brass spacer ⅛ in long, pedal board, grooves cut for valve stems, side lamp mount ³⁄₁₆ in, ¼ in, pedals make 3 ⅛ in, ½ in, ¼ in, African blackwood, brake pedals, location of brass fittings

low enough so tie rod when going across front of car will clear crank hole. Glue in place to back of hubs. Place tie rod on support arms across front of car and trim to length, then glue tie rod to steering supports.

6 On driver side of car steering arm support is glued on top of hub over axle going in the same direction as axle. Dry. Place steering arm on steering box and check to see it reaches steering support that was added to car above axle. Trim to length and glue. Add small grease fittings in locations marked with the letter G on diagram.

7 Place seats over seat block keeping them centered. Place side tanks on side of car just under pedal board hanging just under car rail, one on each side. Mount with tack pins.

8 Add chain guard with a ⅛ in space between guard and pulley. Mount with tack pins. Mount horn on car on driver side with bell even with front edge of seat.

9 Mount levers using a small tack pin and a ⅛-in-long spacer between even with edge of curved part of seat block on driver side, as shown.

10 Use a drill bit the same size as the mounting rod and drill a hole in edge of dash half way up dash between top and bottom edges. Polish light assembly with wire brush in a dremel and glue side lamps in place.

11 With same drill bit, drill mounting holes in top of front rails, as shown. Polish front lights as above and glue in place keeping them at the same height, trimming mounts.

12 Crank should be mounted so handle is pointing towards top edge of car rail. Use small piece of brown leather ⅛ in wide and wrap around car rail and crank handle. This is how it was held when not in use. Glue trunk on back of car.

13 Glue steering wheel into hole with 24-hour epoxy and lift wheel until edge of hand wheel is approximately ⅛ in above side edge of seat. Check it is straight from top view of car. Hold in place with masking tape until dry.

14 Set car for 2 days. Cover with 3-7 coats of clear urethane finish. Clear coat leather trunk as well.

Under - rear axle, drive axle & steering assembly

Top view, location of trunk

Rear gas tank, and how chain goes around rear axle, lock on trunk

1907

Locomobile

The locomobile was a very special car built by the Locomobile Company of America and was one of the first US horseless carriages. The company operated for about 30 years and its slogan was, "The Best Built Car in America." The car were raced with great success and took third place in the Vanderbilt cup in 1905. The last Locomobile was manufactured in 1929.

The model Locomobile in this book is a touring type H model. It was not a production model and was built only on demand with a price tag of $4,500. In its day it was advertised as "A Touring Car DeLuxe" and is called the Mona Lisa of American historic cars. It could carry seven passengers if the buyer elected to have folding seats installed, and came with a 35-horsepower engine driven by a 4-speed selective transmission with a dual chain as a final drive system. The headlights on this car were acetylene and the chassis gears and shaft were made of steel alloy. This car still exists and is a coveted prize for some collectors.

Car Parts

Note Some parts may require pieces of wood to be glued together to obtain proper size.

Car Parts List

Material/Size	Parts		Material	Size
African blackwood			**Brass**	
1 piece 16 in x 5 in x ½ in	Dash Board, Pitman Arm, Support Arm,		¹⁄₁₆ in rod	24 in long
	Mat, Floor Pedals, Buttons, Fan Drive		¹⁄₁₆ diameter tube	1 in long
	Front, Horn Bulb, Tie Rod, Chain		⅛ in rod	8 in long
Guards,	Mat, Fan Drive Rear,		⅛ in tube	6 in long
Floor Pedals, Front	Seat Block, Engine		³⁄₁₆ in rod	6 in long
Cylinder Block,	Running Board Mats,		³⁄₁₆ in tube	3 in long
Rear Door Top	Cushion, Radiator,		¼ in rod	1 in long
Rear Door Inside	Door Panel, Rear		⅜ in rod	6 in long
Door Spacer, Rear Seat	Cushions, Front Seat Cushions		⁷⁄₁₆ in rod	1 in long
Honduras mahogany			½ in rod	1 in long
1 piece 20 in x 8 in x 1¼ in	Side Rails, Wheels, Transmission, Drive		½ in tube	1 in long
	Shaft, Front Axle, Hubs, Steering Box,		½ in strip	20 in long
	Rear Axle Blocks, Rear Axle, Chassis		⅝ in rod	1 in long
	Cross Members, Rear Springs, Chain		¾ in rod	3 in long
	Pulley, Rear Seat Block, Chain Guards		.003 Shim Stock	1⅜ in x 3 in long

Knob, Floor Board, Pedal Board, Chain
Axle, Axle Bearings, Engine Cover, Rear
Seat Bottom, Chain Guards Lever, Dash
Board, Front Seat Block, Rear Seat
Sides, Front Seat Side, Chain Pulley,
Chain Guards Front, Chain Guards End,
Rear Fender, Rear Fender Brackets,
Front Fender, Front, Fender Braces,
Engine Carburetor, Front Seat Block,
Chain Guards Top, Front Fender Braces,
Running Boards, Running Board
Brackets, Rear Door, Rear Door Hinge,
Front Seat Bottom, Engine Fly Wheel

Miscellaneous Materials

Aluminum	⅛ in x ½ in x ¹⁄₁₆ in
Cocobolo	2 in x 3 in x 1¹⁄₁₆ in
Tin	⅛ in x 2 in
Clear plastic disk	⅝ in round
Oak	⅝ in x 2½ in x ¹⁄₁₆ in
Rubber O ring	1½ in diameter
Red Oak	3½ in x 13 in x ⅜ in

Back Wheel

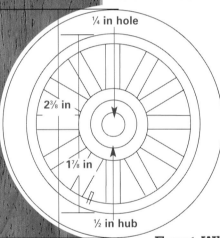

Front Wheel

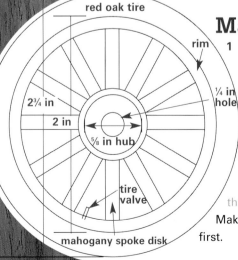

Making Wheels

1 The building process for these wheels is given on p11, but use the following materials: Honduras mahogany 13 in x 3½ in x ¼ in for the wheels and red oak 13 in x 3½ in x ⅜ in for tires.

Note Diagram for this car gives dimensions. Back wheels are smaller than front wheels.

2 Use ½ in diameter brass rod machined to shape for hubs.

Note Back hubs are smaller than front hubs in diameter.

Make from brass starting with back first.

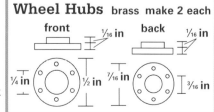

Wheel Hubs brass make 2 each

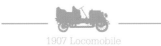

Making Side Rails

1 Use 2 pieces Honduras mahogany 12½ in x 1¼ in x 5/16 in glued (white carpenter's glue) together with paper between to separate (L & R) them after cutting. Transfer (p5) pattern to wood.

2 Cut out between spring and rail first. Drill 4 lightning holes as shown. Cut out the remaining rail and separate rails from each other.

3 Cut notches for cross members. *Note* Cut L & R.

4 On front edge of rail above front spring, dremel small concave shape on both sides just past holes.

5 Shape front springs same as Mercedes, p59. Glue rear springs pieces together as for rails to ensure L & R. Cut out. Cut notch, as shown. *Note* ⅝ in dimension must be exact.

6 Check diagram for size of cross members. *Note* Cross member located towards front of chassis is the only one with a cutout. Glue chassis assembly together. Set aside.

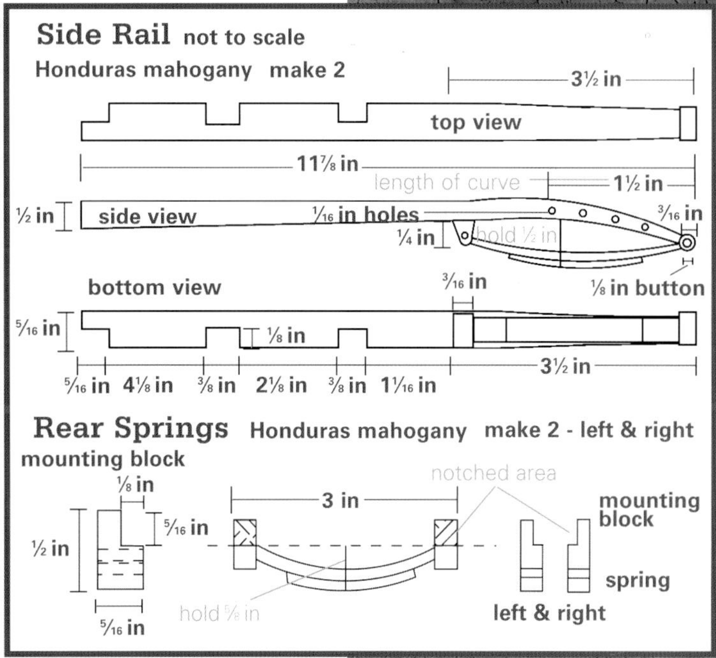
Side Rail not to scale
Honduras mahogany make 2
3½ in
top view
11⅞ in
length of curve
1½ in
½ in
side view
1/16 in holes
3/16 in
¼ in
hold ½ in
bottom view
3/16 in
⅛ in button
5/16 in
⅛ in
3½ in
5/16 in 4⅛ in ⅜ in 2⅛ in ⅜ in 1 1/16 in
Rear Springs Honduras mahogany make 2 - left & right
mounting block
⅛ in
notched area
3 in
mounting block
5/16 in
½ in
spring
hold ⅝ in
left & right
5/16 in

Making Pedal Board

1 Cut Honduras mahogany 2⅞ in long x ¾ in sq to a triangle shape, as shown. Cut and shape 3/16 in flat edge (see diagram) used to butt floorboard against pedal board on assembly. Cut 1/16 in thick African blackwood same size as sloping side of pedal board and glued to pedal board, (shown by dotted lines). Dry.

2 Cut slots with a dremel to fit pedals and drill 3/16 in diameter hole 90° to sloping side of pedal board for steering column.

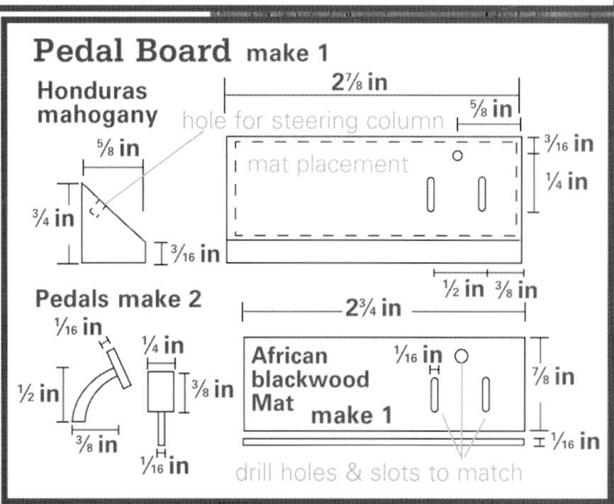
Pedal Board make 1
Honduras mahogany
2⅞ in
⅝ in
hole for steering column
⅝ in
3/16 in
mat placement
¼ in
¾ in
3/16 in
½ in ⅜ in
Pedals make 2
2¾ in
1/16 in
¼ in
½ in
⅜ in
African blackwood Mat make 1
1/16 in
⅞ in
⅜ in
1/16 in
1/16 in
drill holes & slots to match

Making Transmission & Drive Shaft

1 Cut Honduras mahogany 1¼ in x ⅝ in x ½ in thick, to shape (see diagram). Make drive shaft from piece of Honduras mahogany turned to a 3/16 in dowel 2 in long.

2 Rear seal is built from maple dowel ½ in diameter. Drill 3/16 in hole through the maple. Machine outside to shape, as shown. Glue to one end of drive shaft and set aside.

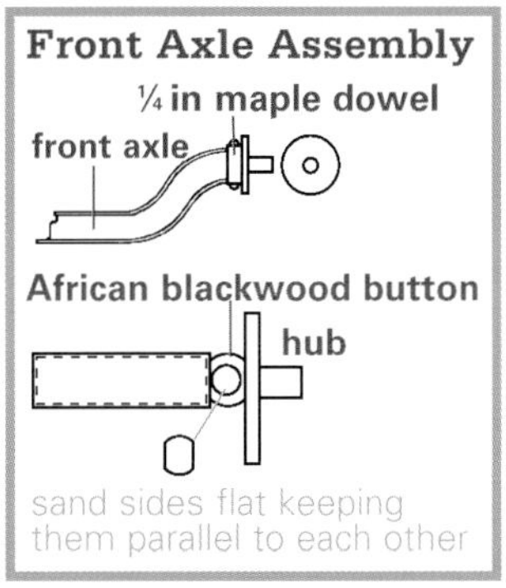
Front Axle Assembly
¼ in maple dowel
front axle
African blackwood button
hub
sand sides flat keeping them parallel to each other

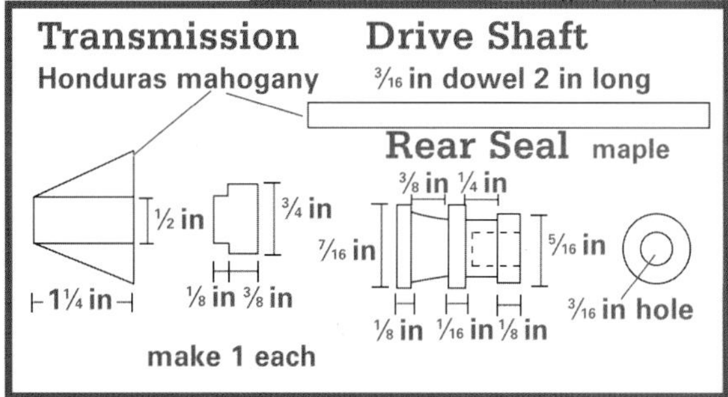
Transmission
Honduras mahogany
Drive Shaft
3/16 in dowel 2 in long
Rear Seal maple
½ in
¾ in
1¼ in
⅛ in ⅜ in
⅜ in ¼ in
7/16 in
5/16 in
3/16 in hole
⅛ in 1/16 in ⅛ in
make 1 each

Making Front Axle

1 Build the same as Mercedes (p59) using these dimensions and Honduras mahogany. Axle hubs are made from ¾ in dowel.

2 Make 4 African blackwood buttons and two ¼ in maple dowels cut ⅜ in long glued to ends of axle between axle and hubs. Maple dowels need 2 flat edges on each side of dowel. These are king pins, in which front wheels pivot on real car.

3 Glue African blackwood buttons on each end of maple dowels used to form king pins. When gluing hubs in place, make sure they are level and straight in all directions.

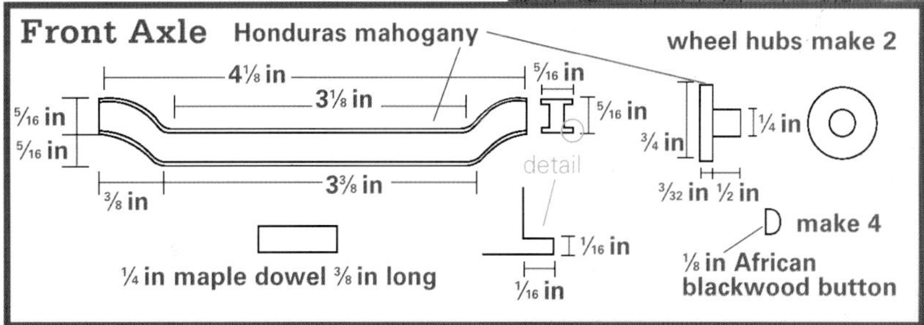
Front Axle Honduras mahogany
wheel hubs make 2
4⅛ in
3⅛ in
5/16 in
5/16 in
5/16 in
5/16 in
¾ in
¼ in
detail
3⅜ in
⅜ in
3/32 in ½ in
make 4
1/16 in
1/16 in
¼ in maple dowel ⅜ in long
⅛ in African blackwood button

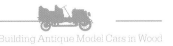

Making Chain Axle

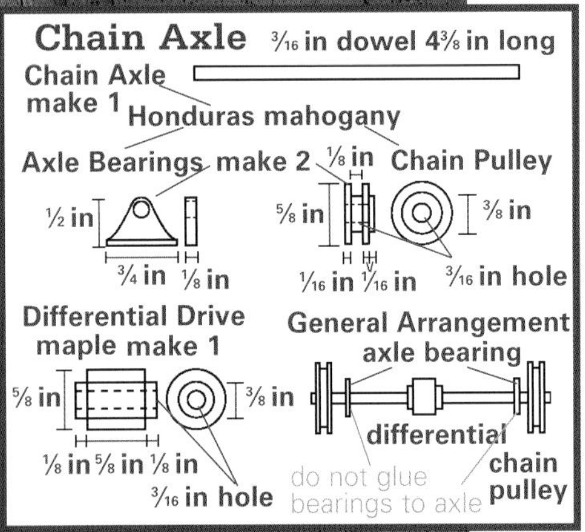
Chain Axle 3/16 in dowel 4 3/8 in long
Chain Axle
make 1
Honduras mahogany
Axle Bearings make 2
1/8 in
Chain Pulley
1/2 in
3/4 in
1/8 in
5/8 in
3/8 in
1/16 in
1/16 in
3/16 in hole
Differential Drive
maple make 1
General Arrangement
axle bearing
5/8 in
3/8 in
1/8 in 5/8 in 1/8 in
3/16 in hole
differential
do not glue
bearings to axle
chain
pulley

1. Build axle from 3/16 in diameter dowel of Honduras mahogany 4 3/8 in long. Build differential from maple dowel 5/8 in round. Drill a 3/16 hole through center then machine outside to shape, as shown. Slide axle through hole.
2. Make chain pulleys from Honduras mahogany dowel 5/8 in diameter and 3/8 in thick. Drill axle hole first then machine outside to shape. Separate pulleys from dowel with a parting tool in lathe. Slide axle through center hole.
3. Make axle bearings from Honduras mahogany. Drill hole first, then draw shape around hole. Cut with scroll saw with a backing board between saw table and working piece so piece won't fall through. Slide parts onto axle, as shown.
4. Glue differential and drive chain pulleys in place. When gluing pulleys on end of axle leave the axle sticking out 1/16 in. Do not glue the axle bearings in place. They will have to be adjusted to line up with the chassis rails on assembly.

Making Floorboard

Transfer (p5) dimensions to Honduras mahogany 7 in x 2 7/8 in x 3/16 in with even grain and color.

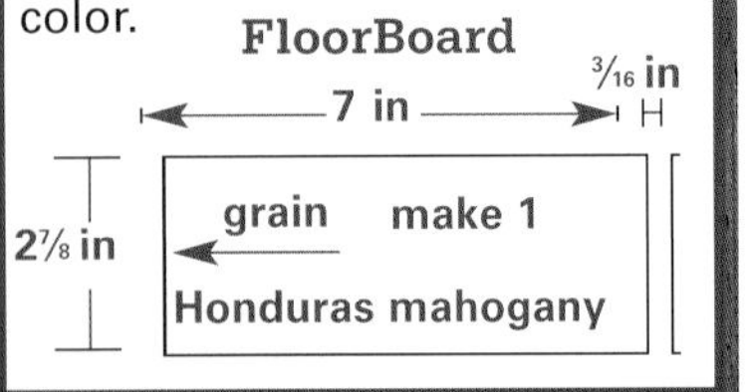
FloorBoard
7 in
3/16 in
2 7/8 in
grain
make 1
Honduras mahogany

Making Steering Parts

1. Tie rod is 4 3/4 in long and 1/16 in sq, built same way as Mercedes tie rod p62 using Honduras mahogany. Build support arms same way as Mercedes, p63.
2. Make steering box 1/2 in x 3/8 in x 1/4 in with hole same size as tack pin. *Note* Hole is same size as pitman arm, mounted to steering box, held in place by a tack pin.
3. Cut notch first on steering arm, then cut to shape. Set aside.

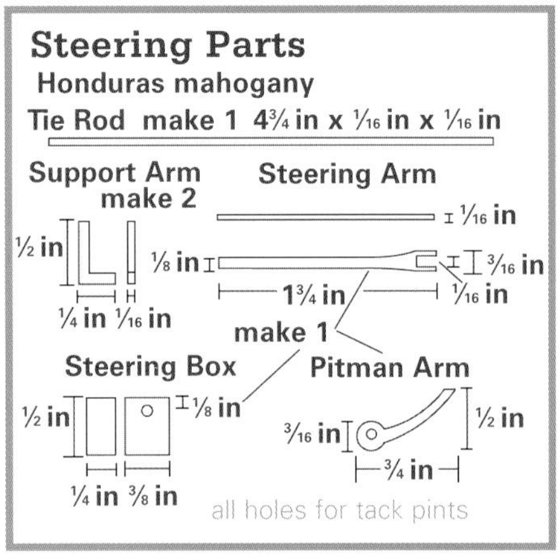
Steering Parts
Honduras mahogany
Tie Rod make 1 4 3/4 in x 1/16 in x 1/16 in
Support Arm
make 2
Steering Arm
1/16 in
1/2 in
1/8 in
3/16 in
1 3/4 in
1/16 in
1/4 in 1/16 in
make 1
Steering Box
Pitman Arm
1/2 in
1/8 in
3/16 in
1/2 in
3/4 in
1/4 in 3/8 in
all holes for tack pints

Making Rear Axle

1. Turn mahogany in lathe to 1/4 in round dowel 4 3/4 in long. Make axle blocks same method as Model A Ford p51.
2. Make chain pulleys same as Mercedes following dimensions as shown. Glue to axle. Set aside.

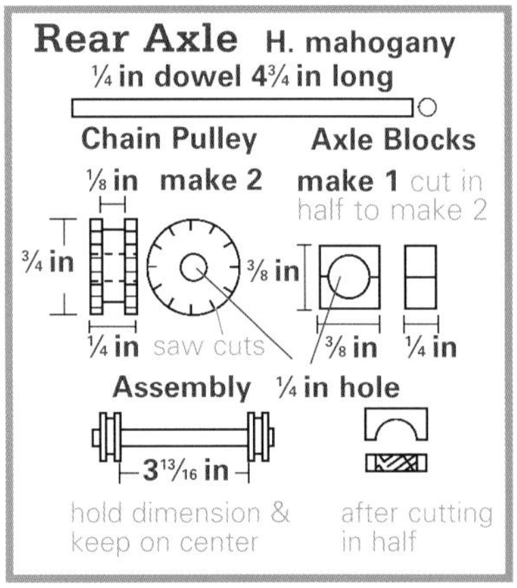
Rear Axle H. mahogany
1/4 in dowel 4 3/4 in long
Chain Pulley
Axle Blocks
1/8 in make 2
make 1 cut in half to make 2
3/4 in
3/8 in
1/4 in saw cuts
3/8 in 1/4 in
Assembly 1/4 in hole
3 13/16 in
hold dimension & keep on center
after cutting in half

Making Dash

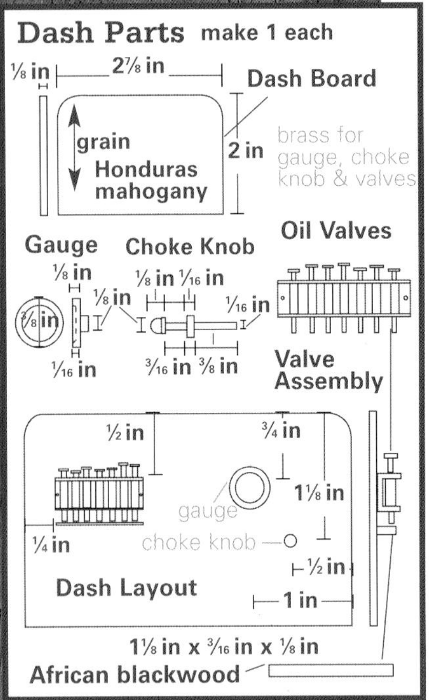
Dash Parts make 1 each
1/8 in
2 7/8 in
Dash Board
grain
Honduras mahogany
2 in
brass for gauge, choke knob & valves
Gauge
Choke Knob
Oil Valves
1/8 in
1/8 in
1/8 in 1/16 in
1/16 in
3/8 in
1/16 in
3/16 in 3/8 in
Valve Assembly
1/2 in
3/4 in
1 1/8 in
gauge
1/4 in
choke knob
1/2 in
Dash Layout
1 in
1 1/8 in x 3/16 in x 1/8 in
African blackwood

1. Use flat Honduras mahogany 2 7/8 in x 2 in x 1/8 in. Check grain. Make oil valves same as Mercedes, p60, but position differently when mounting.
2. For gauge turn 3/8 in diameter brass rod to shape in lathe starting with small diameter. Machine small recess in face side of gauge body for paper gauge.
3. Machine choke knob from brass rod 1/8 in diameter. Separate pieces using a parting tool.
4. Glue (5 minute epoxy) parts to dash as shown. Place African blackwood strip 1 1/8 in x 3/16 in x 1/8 in thick under valve assembly to finish dash. Set aside.

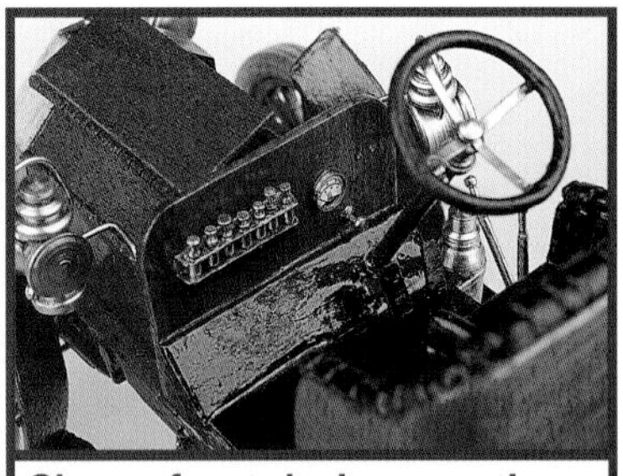
Shows front dash, mounting side lamp, steering wheel

Making Radiator

1. Cut African blackwood to 2 1/2 in x 2 3/8 in x 7/16 in. Bend

½ in wide brass strip tightly around edge of radiator, as shown.

2. Drill 4 holes in strip to fit tack pins. Also bend brass strip for bottom of radiator.

3. Cut triangle pieces for top of radiator from same strip. Position by letters on diagram.

4. Solder brass pieces to side trim of radiator. Remove excess solder, polish with wire brush in dremel at medium speed.

5. Drill 4 small holes into radiator block and place in tack pins. Glue bottom trim and bottom front and back plates to radiator block. Dry.

6. Drill ⅛ in diameter hole in the top through brass to fit radiator fill cap in and drill ⅛ in diameter crank hole through bottom of radiator. For radiator cap machine ¼ in diameter brass rod, as shown. Glue cap in top hole and set aside.

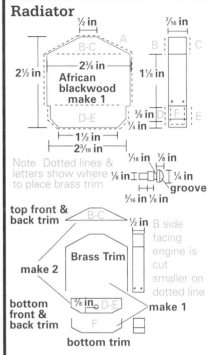

Radiator

Making Engine Cover

1. Use 3 pieces Honduras mahogany each 2⅝ in x 1⅛ in x 1/16 in thick and one piece 2⅝ in x 1¼ in x ⅛ in thick. Make small saw cuts in one edge and a groove cut in the center of edge along length of ⅛ in thick piece for hinge. Center groove looks like 2 panels.

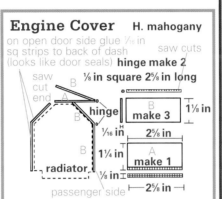

Engine Cover H. mahogany

2. Make hinge same as Mercedes (p60). Letters on diagram show position. The 1/16 in square pieces are glued to back of dash after radiator and engine are glued to car to form door seal.

3. Complete the engine detail parts before gluing covers in place. *Note* If building car without engine make engine cover go around radiator adding hinges as required.

Making Front Seat Block

Use same method as Mercedes (p61). Make design from African blackwood ⅛ in sq and glue to front of block ¼ in away from all outside edges. Dry. Sand to 1/32 in thickness to give effect of pieces inlaid into seat block. Glue side pieces to seat block keeping them flush with back of seat block. Set aside.

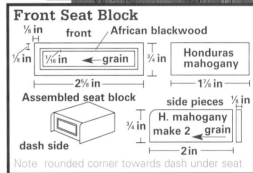

Front Seat Block

Making Rear Seat

1. Make seat block from Honduras mahogany 2⅞ in x 1¾ x ¾ in. *Note* Block has 3 edges curved towards top of block with curves the same. Front of block is flat to attach seat panel. Make single panel from oak 2½ in x ⅝ in x ⅛ in using the same method as Model A Ford seat, (p47). *Note* Seat must have finished size given on diagram so doors will line up. Cut bottom to exact size. Cut back and sides of seat ¼ in thick and glue to bottom with sides and back sticking out ⅛ in from edge of bottom pieces. Sand back and side pieces until flush with bottom seat. Sand curve on back corners.

2. Make bottom seat cushions from African blackwood 3/16 in thick and fit on the bottom piece inside seat sticking out ⅛ in on leg side of seat. Make cushions that go along back and sides of seat from pieces of blackwood cut and sanded to shape. Glue. Make back cushions in 2 pieces with top cushion slightly shorter than bottom ones. Cushions along top edge of seat are also made as individual pieces sanded to shape then cut to length. The length of

Cushions fit & door fits against seat & front, floor mats, side lamp mounts into dash

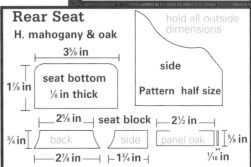

Rear Seat

Running Board & Mats

Running Board

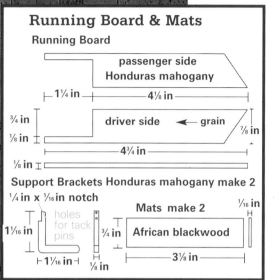

passenger side
Honduras mahogany

1¼ in — 4⅛ in

¾ in — driver side ← grain — ⅞ in

⅛ in — 4¾ in

⅛ in

Support Brackets Honduras mahogany make 2

¼ in x ¹⁄₁₆ in notch

holes for tack pins

1¹⁄₁₆ in — ¾ in — **Mats make 2** — ¹⁄₁₆ in

African blackwood

1¹⁄₁₆ in — ⅛ in — 3⅛ in

Chain Guard — Honduras mahogany make 2

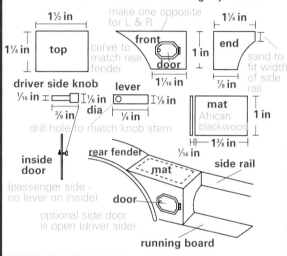

1½ in — make one opposite for L & R — 1¼ in

1¼ in — **top** — curve to match rear fender — **front** — **door** — 1 in — **end** — sand to fit width of side rail

1¹⁄₁₆ in — ⅞ in

driver side knob — **lever**

¹⁄₁₆ in — I1⅛ in — I1⅛ in

⅜ in — dia — ¼ in — **mat** African blackwood — 1 in

drill hole to match knob stem — 1⅜ in — ¹⁄₁₆ in

inside door — **rear fender** — **side rail**

(passenger side - no lever on inside) — **mat**

optional side door is open (driver side) — **door** — **running board**

Rear Fender make 2

Honduras mahogany

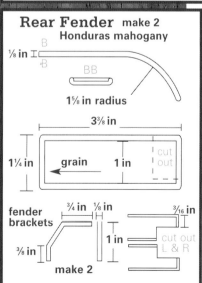

⅛ in — B B — BB

1⅝ in radius

3⅜ in

1¼ in — grain — 1 in — cut out

fender brackets — ¾ in — ⅛ in — ³⁄₁₆ in

⅜ in — 1 in — cut out L & R

make 2

---

this cushion is equal to the width of 2 cushions running across back of seat.

3 When attaching, make first joint of cushions in the middle of back of seat. Then add cushions on each side of first cushion. Top of cushions must be flush with top edges of seat edges and back. Then add top edge cushions keeping them flush with front edge of vertical cushions and even with back of seat and sides.

4 Repeat above method for FRONT seat following dimensions on front seat diagram (p73). Keep outside dimensions exact. Set aside.

Making Running Boards & Mats

1 Use 2 flat pieces of Honduras mahogany 4¾ in x ⅞ in x ⅛ in. *Note Match grain on both sides.* Cut piece thicker than required then cut in half down the length. Cut pieces to shape. Sand to proper thickness.

2 Make mounting brackets from Honduras mahogany. Shape, then cut into slices to proper thickness. Drill holes in brackets with a drill bit and pin vice to fit tack pins (look like rivets).

3 Make 2 mats from African blackwood 3⅛ in x ¾ in x ¹⁄₁₆ in, glued to running board on final assembly.

Making Chain Guards

1 Make from Honduras mahogany grain direction same as running boards. Make 2 of each. Front pieces of chain guards matching curve of rear fender so no gaps are in the joint between guard and fender. Door is carved into panel on passenger side.

2 Make hinge from ⅛ in round dowel and glue to face of front piece beside edge of carved door. *Note You can make a small panel and glue it to this panel to look like a door.*

3 Turn a small knob and glue to door on both front panels. Machine stem of knob first then cut to length. Drill hole into a piece of wood to fit knob stem into. Sand on belt sander to final size holding with needle nose pliers.

4 Cut out front panel of door (driver's side) and glue in open position to show chain drive pulley under the guard. *Note If driver door is not open, make sure L and R are carved in front pieces.* Make a small groove with dremel around front panel opening to look like a stiffening edge on front piece. Cut groove on passenger side also, even if door is closed.

5 Cut remaining parts as shown, and sand smooth. Make mats from African blackwood and glue to top pieces. Set aside.

Making Rear Fenders

1 Use 2 pieces of Honduras mahogany each 3½ in x 2½ in x 1¼ in. Build as Cadillac (p35). *Note Cut notches on each fender for L and R.*

Rear Seat

Seat Cushions

African blackwood

(fits in between sides)

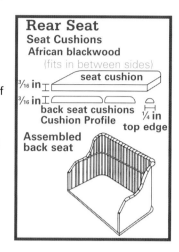

³⁄₁₆ in — seat cushion

³⁄₁₆ in — back seat cushions — ¼ in

Cushion Profile — top edge

Assembled back seat

Chain guard, chain pulleys, side with chain guard open, rear wheel hubs, rear fender brackets, 3 rivets in side rail

2. Fender brackets are made from a larger piece cut to shape then cut to proper thickness in band saw. *Note* Thinner brackets look better.

Making Front Fenders

1. Honduras mahogany 5 in x 3 in x ¾ in will make both front fenders. Draw 4½ in diameter circle on the wood using center point for circle along the 5 in side and ¼ in from the edge. Draw another circle ³⁄₁₆ in outside first circle.

2. Set band saw table to 45° angle and cut inside circle first then cut outside circle. Cone shape piece remains. Sand on both sides with drum sander in drill press. Cut 2 fenders L and R from the cone shape piece using 2¾ in measurement on diagram. Sand top corners round.

3. Cut strips (see diagram) for mounting brackets and reinforcement braces on fender.

Making Rear Doors

1. Draw outline of door on Honduras mahogany 2 in x 1½ in x ⅛ in. Glue (white carpenter's glue) another piece of wood same size on bottom with paper between. Cut out leaving pattern line visible. Sand to final size on belt sander drum sander for curved part of door. Separate doors L and R and sand off paper and glue.

2. Cut 2 pieces of African blackwood the same size as doors and thin as possible and glue to one side of doors (L and R) for inside panels.

3. Use two strips of African blackwood (sizes on diagram) and round cushion shape for top door edge cushions. Glue to top edge of door.

4. To make hinge use Honduras mahogany ½ in x ⅛ in x ⅛ in and cut piece ⅛ in sq and long enough for 2 pieces. Make several saw cuts into piece (not all the way through). Cut hinge piece to proper length and set aside.

5. Make door spacer as shown to attach door to side of front seat from African blackwood ¾ in x ⅛ in sq.

6. Make doorknob assembly from brass rod ³⁄₁₆ in diameter for handle plate and another brass rod ⅛ in diameter for handle. Handle plate has ¹⁄₁₆ in diameter pin machined on one side to solder door handle to door plate. Other side of door plate needs only a pin so that it can be glued to door. *Note* This side of plate can actually be any size smaller than ³⁄₁₆ in diameter with hole drilled in door to match.

7. Handle is machined to size, as shown. Drill ¹⁄₁₆ in hole by hand using a pin vice to hold drill bit. Solder handle to plate then polish both assemblies with wire wheel in dremel at medium speed. Glue handles to doors (L and R).

8. Place doors on table with ⅝ in side facing each other and glue handles to doors. Set aside.

Making Engine

1. Make oil pan from 2 in x 1½ in x 1¹⁄₁₆ in of cocobolo. Cut ³⁄₁₆ in x ⅛ in notch in top on both sides, then cut bottom to proper width, as shown. Cut bottom of

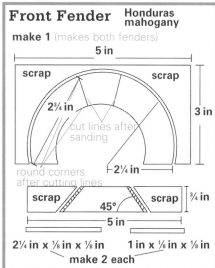

Front Fender Honduras mahogany
make 1 (makes both fenders)

5 in

scrap   scrap
2¾ in
3 in
cut lines after sanding
round corners after cutting lines
2¼ in

scrap   45°   scrap   ¾ in
5 in

2¼ in x ⅛ in x ⅛ in   1 in x ⅛ in x ⅛ in
make 2 each

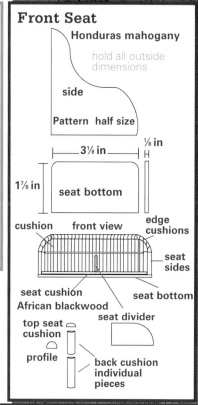

Front Seat

Honduras mahogany
hold all outside dimensions

side

Pattern half size

3⅛ in   ⅛ in

1⅞ in   seat bottom

cushion   front view   edge cushions

seat sides

seat cushion   seat bottom

African blackwood   seat divider

top seat cushion

profile   back cushion individual pieces

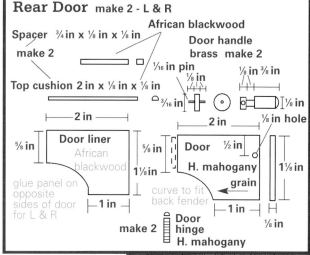

Rear Door make 2 - L & R

African blackwood

Spacer ¾ in x ⅛ in x ⅛ in   Door handle brass make 2
make 2

¹⁄₁₆ in pin   ⅛ in ⅜ in
⅛ in

Top cushion 2 in x ⅛ in x ⅛ in   ³⁄₁₆ in   ⅛ in

2 in   2 in   ⅛ in hole

⅝ in   Door liner   ⅝ in   Door   ½ in
African blackwood   H. mahogany   1⅛ in
1⅛ in   grain

glue panel on opposite sides of door for L & R   curve to fit back fender

1 in   1 in   ⅛ in

make 2   Door hinge   H. mahogany

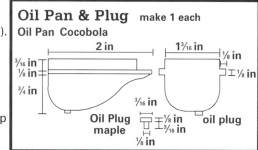

Oil Pan & Plug make 1 each

Oil Pan Cocobola

2 in   1³⁄₁₆ in   ⅛ in

³⁄₁₆ in
⅛ in   ⅛ in

¾ in

³⁄₁₆ in

Oil Plug maple   ⅛ in   oil plug
³⁄₁₆ in
⅛ in

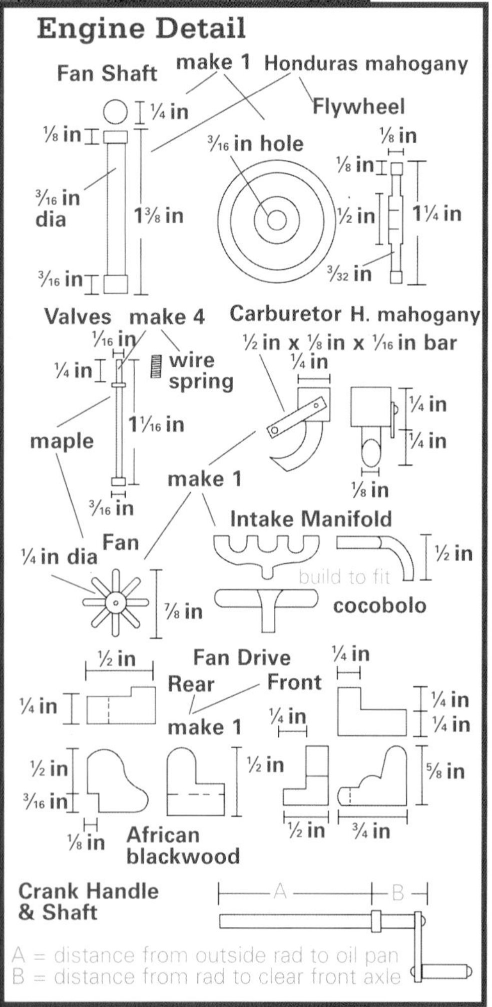
Engine Detail
Fan Shaft
make 1 Honduras mahogany
Flywheel
1/4 in
1/8 in
3/16 in hole
1/8 in
1/8 in
3/16 in dia
1 3/8 in
1/2 in
1 1/4 in
3/16 in
3/32 in
Valves make 4
Carburetor H. mahogany
1/16 in
1/2 in x 1/8 in x 1/16 in bar
1/4 in
wire spring
1/4 in
1/4 in
1/4 in
maple
1 1/16 in
make 1
1/8 in
3/16 in
Intake Manifold
1/4 in dia
Fan
1/2 in
build to fit
7/8 in
cocobolo
1/2 in
Fan Drive
1/4 in
Rear
Front
1/4 in
1/4 in
1/4 in
make 1
1/4 in
1/2 in
1/2 in
5/8 in
3/16 in
1/8 in
African blackwood
1/2 in
3/4 in
Crank Handle & Shaft
A
B
A = distance from outside rad to oil pan
B = distance from rad to clear front axle

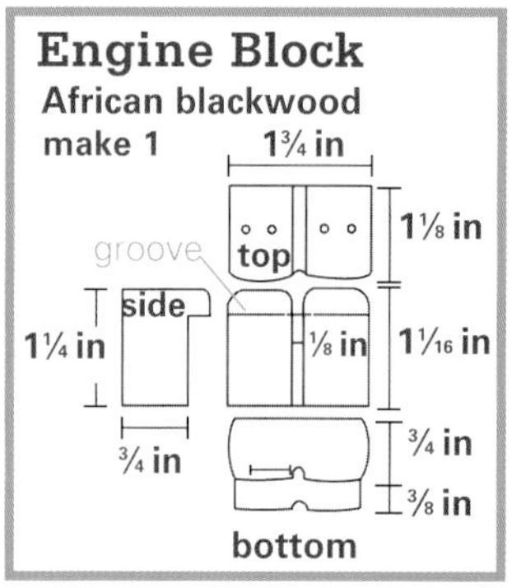
Engine Block
African blackwood
make 1
1 3/4 in
groove
top
1 1/8 in
side
1 1/4 in
1/8 in
1 1/16 in
3/4 in
3/4 in
3/8 in
bottom

block to shape, draw profile of oil pan, and cut out on scroll saw. Round bottom edges with sandpaper and small drum sander in dremel.

2 Cut cylinder block from African blackwood 1 3/4 in 1 1/4 in x 1 1/16 in. First cut L shape shown on diagram and dremel the small 1/8 in deep groove through the center of the block going across the top and down the side as shown, and used to show that the cylinders were made in two sets.

3 Drill four 1/8 in diameter equally spaced 1/4 in deep holes shown on top view. *Note* Hole must be deep enough to hold round toothpicks, used to make spark plugs and glued into these holes. Round all edges of block to shape,using dremel and drum sander.

4 Make top of block where spark plugs go look like cast iron by using a fine steel cutter in dremel to rough the wood, carving top to curve down towards edges of block. Curve inside of L shape working from edge towards center groove. Bottom of the block has an oval shape.

5 Make fan shaft from Honduras mahogany dowel turned to shape in lathe. Make flywheel from Honduras mahogany the same as flywheel on Ford Model A (p47).

6 Turn valve stems from 3/16 in diameter maple dowel in lathe, 1/4 in dimension from top of valve to first ring. Total length is exact as shown on diagram.

7 Make spring by coiling a fine wire around a drill bit that matches the diameter of stem on top of valve. Pull wire apart, then cut spring to length to go from support ring to just below top of stem. No glue required to hold in place.

8 Make oil plug from maple dowel turned to shape or use a button glued to bottom of oil pan.

9 Make carburetor from 1/4 in Honduras mahogany and 1/8 in maple dowel cut to shape. *Note* Maple dowel is used to show intake of carburetor and small level is used to show choke. Lever is attached to carburetor with a tack pin cut to length and block has a hole drilled to match the tack pin. Location of hole is not critical as long as it is in same area of block as shown on diagram. Make fan from maple dowel cut to the proper thickness. Draw blades on the face of dowel and cut out in scroll or band saw.

10 From African blackwood cut L-shape then cut face to shape. *Note* Height and width of front fan drive must be exact for the fan drivers. Intake manifold cannot be made until the engine is partially assembled.

11 Make crank same method as Mercedes (p62), but use measurements found once the radiator and front axle are attached to the car. Make crank handle and support arm same way as Mercedes (p62) with same measurements, but use Honduras mahogany for support arm and shaft and cocobolo for handle.

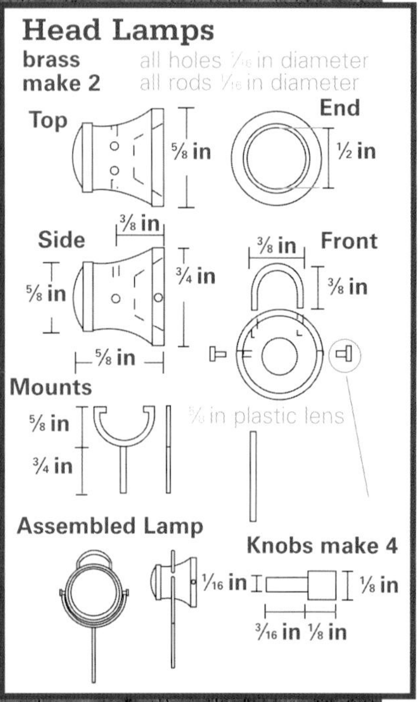
Head Lamps
brass
make 2
all holes 1/16 in diameter
all rods 1/16 in diameter
Top
5/8 in
End
1/2 in
Side
3/8 in
5/8 in
3/4 in
3/8 in
Front
3/8 in
5/8 in
Mounts
5/8 in
3/4 in
5/8 in plastic lens
Assembled Lamp
Knobs make 4
1/16 in
1/8 in
3/16 in
1/8 in

Making Head and Side Lamps

1 Make same as for Mercedes, using dimensions (see diagram). Drill all holes in solid brass rod before starting machining process. Shape curved part of light body with a round file while piece is spinning in lathe. Make both

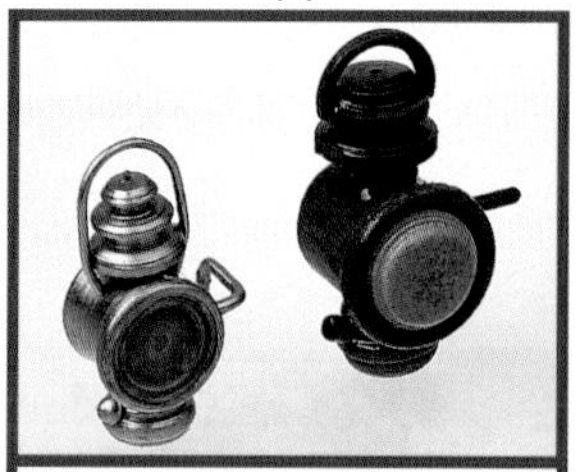

Brass & optional wood used for side lamp

measurements same. Make mounting brackets same as Mercedes, p64.

2. Align all lamp parts (see diagram), and solder in place. Polish to bright finish, then glue plastic lens to light assembly with 5-minute epoxy.

3. Make side lamps same as Model A Ford, p52, but shape as shown. Drill all holes into a solid piece of brass rod. Machine to shape, working around holes by keeping them in middle of part.

4. Make 2 mounting brackets by drilling holes into piece of brass shim, then draw pattern of bracket around holes and shape using a tiny drum sander in dremel at slow speed. *Note* Hold bracket with pliers while sanding, as brass will get hot. Discoloring of brass can be polished to original color.

5. Cut a small tube to fit over ¹⁄₁₆ in diameter mounting rod and solder to edge of mounting bracket as shown. Mounting rod is bent in two 90° angles as shown. Make L & R. Do not solder mounting brackets to mounting rods.

6. Assemble lights and solder parts together. Polish to bright finish and glue lens in place. Set aside.

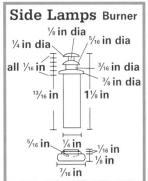

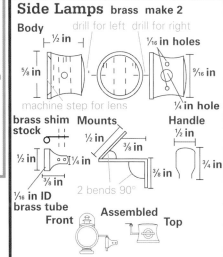

Gas Generator and Horn

1. Using miniature tube cutter, cut ½ in diameter brass tube ¾ in long. Make top piece of generator from ½ in diameter brass rod, and drill 2 holes on top of piece in drill press. Place in lathe and turn end to fit into tube. Turn piece around in lathe (end with the holes sticking out) and machine part to shape. Machine 2 knobs to fit into holes. *Note* Make both knobs same length then sand one slightly shorter.

2. Using smooth part of tin can cut a strip with snips longer and wider than required. Hold with pliers and sand to proper width. Strip fits tightly against tube of generator. Drill 2 holes by hand to fit tack pins using pin vice.

3. Assemble all parts as shown and lightly solder in place. Cool. Polish with wire brush in dremel at medium speed. Set aside.

4. Make horn and bulb using same method as Mercedes, (p64). Machine parts to dimensions as diagram. *Note* Bulb will be joined to horn later by 4 in long ¹⁄₁₆ in diameter brass rod. Set parts aside.

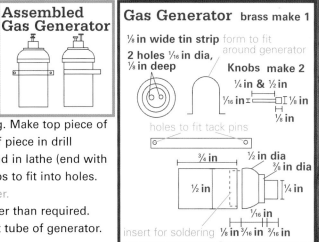

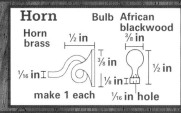

Brake and Shift Lever

1. Use ⅛ in diameter brass tube for main part of lever and build same method as Mercedes levers. *Note* Levers not same length. Turn handles from ³⁄₁₆ in diameter brass rod machined to shape, as shown. Handles fit into one end of brass rod and both handles are the same. On end of one lever, machine another piece of brass rod, as shown (used as pivot point of lever as seen on real car). Solder handles to one end of each brass tube and solder pivot point to the end of longest brass tube.

2. With a small hammer flatten handles, pivot part, and brass tube to an oval shape. By hand drill small hole in

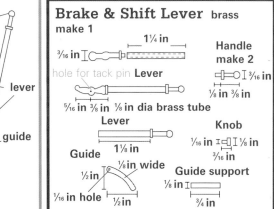

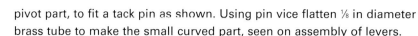

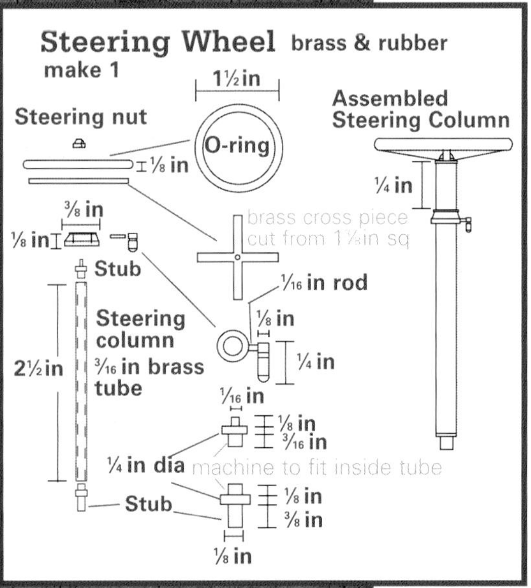
Steering Wheel brass & rubber
make 1
1 1/2 in
Steering nut
O-ring
1/8 in
Assembled Steering Column
1/4 in
3/8 in
1/8 in
brass cross piece cut from 1/8 in sq
Stub
1/16 in rod
Steering column
3/16 in brass tube
1/8 in
1/4 in
2 1/2 in
1/16 in
1/8 in
3/16 in
1/4 in dia machine to fit inside tube
Stub
1/8 in
3/8 in
1/8 in

pivot part, to fit a tack pin as shown. Using pin vice flatten 1/8 in diameter brass tube to make the small curved part, seen on assembly of levers.

3 Drill 1/16 in diameter hole in one end of this curved piece to mount knob to assembly. Use side cutters to separate curved part from brass tube, as shown.
4 Machine knob to shape in lathe, starting with small diameter of knob. Guide support is made from brass shim stock cut to shape with tin snips.
5 Hold parts together with third hand, begin to solder assembly, using as little solder as possible. Cool. Place in alcohol to clean off solder resin.
6 Polish assembly with wire brush in dremel at medium speed. Coat assembly with clear gloss and set aside to dry.

Making Steering Wheel

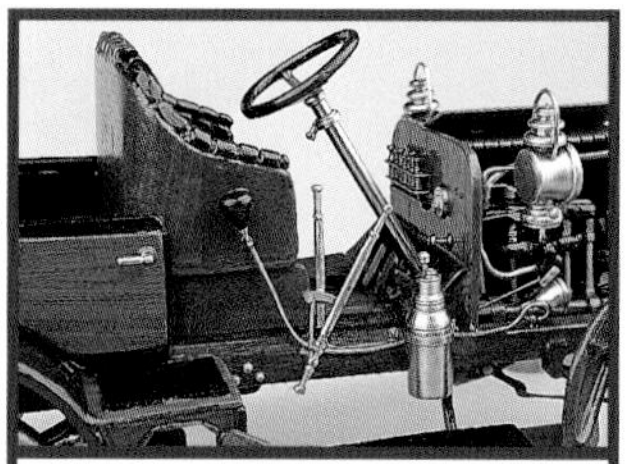

Shows levers on steering wheel, horn, rear door handle, rubber O-ring on steering wheel

1 Cut 3/16 in diameter brass tube 2 1/2 in long for steering wheel column. Machine 2 stubs to fit into end of tube. *Note* Stubs are different sizes. Large one goes into hole in pedal board and small one used to hold steering wheel to column.
2 Machine lever ring and lever as shown, to slide onto steering column. Place ring onto brass tube in position and drill 1/16 in diameter hole through ring into tube. Place short length brass tube into hole leaving it sticking out enough to solder lever handle to it.
3 When building handle, drill 1/16 in diameter hole first then machine part around it. Machine steering nut from 3/16 in diameter brass rod. Drill recess in end of rod first, then machine to shape.
4 Cut out crosspiece same way as Model A Ford p54. Assemble all parts as shown and solder in place. Polish with wire wheel in dremel at medium speed.
5 Steering wheel is made from rubber O-ring 1 1/2 in diameter. To attach, lay crosspiece over O-ring. Cut slits through the ring where the cross pieces touch. Slide crosspiece into slits to hold ring to crosspiece. Pull ring to round shape. No glue is needed. Set aside.

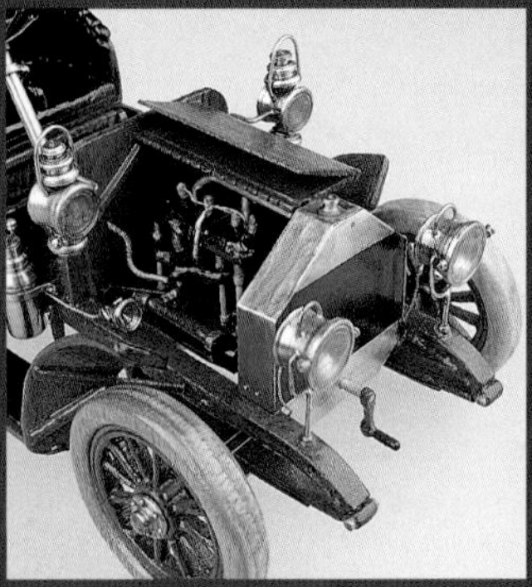

Shows top of front, engine compartment, valves, intake manifold, fan shaft, spark plugs, engine cover

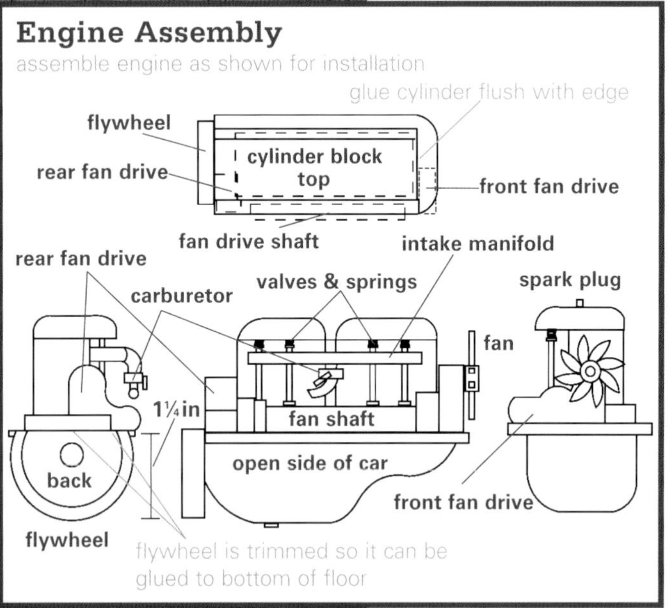
Engine Assembly
assemble engine as shown for installation
glue cylinder flush with edge
flywheel
cylinder block top
rear fan drive
front fan drive
fan drive shaft
intake manifold
rear fan drive
valves & springs
spark plug
carburetor
fan
1 1/4 in
fan shaft
open side of car
back
front fan drive
flywheel
flywheel is trimmed so it can be glued to bottom of floor

Assembling Engine

1 Cylinder block is flush with raised edge of oil pan, 1/8 in from each end and 3/8 in space between valves leaving 3/4 in gap in middle of valves. Mark valves and glue in place. *Note* If valves are too long to fit between oil pan and overhang of cylinder block, sand bottom of valve.
2 Glue front fan drive to engine assembly over lip on oil pan keeping corner notch against corner and front of cylinder block.
3 Glue fan shaft in place at end of front drive along edge of oil pan. Glue rear fan drive to end of fan shaft, gluing to back of cylinder block.
4 Cut flywheel as shown and glue to back of oil pan with cut edge level with the edge of oil pan.
5 Make a cardboard cutout of design of intake manifold parts that fits between (not touching) valves with center prongs fitting between 2 middle valves. Valves fit into U-shaped cutouts on manifold. Cut a piece of cocobolo in L-shape with

the shorter side ½ in long. Place pattern on wood and trace. Cut out U-shapes in manifold with small cutter in dremel.

6 Round off all edges of manifold inside and out. The part that hangs down (where the carburetor is attached to manifold) is also rounded. Glue manifold to cylinder block keeping it at a 90° angle from cylinder block. Dry. Add carburetor to manifold, as shown. Dry. Coat engine with clear urethane but don't cover top edge of flywheel at rear of engine. This will be glued to underside of dash to hold engine in place.

7 Spark plugs are made from round toothpicks glued to holes that were drilled in top of cylinder block, sticking out ¼ in. *Note* If you do not build the engine the flywheel and oil pan are still required. The ⅛ in thick piece of wood that oil pan is glued to will fit between chassis rails and the dash and radiator. Placement must be high enough so crankshaft can go through radiator and into oil pan. It is easier if the part is glued in place. Drill ⅛ in diameter hole for crank using hole in radiator as a guide. Drive shaft is attached to flywheel. Engine cover will have to go all around the radiator to cover the missing engine.

First Stage Assembly

1 See chassis diagram. Glue cross members to side rails as shown. *Note* Cross member towards front of chassis has notch, which must face towards bottom of car. Sand all edges flat and smooth so cross members are flush with top and bottom of edges of rails.

2 Glue floor to chassis assembly. Notch in front cross member is not glued to floor side. *Note* Chassis assembly is not even with back edge of floorboard which sticks ¼ in past chassis. Dry overnight.

3 Add rear axle and front axle to stick out same distance on each side of car. Glue chain axle drive assembly to car and axle bearing to center of rails. Do not install transmission until engine is attached to car.

4 Glue steering block to side rail to same side as shown on diagram.

5 Attach small wheels on back of car and large wheels on front. Must be straight vertically and horizontally. Add rod supports to front hubs and install tie rod and steering arm. Add chains to rear drive system. Chain is wrapped around chain drive pulleys and around rear drive pulleys located beside rear wheels on each side of the car. Tie ends of chain together on the bottom edge of drive axle assembly. Set aside.

Second Stage Assembly

1 Add rear seat block flush with end of floorboard. Add front seat block placed on floor (see diagram). Place pedal board on end of floorboard, gluing to car rails.

2 Glue floor mats to floorboard between seat blocks and pedal board keeping them flush with outside edges of floorboard. Attach dash to pedal board. Dry.

3 Add radiator (2⅝ in dimension must be exact). See diagram for placement. Add engine. Place top edge of flywheel at underside of dash. Keep engine in middle of car rails. Place ⅛ in drill bit through hole in radiator and drill into oil pan.

4 Place crankshaft through hole in radiator into hole of oil pan to hold engine in place.

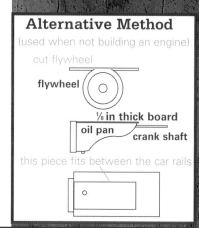

Alternative Method
(used when not building an engine)
cut flywheel
flywheel
⅛ in thick board
oil pan
crank shaft
this piece fits between the car rails

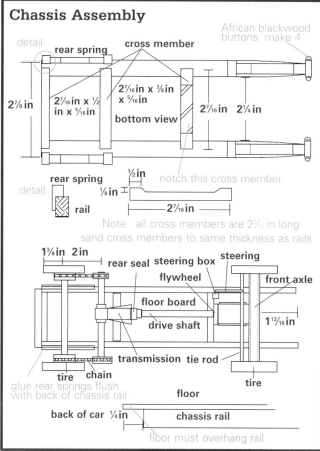

Chassis Assembly

detail
rear spring
cross member
African blackwood buttons make 4
2⅞ in
2⁷⁄₁₆ in x ½ in x ⁵⁄₁₆ in
2⁷⁄₁₆ in x ⅜ in x ⁵⁄₁₆ in
bottom view
2⁷⁄₁₆ in 2¼ in
½ in
notch this cross member
rear spring
detail
⅛ in
rail
2⁷⁄₁₆ in
Note all cross members are 2⁷⁄₁₆ in long
sand cross members to same thickness as rails
1⅜ in 2 in
rear seal steering box steering
flywheel
front axle
floor board
1¹³⁄₁₆ in
drive shaft
transmission tie rod
tire chain
glue rear springs flush with back of chassis rail
tire
floor
back of car ¼ in
chassis rail
floor must overhang rail

Shows underside, drive axles attach to car, axles for wheels, alignment of chain pulleys to drive pulleys, tie rod, steering box, shape of oil pan

Engine Final Assembly — driver side view

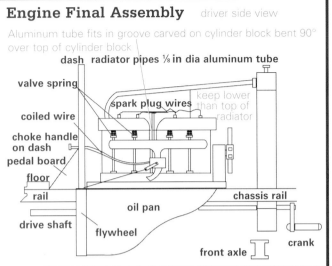

Aluminum tube fits in groove carved on cylinder block bent 90° over top of cylinder block

- dash
- radiator pipes ⅛ in dia aluminum tube
- valve spring
- spark plug wires
- keep lower than top of radiator
- coiled wire
- choke handle on dash
- pedal board
- floor
- rail
- oil pan
- chassis rail
- drive shaft
- flywheel
- front axle
- crank

Fan shaft should be level with side rail. Hold in place while drilling hole for crank. Glue engine in place. Dry overnight.

5 Turn car over and add transmission and drive shaft to chassis. Check direction of transmission when gluing in place. Drive shaft will fit in hole of flywheel, and then attach to end of transmission. Underside of car chassis is finished

6 Check engine diagram and add radiator pipes, choke cable, spark plug wires, and throttle rod. Radiator pipes are made from ⅛ in diameter aluminum tube bent around ½ in drill bit for shape and glued in place. Pipe assembly is lower than top edge of radiator so engine cover will fit.

7 Cut small vertical tube to shape on one end with dremel to fit top pipe into. Make a nice joint. Add detail to pipe on radiator, by sliding small rubber ring cut from electrical wire over pipe. Wrap a small wire around rubber to look like a hose clamp.

8 Bend tube that will fit in groove that was cut into the side of the engine cylinder block. Glue this tube in groove and attach to spark plugs wires. Tube is bent around ⅜ in drill bit to go over top of the cylinder block and fit down past intake manifold. Attach a fine wire to the spark plugs and other end into tube.

9 Make choke cable by wrapping a thin wire around a rod same size as stem of choke knob that is sticking out of dash. Wire goes from dash to side of carburetor. Cable has slight curve.

10 Throttle rod (made from 1/32 in brass rod or straight fine wire) goes from lever on carburetor to bottom edge of dash. Glue.

Final Assembly

1 Rear seat should overhang seat block and flush with the end of the car. Front seat is flush with back of front seat block.

2 Place a door on car, as shown. Insure front seat is in right place. Glue. Dry overnight. Add rear doors (see diagram). *Note* Under seat glue a spacer wide enough to go from back edge of seat block ⅛ in past edge of door and to front seat block on edge under seat. Place door on car. Make a small mark on seat then measure from end of seat block ⅛ in past mark to get proper width of spacer. Repeat this on other side of car. Glue spacers in place. Glue doors in place over spacer and running

Shows chain guard on passenger side without door open, rear wheel

Shows front, mounting of lamp, crank, how front rails are carved

Shows side, back door fits into car, with front seat block

Finished Locomobile

board, attach them to edge of back seat. Cut a small filler piece for the gap on the inside of door and seat block. Cut a pattern out of cardboard to get the proper shape. Make from Honduras mahogany ¹⁄₁₆ in thick.

3 Glue rear fenders (R and L) to rail under doors. Notch on fenders faces towards car body clearing drive pulleys. Line up fenders with bottom edge of rear seat with ¼ in gap between seat and fender and flush with back of car. Use masking tape with ¼ in spacer under seat to hold fenders in place.

4 Place running board level on bracket against rear fender flush with bottom. Repeat on other side. Glue running boards in place. Glue chain guards in place over hole in fender attaching them to side rails and running board with door facing, as shown.

5 Glue front fenders to ends of running board. Glue support bar from car rail to inside of fender using angle of fender to find location. Cut support bar to go from rail to outside edge of fender. Glue cross brace to fender for decoration. Repeat on other side.

6 Add engine cover, and glue hinges in place. Add side lamps mounted to outside dash ½ in from top edge and ¼ in from edge. Attach head lamps to front rails drilling holes in proper place and gluing mounts into these holes. Attach gas generator to rail with center of generator lining up with joint of pedal board and floor.

7 Attach brake lever to rail even with front edge of front seat block. Glue horn bulb to side of front seat. Glue horn in place on top of rail in front of dash. Run ¹⁄₁₆ in diameter brass rod from bulb to horn, as shown. Three small buttons seen on rail in front of chain guards are optional but resemble rivet heads seen on real car.

8 Add steering wheel using same method as Mercedes (p66). Hold in place with masking tape until glue dries. Check for excessive glue joints and remove glue with a wire brush in dremel at medium speed. Set aside to cure. Coat car with a clear gloss finish.

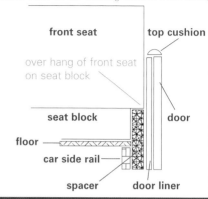

Front Door Assembly
(back view of car looking behind front seat)

Shows rear curve in seat block, axle attached to springs, chains on rear axle, fender bracket fits from body to fender

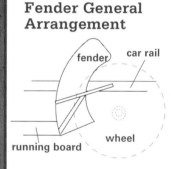

Fender General Arrangement

Shows side of motor mounted into car, choke cable attached

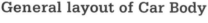
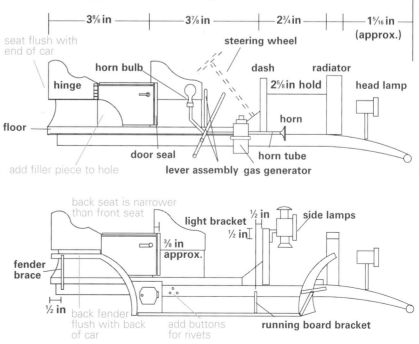

General layout of Car Body

De Dion-Bouton

The De Dion-Bouton Car Company of France started with a variety of steam engines in the 1880s and 90s for 2-seater cars and tractors. It was for these vehicles that engineer Tre'pardoux designed the De Dion axle that had gears attached with a rigid beam known as the De Dion tube, patented in 1893. This system took up little room and gave the car individual wheel suspension, an advantage that made it cost effective.

The first single cylinder engines were designed by George Bouton who convinced Comte Albert De Dion to use this form of power. These test engines ran at 3500 rpm but in production they ran at 1800 rpm, quite fast for their time. The engines were very popular and by 1900 more than 20,000 had been sold to other companies.

The R De Dion model in this book was the most popular, but models N, Q, and Y used the engine as well, even when it was outdated. The cars were available in 6 hp and 8 hp and were still found in open cars and vans up to 1912. Several of these cars are still running today. The simple single cylinder engines took up very little space under the hood of the car. However, they didn't make the cars easier to operate. The cars had pedals on the floor to engage the reverse gear and operate the decelerator which slowed the car down by an exhaust lifter and transmission brake. Hand controls included a combined gear lever and clutch with ignition. The car had a throttle and exhaust valve lever and brake lever. Operating these pedals and levers to keep the car going and stopping was a test to any driver's dexterity. Yet these little cars provided a significant step towards the production and standardization of the automobile and brought motoring to the popularity it enjoys today. At the time the De Dion-Bouton Car Company was the largest in the world.

1903 De Dion-Bouton

Car Parts

Note Some parts may require pieces of wood to be glued together to obtain proper size.

Car Parts List

Material/Size	Parts
African blackwood	
1 piece 4 in x 6 in x 1 in	front and rear wheel hubs, chassis buttons, rear brake drums, rear axle seals, tie rod arm, pins, pressure valve, foot pedals, radiator, mats, drain plug, cross bar, center cap pin
Cocobolo	
1 piece 10 in x 12 in x ⅞ in	floor, side panels, seat, engine cover, trunk, front and rear fender, dash, under seat panel
Honduras mahogany	
1 piece 6 in x 8 in x ¾ in	spring mounts, dion tube, grease fittings, front axle, filler can, carburetor connector, bolt heads, engine cylinder, valve, muffler support
Maple	
1 piece 4 in x 12 in x ½ in	wheel spokes, chassis rails, front & rear springs, shift rod, seal shaft seals, coil box, steering box, steering arm & rod, license plate, fender brace, various engine parts
Oak	
1 piece 5 in x 5 in x 1 in	differential, transmission
Walnut	
1 piece 3 in x 14 in x ⅜ in	tire, muffler
Holly wood	
1 piece 5 in x 6 in x ¼ in	seat cushions
Teak	
1 piece 1 in x 2½ in x ¼ in	gas tank strap

Material	Parts / Size
Bamboo	
2 barbeque skewers	drive shaft & axles
Maple dowels	chassis rails & various engine parts including exhaust pipes
⅛ in x 36 in long	
¼ in x 36 in long	
Brass	rear lamp, side lamp, steering wheel, brake lever, lever details, horn, mirror, engine cover rod
1/16 in rod	24 in long
1/16 id tube	6 in long
⅛ in rod	6 in long
⅛ id tube	12 in long
3/16 in rod	8 in long
⅜ in rod	6 in long
½ in rod	12 in long
.003 Shim Stock	⅛ in x 2 in x 1/32 in
Aluminum rod	
⅛ in x 1 in	knob
⅜ in x 2 in	switch plate
Aluminum strip	
¼ in x 5 in x 1/32 in	hinges

Making Wheels

1 Follow same procedure as described on p11, but use these dimensions.
2 Machine center caps from long piece of brass in lathe. Make 4 the same. Hole must be ⅛ in to fit ⅛ in hole of wheel hub.

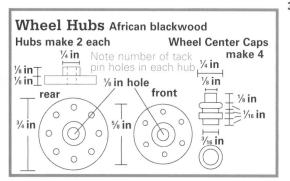

Wheel Hubs African blackwood

Hubs make 2 each
Note number of tack pin holes in each hub
¼ in
⅛ in
⅛ in
⅛ in hole
rear
front
¾ in
⅝ in

Wheel Center Caps make 4
¼ in
⅛ in
⅛ in
1/16 in
3/16 in

3 Glue (24-hour epoxy) stud into ⅛ in hole of wheel. *Note* Rear wheels have 8 tack pins, front wheels have 6 and one set of hubs for front wheels has no tack pins. These will be glued to inside of front wheels. (Locate valve stems in different areas).

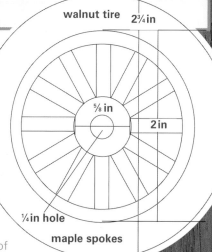

walnut tire 2¾ in
⅝ in
2 in
¼ in hole
maple spokes

Main Floor make 1

pattern half size

$3/16$ in

$3/4$ in

$2^1/4$ in

cut out square

$1/16$ in pedal holes

$1/4$ in

$7/8$ in — 1 in

$3/4$ in — $1/8$ in steering column hole

$1/16$ in lever holes $1/4$ in

$7/8$ in

$1/16$ in fender mounting rod holes

grain cocobolo

Front Spring pattern half size

maple make 2

3 in

$1/8$ in x $1/16$ in in strips

$1/2$ in

$1/4$ in

$3/16$ in $1/4$ in

Front Spring Detail

Spring Mounts

Buttons make 8 $1/8$ in

$1/4$ in $5/16$ in

$3/8$ in $1/8$ in

$3/16$ in

A. blackwood buttons

H. mahogany make 2

Making the Floor

1 Use cocobolo $3/16$ in thick and use stencil ink to transfer (p5) pattern.

2 Cut out large square hole for engine. Drill remaining holes in drill press (see diagram). Drill $1/16$ in diameter holes $1/4$ in deep by hand using pin vice in edge of wood after piece is cut to shape.

3 Make holes for steering column and levers. Make $3/4$ in dimension exact.

4 Sand both sides of wood removing stencil ink. Do not round edges.

Making the Chassis

1 Machine $1/4$ in maple dowel to $3/16$ in diameter leaving small rings $1/4$ in diameter to represent joints of tubing (optional).

2 Cut V in long dowel. Bend to close V, making angle for front main rail. Make 2. Both rails must have same angle. Trim dowel to length after bending. *Note   While building parts have floor of car on bench. Place parts as built to check fit.*

3 Glue (5-minute epoxy) cross member between front side rails to ensure width. Glue pieces to floor. Hold with spring clamps.

4 Use dremel with fine $3/16$ in diameter grindstone and grind small curve in both dowels (level with each other).

5 Add front dowels to ends of bent dowel to represent connection bolts for suspension. Glue buttons on end of these dowels, as shown.

6 To keep dowels level on ends of bent chassis tubes, place floor assembly on flat surface with bent dowels pointing towards flat surface. Place small dowels under ends of these tubes into grooves already cut in small tube. Place strip of scrap wood across front, touching each dowel to align.

Chassis Detail

Front Cross Member make 1

$2^5/8$ in

$1/4$ in

$3/16$ in

maple

$3/16$ in

Front Main Rail make 2

$3^3/8$ in

$1/2$ in

$3/16$ in $1/8$ in

glue dowel in place on end note direction keep level

notch in saw bend

Buttons

buttons

make 4 $1/4$ in

African blackwood buttons

$3/16$ in

Side Members maple make 2

$4^3/4$ in

$1/2$ in

Note hole location

$3^1/4$ in

Car floor underside

cut out

hold this dimension so axle fits

Side View under front of car

car floor

Making Front Springs

1 Transfer (p5) front springs pattern to 2 pieces maple $1/4$ in thick.

2 Draw lines to form different layers of spring and cut a groove along lines with a fine cutter. Cut small flat toothpicks, glue to spring to form clamps that hold layers together on real car. Make both springs the same.

3 From maple $5/16$ in wide x $1/4$ in thick x $3/8$ in long, use scroll saw to cut notches in ends of pieces to form H shape. Notches fit over chassis rail and spring fits in the other. *Note   One end of spring is slightly thinner than other end and fits into spring mount, as shown.*

4 Springs align with chassis rails. Glue (5-minute epoxy) against front pivot dowel glued to end of bent dowel. At same time glue 4 buttons (bolts) onto sides of spring mounts, as shown. Dry overnight.

1903 De Dion-Bouton

Making Rear Springs

1. Transfer (p5) rear springs pattern to 2 pieces of maple ¼ in thick and cut out on scroll saw. *Note* Narrow end of spring fits into spring mount. Cut grooves in side of springs same way as front springs.

2. Mounts on 'B' end of spring built same as front spring mounts. Mounts for 'A' end are two flat pieces cut to shape, as shown. Rear of spring is glued to rail while front end is glued to mount and mount is glued to rail. Flat spring mounts are glued to side of springs and sides of chassis rail. *Note* Measurement from end of chassis rail to spring must be exact.

3. Glue buttons to both sides of mounts on each end to finish spring. Fit spring mounts on front springs and chassis rail. Use needle file to adjust fit of notch in mount.

4. Mark location of rear spring mount on chassis rail. Both are same distances from end of rail. Glue with 5-minute epoxy. Distance between bottom of spring attached to chassis rail is same distance across top of springs so springs are straight. Dry.

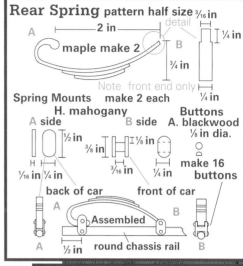

Making Differential

1. In lathe drill ⅛ in hole through center of oak disk 1¼ in diameter and ¾ in thick.

2. Machine different sizes of steps into disk, as shown. Turn disk around and repeat machining of steps on this side (maintain thickness by facing off small diameter of part on both sides of disk until final thickness is reached).

3. Small triangle pieces can be left as 5/16 in sq and ⅛ in thick. Make 4. Glue (5-minute epoxy) in place, as shown, to one side of differential. Dry. Use dremel with a drum sander to sand squares to a triangle shape. Saw flat surface across edge of part 1 in long. Place triangle pieces in proper position before marking and cutting. Use wire brush in dremel at slow speed to brush part to a smooth finish. Set aside.

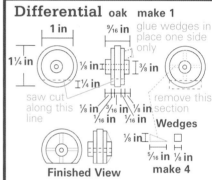

Making Drive Axle Assembly

1. Machine ⅛ in bamboo barbecue skewers 2 in long in lathe to shape, as shown. With belt sander, sand 2 axles to proper length from one end of axle.

2. Make tube brackets from Honduras mahogany 1 in x 5/16 in x ⅛ in thick. Mark and drill the holes as shown. *Note* Piece is cut wider than diagram to drill ¼ in hole and sand to width on belt sander. Cut piece in half cutting through center of hole.

3. Make 2 axle seals from one long piece of African blackwood turned in lathe and machined to shape.

4. Make drive shaft from bamboo barbecue skewer and sand edges flat on one end only. Use hand file or drum sander in dremel. Do not cut skewer at this time.

5. Draw shape of De Dion tube on flat Honduras mahogany ¼ in thick. Cut out on scroll saw and sand ¼ sq piece to ¼ in round shape. *Note* To check shape, drill ¼ in hole in wood and slide piece along tube through hole. Sand tube wherever piece will not pass over tube. Make brake drums from 2 pieces of African blackwood, ⅞ in diameter and 3/16 in thick with 3/32 in hole in middle of the disk.

Making Rear Axle Assembly

1. Slide axle through holes in center of seals. Slide axles into center hole of differential (axles stick out same on both sides of seals). Slide brackets onto axles over from each end. Place Dion tube into ¼ in hole cut in half. *Note* Diagram 3¼ in

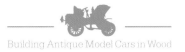

Rear Axle Assembly

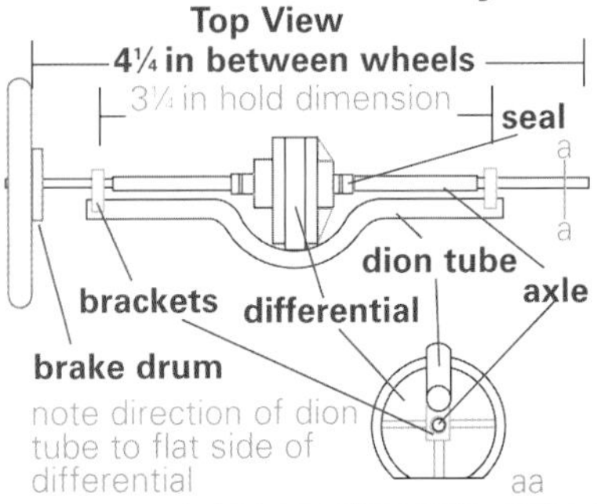
Top View
4¼ in between wheels
3¼ in hold dimension
seal
a
a
dion tube
axle
brackets
differential
brake drum
note direction of dion tube to flat side of differential
aa

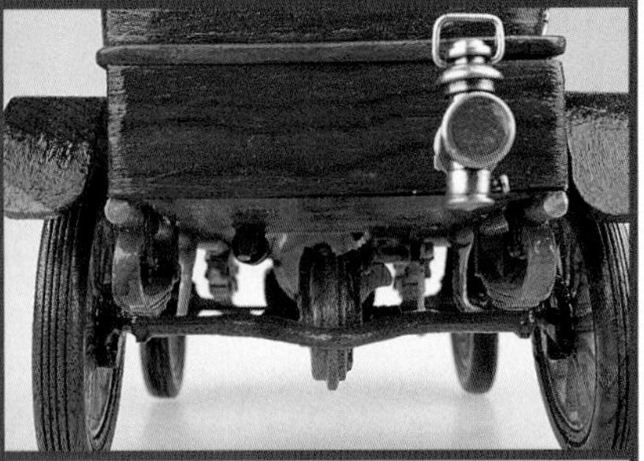
Shows rear axle and rear light

Transmission make 1 each

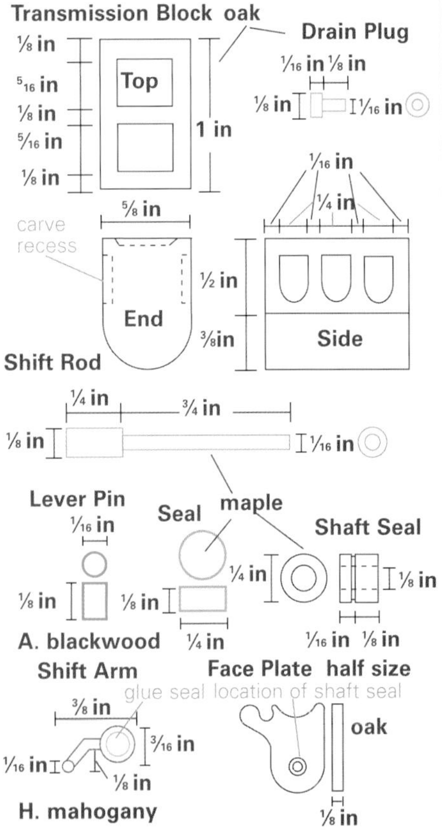
Transmission Block oak
Drain Plug
⅛ in
5/16 in
⅛ in
5/16 in
⅛ in
Top
1 in
1/16 in ⅛ in
⅛ in
1/16 in
⅝ in
carve recess
End
½ in
⅜in
1/16 in
¼ in
Side
Shift Rod
¼ in
¾ in
⅛ in
1/16 in
Lever Pin
1/16 in
⅛ in
A. blackwood
Seal
maple
⅛ in
¼ in
¼ in
Shaft Seal
⅛ in
1/16 in ⅛ in
Shift Arm
⅜ in
1/16 in
3/16 in
⅛ in
H. mahogany
Face Plate half size
glue seal location of shaft seal
oak
⅛ in

measurement must be exact. Differential must be in center of assembly.

2 Lay assembly on chassis assembly. Brackets sit on top of rear springs in center of each spring. Mark location of brackets on axle and glue assembly with 5-minute epoxy. Keep straight. Dry. Slide rear brake drums and wheels onto end of each axle with 8 pins. Distance between wheels is 4¼ in. Glue brake drums and wheels to axle.

Making Transmission

Assembled Transmission

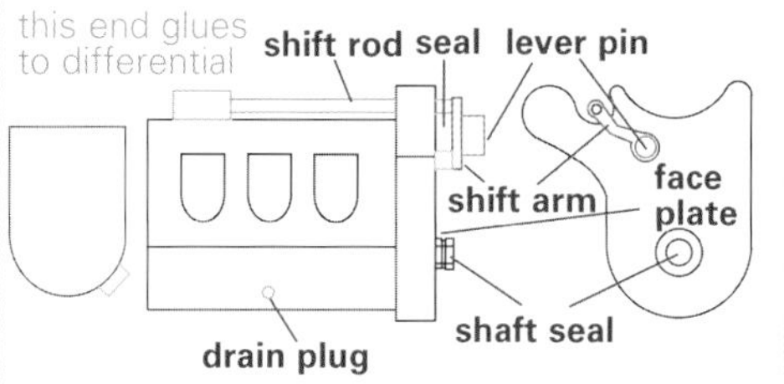
this end glues to differential
shift rod seal
lever pin
face plate
shift arm
shaft seal
drain plug

1 Use oak 1 in long x ⅞ in high x ⅝ in wide. Sand bottom round across the ⅝ in width leaving ends straight. Draw and carve shallow panels on both sides of block with dremel and small ball cutter. Make top panel on block and carve two recesses as above. Machine drain plug from ⅛ in diameter oak dowel to fit into hole drilled in bottom of block. Machine ⅛ in diameter maple dowel 1 in long for shift rod. Shape small diameter first.

2 Make shaft seal from ¼ in diameter maple dowel. Place in lathe and drill ⅛ in diameter hole through center of dowel. Machine groove in end as shown using thread-cutting tool. Cut piece to 1 in length in band saw or cut to length with thread cutting tool.

3 Make lever pin from African blackwood 3/16 in round and ⅛ in long. Trace pattern for faceplate on oak and cut out, long sides first, in band saw, then trim wood across bottom below curve. Sand curve to shape with belt sander and use drum sander in dremel to shape curves on top edge. Use different fine edge cutters as the curve changes on top edge.

4 Draw shape of shift lever on Honduras mahogany ⅜ in wide x 1/16 in thick and approximately 6 in long. Remove excess wood with dremel with small cutters. Leave one end attached to the piece. Sand edges lightly then remove from larger piece and sand end by hand.

5 Assemble transmission by gluing (5-minute epoxy) faceplate to one end of block slightly overhanging bottom edge. Glue shift rod in small curved section on top of faceplate resting on top of transmission towards the back. *Note Larger end of shift rod is towards back of transmission. Small diameter protrudes past faceplate same distance as thickness of seal.*

6 Glue seal to one end of shift arm with seal glued to it towards center of faceplate. Glue shaft seal as shown. Keep hole in center clear of glue.

7 Dry completely. Glue (24-hour epoxy) assembly to flat side of differential as shown (see p86). Shaft seal is in center of assembly. Adjust before glue dries.

Making Front Axle

1 Draw axle shape on Honduras mahogany 5 in x ¾ in x ¼ in thick and cut out on lines with scroll saw. Sand axle round. Use piece of wood with ¼ in hole to slide along axle to ensure it is round and even from end to end. Make tie rod from African blackwood 1/16 in and 4 in long (length trimmed later).

2 Make support and rod arms from African blackwood 3 1/16 in wide and long enough to cut 4 parts. Spray wood with marking ink before drawing shapes. Drill 1/16 in diameter holes using pin vice. Machine grease fitting from ⅛ in diameter Honduras mahogany dowel long enough for 4 fittings. Make one, then next, using first as pattern.

3 To assemble front axle, slide wheels to end of axle (distance between wheels is 4¼ in). Trim axle from both ends on belt sander. Glue wheels to axle with 5-minute epoxy. Dry 10 minutes then add remainder of parts.

4 Glue tie rod arms to one side and support bars to other side of axle.against inside wheel hub, and parallel to each other. Glue grease fittings into ⅟₁₆ in holes drilled into tie rod arm and support bars. Dry 10 minutes then trim tie rod to fit across axle resting on end of each tie rod as shown. Dry overnight.

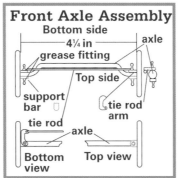

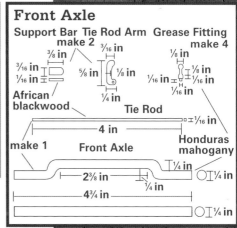

Making the Dash

1 Cut cocobolo 3 in x 1¾ in x ⅛ in for dashboard in band saw. Sand both sides smooth.

2 Make fuel tank from solid maple ⅜ in x 1⅛ in x ¾ in thick. Make strap from teak to fit around fuel tank as shown. Drill 4 holes to fit tack pins.Make coil box on band or scroll saw. Make angled groove in side with small hacksaw or dremel.

3 Cut front lock on box from aluminum and sand smaller with belt sander holding piece with pliers. Make filler cap from Honduras mahogany ⅜ in round and long enough to hold in lathe while shaping. Cut to ¾ in long with parting tool or wood saw.

4 Make pressure valve from African blackwood using same method as filler cap. Make small notch across top ⅛ in deep with fine saw blade in dremel.

5 Draw lever on African blackwood ⅟₁₆ in thick. Cut out with dremel and a fine cutter or grindstone. Glue (5-minute epoxy) fuel tank to one side of dash centered and flush with bottom edge. Glue gas tank strap over fuel tank onto dash. Trim tack pins so heads are flush with tank strap. Glue.

6 Glue filler cap "a" to top of tank. Glue carburetor connector "b" in center of fuel tank on top edge. Glue pressure valve "c" to top, on opposite side of carburetor towards edge. Glue coil box to other side of board. Dry overnight.

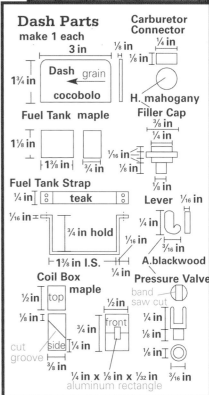

Steering Parts

1 Machine (small diameter first) ⅛ in diameter maple dowel in lathe, as shown.

2 Drill small holes in one end with pin vice to fit a tack pin. Make control arm from maple 1 in x ¼ in x ⅟₁₆ in thick, using method for lever on fuel tank valve. Make steering box from maple ¾ in x ½ in x ½ in thick. Drill ⅟₁₆ in diameter hole through piece ⅛ in from top edge of center of block. Draw curve on top and carve round as shown in top view of block.

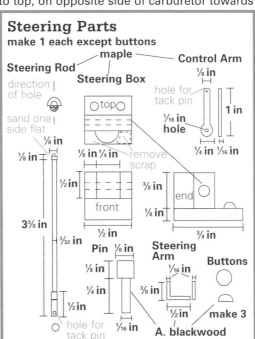

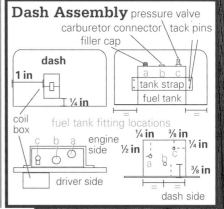

Steering Parts Assembled

buttons | Top View

steering box

steering arm

steering rod

pin

car floor top side

Side View | driver side

tack pin | this end to arm on wheel

Floor boards, dash showing coil box, levers, steering wheel, horn, mirror

3 Make steering arm from African blackwood, cut to shape as shown.

4 Make pin from African blackwood using same method as filler cap on fuel tank. Make 3 buttons from African blackwood. Glue only two buttons to steering box. DO NOT assemble other parts at this time.

Underside Assembly

1 Add front axle assembly to undercarriage of car. Place front axle in middle of springs on both sides (wheels stick out same distance). Tie rod should not hit anything. Glue with 5-minute epoxy. Let set.

2 Glue steering arm to front of front axle pointing towards center of car on same side holes were drilled into floor. Part hangs down past bottom of front axle. Glue steering box over holes drilled for steering column and levers. Add rear axle to car. See placement of brackets onto springs. Keep transmission shaft seal in middle of car.

3 Sand brackets at angle if needed, for transmission to sit at proper angle and to place scrap piece of wood ¼ in thick between transmission and floor. Dry overnight.

Body Side and Under Seat Panels

1 Place partly assembled car on workbench for reference. For side panels cut 2 pieces cocobolo 3½ in x 1¼ in x ½ in thick. Transfer (p5) pattern of side view onto wood and mark L and R on opposite sides. Also mark angle cut on edge of wood and cut along this line with band saw stopping at angle mark. Remove saw blade from cut and cut angle starting from outside edge cutting towards end of last cut for a sharp corner. Repeat for other panel. Use scroll saw to cut side view of panel traced on side of wood. With small drum sander in dremel sand curved edge of panel. Leave corners square and measure distance between them.

2 Place body side panels flush with edge of floor and measure distance between them to check length of under seat panel (oak) and piece of cocobolo that goes across back of side panels. Under seat panels have ¼ in space around outer edge and between the panels.

3 Glue (5-minute epoxy) panels to oak. Dry. Drill hole into panel for switch plate. Glue switch into hole in panel and knob in switch plate hole.

4 Machine switch from ⅜ in diameter aluminum rod and drill hole by hand with pin vice. Machine knob from aluminum.

5 Sand rear edge of side panel rounded towards inside edge. Glue dash assembly on body assembly. Dry. Check fit of side panels and glue to floor. Check fit of under seat panel and back piece between panels. Glue. Dry overnight.

6 Build trunk section from wood with tiny knot or uniform grain. Cut pieces to form side and back panel first. Tape pieces together with masking tape and place on back of car behind body panels. Check it is not wider than floor and back panel is flush with end of

Underside Assembly

Front View

front axle

floor

spring

mount front axle in this direction

steering rod

steering arm

detail

note where brackets fit into springs

radiator

steering box fits over holes

transmission

tie rod

rear axle assembly

front axle assembly

place front & back axle in middle of springs

¼ in block

front axle detail

grease fitting

support bar | front axle

tilt transmission to leave ½ in space between floor & transmission

tie rod

tie rod arm

steering arm

steering rod

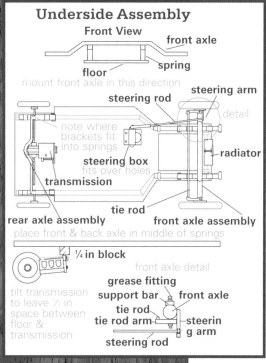

Body Side Panels   cocobolo

make left & right

1¼ in

grain

Pattern half size

⅝ in

3⅝ in

Top View 3⅝ in x 1¼ in x ½ in

3/16 in

½ in

½ in

shows left & right

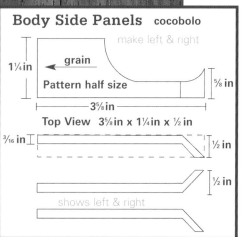

Foot Pedals

African blackwood make 2

⅜ in

½ in

¼ in | 1/16 in | 1/16 in dowel

floorboard. Glue back panel and sides of trunk together. Dry completely.

7 Make trunk lid from 2 pieces cocobolo. Small strip at top edge of trunk is same size as lid. Lid is wider and longer than side pieces to form a drip edge to keep rain out. Cut lid from one piece including small strip. Sand all edges round, then cut small strip in band saw making 2 pieces. Glue lid and strip to trunk area of car leaving no space between lid and small strip. Make hinge from bent aluminum strip using same method as hinges on other cars. Drill holes by hand to fit tack pins. Dry. Make pedals from African blackwood ¼ in wide x 1 in long. Round ends then cut piece in half. Sand ends round in belt sander maintaining proper length of each pedal. Turn blackwood ¹⁄₁₆ in diameter. Set all aside.

Making the Seat

1 Cut seat sides from 2 pieces cocobolo 2 in x 1½ in and ¼ in thick, as shown. Tack glue (hot glue gun) together (grain same as 2 in side). Trace pattern, cut out sides of seats (L & R). Sand edges with drum sander in dremel.

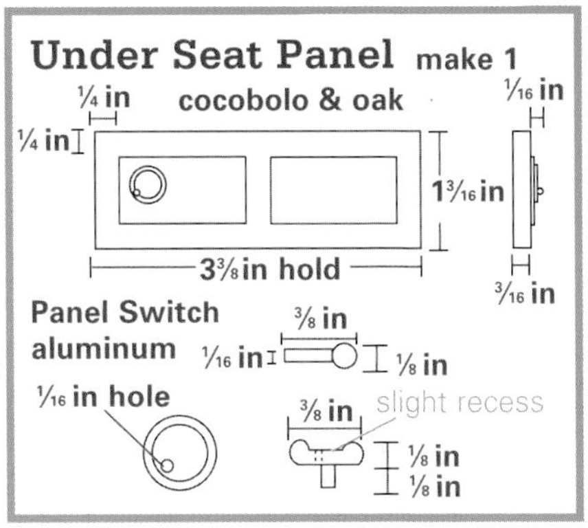

2 Separate pieces and glue (24-hour epoxy) to seat bottom so pieces go ⅛ in past edge of seat bottom. Measure distance between side panels and cut back of seat ⅛ in past seat bottom. Glue with 24-hour epoxy. Dry, then sand to finished size shown on diagram.

3 Cut holly wood into strips wide enough to fit evenly across seat bottom. Glue (5-minute epoxy). Then glue back seat cushions. Cut angle pattern on cushion. Side cushions are flat.

4 Make a cardboard pattern of seat side cushions to get proper shape. Cut pattern from holly ¹⁄₁₆ in thick and glue. Dry overnight. With round ball cutter in dremel at slow speed cut grooves in all joints of cushion on seat to give soft deep appearance. Cut and bend ¹⁄₁₆ in diameter brass rod to form rails. Place on seat sides and mark location of ¹⁄₁₆ diameter holes. Drill into side panels by hand. Glue rails in place with 5-minute epoxy. Dry. Glue (5-minute epoxy) seat on car ¹⁄₁₆ in overhang in front of seat panel. Dry. Place pedal dowels into holes with sloping side of dowel facing seat. Glue pedal on top of slopping part of dowel. Hold in place until glue sets.

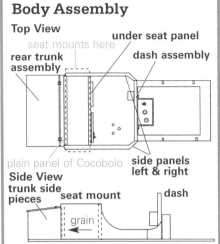

Body Assembly

Top View

seat mounts here
rear trunk assembly
under seat panel
dash assembly
plain panel of Cocobolo
side panels left & right

Side View
trunk side pieces
seat mount
dash
grain

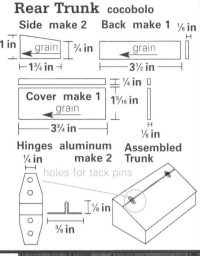

Rear Trunk cocobolo

Side make 2   Back make 1   ⅛ in
1 in   grain   ¾ in   grain
1¾ in   3½ in
¼ in
Cover make 1   1⁵⁄₁₆ in
grain
3¾ in   ⅛ in

Hinges aluminum make 2   ¼ in   Assembled Trunk
holes for tack pins
⅛ in   ⅜ in

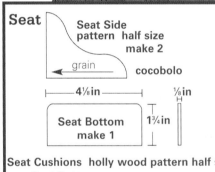

Under Seat Panel make 1

¼ in   cocobolo & oak   ¹⁄₁₆ in
¼ in
1³⁄₁₆ in
3⅜ in hold   ³⁄₁₆ in

Panel Switch aluminum   ⅜ in
¹⁄₁₆ in   ⅛ in
¹⁄₁₆ in hole   ⅜ in   slight recess
⅛ in
⅛ in

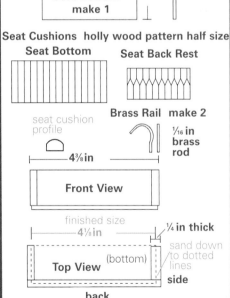

Seat

Seat Side pattern half size make 2
grain   cocobolo
4⅛ in   ⅛ in
Seat Bottom make 1   1¾ in

Seat Cushions holly wood pattern half size
Seat Bottom   Seat Back Rest
seat cushion profile   Brass Rail make 2
¹⁄₁₆ in brass rod
4⅜ in

Front View

finished size
4⅛ in   ¼ in thick
sand down to dotted lines
Top View   (bottom)   side
back
Assembled Seat
top cushion on top seat edge up to rails   flat cushion on side pieces
brass rail
4⅛ in
1¾ in

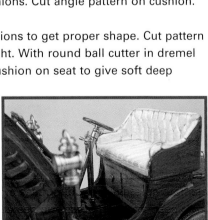

Shows panel under seat & hand rails on seat, seat cushions

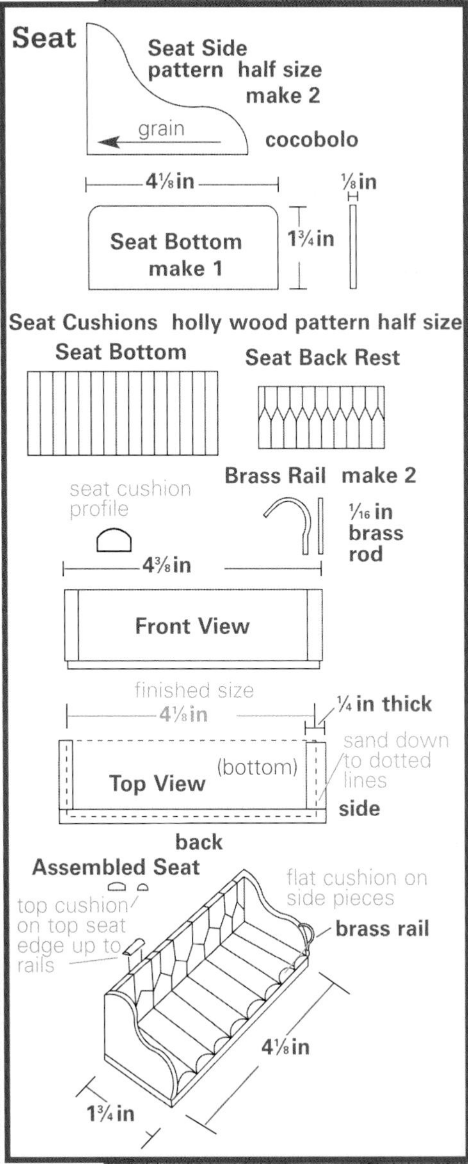

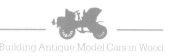

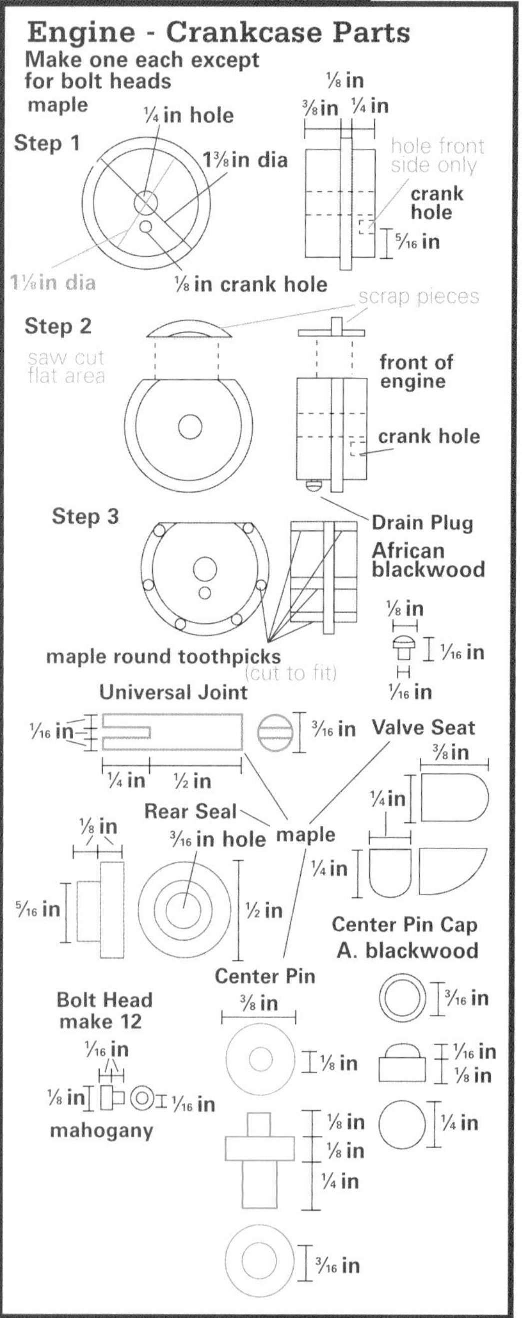
Engine - Crankcase Parts
Make one each except for bolt heads
maple
Step 1
¼ in hole
1⅜ in dia
1⅛ in dia
⅛ in crank hole
⅛ in
⅜ in ¼ in
hole front side only
crank hole
5/16 in
Step 2
saw cut flat area
scrap pieces
front of engine
crank hole
Drain Plug
Step 3
African blackwood
maple round toothpicks
(cut to fit)
⅛ in
1/16 in
1/16 in
Universal Joint
1/16 in
¼ in ½ in
3/16 in
Valve Seat
⅜ in
¼ in
Rear Seal
maple
⅛ in
3/16 in hole
5/16 in
½ in
¼ in
Center Pin Cap
A. blackwood
Center Pin
⅜ in
Bolt Head
make 12
1/16 in
⅛ in
1/16 in
mahogany
⅛ in
3/16 in
1/16 in
⅛ in
⅛ in
⅛ in
¼ in
¼ in
3/16 in

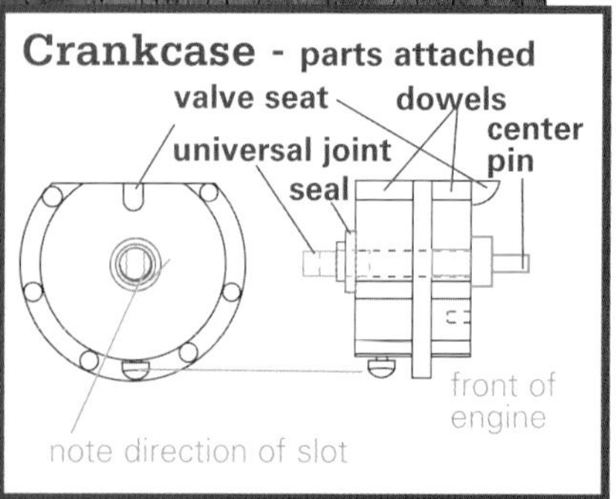
Crankcase - parts attached
valve seat
dowels
center pin
universal joint
seal
front of engine
note direction of slot

Making the Radiator

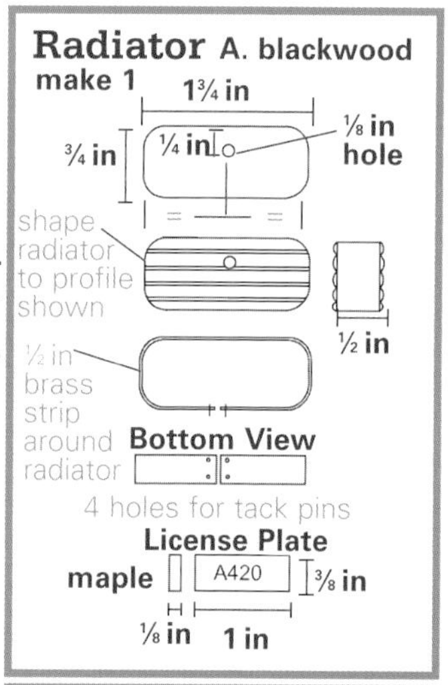
Radiator A. blackwood
make 1
1¾ in
¾ in
¼ in
⅛ in hole
shape radiator to profile shown
½ in
½ in brass strip around radiator
Bottom View
4 holes for tack pins
License Plate
maple
A420
⅜ in
⅛ in
1 in

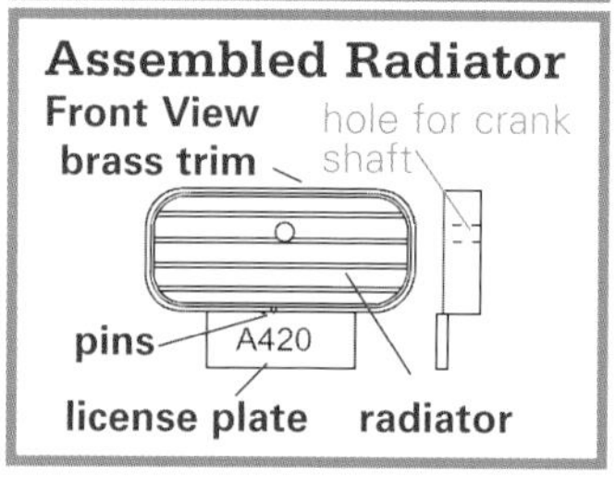
Assembled Radiator
Front View
brass trim
hole for crank shaft
pins
A420
license plate
radiator

1 Cut out African blackwood 1¾ in x ¾ in x ½ in thick with sq corners and sand ends round on belt sander.

2 Cut small grooves across front and back of wood with cut-off disk in dremel at slow speed. Wear safety glasses. Drill hole through radiator for crank in drill press using ⅛ diameter drill bit.

3 Place brass strip on flat surface in front of radiator and mark radiator half way along bottom edge. Place end of strip at mark and roll radiator along brass strip back to mark. Mark brass at this point and cut. Form strip around radiator.

3 Drill 4 holes in radiator for tack pins.

4 Put 5-minute epoxy inside of brass strip and glue onto radiator. Stick pins into drilled holes. Set aside to dry.

5 Make numbers and letters for license plate from vinyl stick-on.

6 Crank handle is made from ⅛ in maple dowel turned to shape, as shown. Small diameter stub is 1/16 in diameter and ⅛ in long. Crank arm made from mahogany ¼ in wide and long enough to hold and 1/16 in thick. Drill (by hand) holes into ends of crank arm, as shown, ⅛ in diameter on larger end and other end fits stub on crank handle (1/16 in diameter). Draw shape around holes. Place a cutter into dremel and cut out. Set aside. Glue radiator in place, as shown on diagram. Hole in radiator is towards floor of car, otherwise engine will sit too low in car when crank is installed.

Making the Engine (Optional)

1 Make crankcase from 1⅜ in round maple disks ¾ in thick. Cut disk with a hole saw 1⅜ in inside diameter making ¼ in diameter hole in center of disk.

2 Turn 1⅛ in diameter ⅜ in long on one side of disk. Remove disk from lathe and turn it around, replace in lathe. Machine 1⅛ in diameter on this side. Disk has ⅛ in thick ring around. Remove disk, drill ⅛ in hole for crankshaft. Make 1 in long cut across top of crankcase to form base for cylinder head.

3 Place crankshaft with flat side on table and drill 1/16 in hole, ¼ in deep on ⅜ in side of ring. Fit round toothpicks (bolts) onto edge of crankcase on each side of ring, not past face of crankcase. Place ½ in maple dowel 1 in long into lathe. Using a center drill mark center of dowel, then with 3/16 in drill bit drill ¼ in deep hole. Shape rear seal using parting tool and use it to remove seal.

4 Make universal joint from 3/16 in maple dowel ¾ in long. Cut notch in one end on band saw. Make center pin with ⅜ in round dowel 1 in long. Machine to shape starting at small diameter. Machine bolt heads to shape from mahogany dowel ⅛ in diameter and 4 in long. Make 12. They will be glued to ends of toothpicks on crankcase.

5 Make valve seat from maple ¼ in sq and long enough to hold. Cut to length. Glue rear seal and universal joint on back of crankcase. Glue center pin on other side of crankcase

6. Make engine cylinder from mahogany 1¹¹⁄₁₆ in x 1 in x ¾ in. Round top of block using belt or disk sander, to shape as shown. Draw ½ in sq on bottom of block and mark ³⁄₁₆ in line around block. Using band saw cut bottom along lines, stopping at marks at bottom. Square will stick out ³⁄₁₆ in from bottom.

7. Use dremel and small cutter on front of cylinder to make notch cutout ½ in high and ¼ in deep leaving ⅛ in lip down side.

8. Use a drum sander in dremel to finish shaping block. Glue cylinder to crankcase, cutout is past front of crankcase for placement of valve.

9. Make valve from ⅛ in mahogany dowel. Measure distance between valve seat and notch in engine for length of valve dimension. Shape remaining parts with small needle files. Cut dowels longer than required to hold in lathe while spinning. Machine pressure valve from maple dowel ⅛ in diameter. Machine carburetor from ⅜ in maple dowel. Make ⅛ in round flat spot with small grindstone in dremel.

10. Machine exhaust connector from ¼ in maple dowel. Machine valve from ⅛ in mahogany dowel. Machine spark plug from ⅛ in maple dowel ⅜ in long from one of small diameters to prevent breaking. Turn part around and machine other end. Machine cable clamp from ³⁄₁₆ in maple dowel. Assemble parts to engine cylinder as shown. Carburetor and exhaust connector must be located exactly.

11. Front cover is made from ⅛ in thick maple. Draw shape of piece on wood ¾ in long. Cut out with dremel and small cutter. Glue on front of engine with 5-minute epoxy. Machine idler to shape from ¼ in diameter maple dowel and glue in place on crankcase, as shown. Make lever support from maple cut in L shape. Glue in place with L shape pointing outward from crankcase. Make swing arm from maple ¹⁄₁₆ in thick and long enough to fit on crankcase. Hole in center of swing arm must be large enough to slide onto center pin. Draw shape on ¹⁄₁₆ in thick and large enough to hold. Drill center hole first then use dremel and cut out the shape of part. Glue in place sliding onto center pin, as shown.

12. Glue rod support on end of swing arm. Machine lever arms ⅛ in maple dowel. Small diameters must fit into holes to be drilled in larger diameters. Finished assembly should be L shape. Place end of lever with no holes on lever support. Then measure distance from lever arm assembly across front to rod support glued onto swing arm.

13. Cut cross bar to this length and glue lever assembly and cross bar in place. Dry. Machine lever handle from ⅛ in maple dowel to shape as shown. Place lever handle between cross bar and crankcase with small end of swing arm. Larger diameter goes just above cross bar. Sand to length. Then glue lever handle in place. Larger end of lever handle is towards top of engine. Dry completely.

14. Use small nylon brush in dremel at slowest speed and carefully brush entire engine.

Installing the Engine

1. Cut ⅛ in diameter bamboo 2 in long. Slide through radiator hole into crank hole in crankcase. Engine is 1 inch from edge of square hole to crankcase.

2. Measure from transmission shaft seal to universal joint on back of engine and cut bamboo drive shaft to this length measuring from end with flat edges. Place bamboo drive shaft back into position. Glue these to crank hole with 5-minute

keeping this in center of engine case. Center pin cap is glued in place when all of crankcase is assembled. Dry.

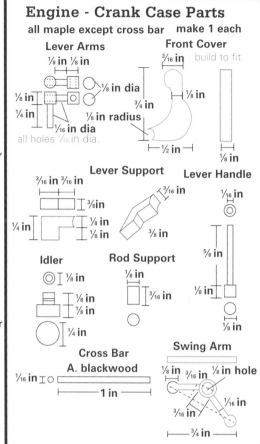

Engine - Crank Case Parts
all maple except cross bar   make 1 each
Lever Arms   Front Cover
Lever Support   Lever Handle
Idler   Rod Support
Cross Bar   Swing Arm
A. blackwood

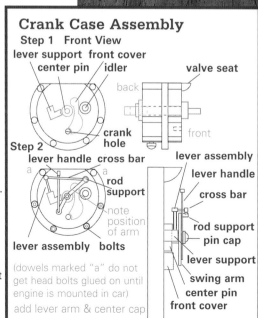

Crank Case Assembly
Step 1 Front View
lever support front cover
center pin idler   valve seat
back
crank hole
Step 2
lever handle cross bar
a   a
rod support
note position of arm
lever assembly bolts
lever assembly
lever handle
cross bar
rod support
pin cap
lever support
swing arm
center pin
front cover
(dowels marked "a" do not get head bolts glued on until engine is mounted in car)
add lever arm & center cap

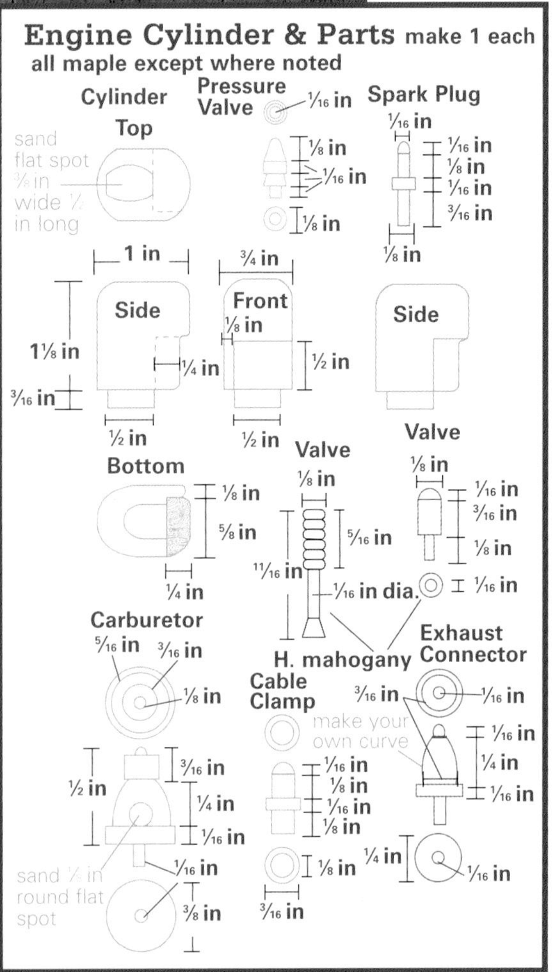
Engine Cylinder & Parts make 1 each
all maple except where noted
Cylinder
Top
sand flat spot 3/8 in wide 1/2 in long
Pressure Valve
1/16 in
1/8 in
1/16 in
1/8 in
Spark Plug
1/16 in
1/16 in
1/8 in
1/16 in
3/16 in
1/8 in
1 in
3/4 in
Side
Front
1/8 in
Side
1 1/8 in
1/4 in
1/2 in
3/16 in
1/2 in
1/2 in
Bottom
1/8 in
5/8 in
1/4 in
Valve
1/8 in
5/16 in
11/16 in
1/16 in dia.
Valve
1/8 in
1/16 in
3/16 in
1/8 in
1/16 in
Carburetor
5/16 in
3/16 in
1/8 in
H. mahogany
Exhaust Connector
Cable Clamp
3/16 in
1/16 in
make your own curve
1/16 in
1/4 in
1/16 in
1/2 in
3/16 in
1/4 in
1/16 in
1/16 in
1/8 in
1/16 in
1/8 in
sand 1/4 in round flat spot
1/16 in
3/8 in
1/8 in
1/4 in
1/16 in
3/16 in

epoxy. Place engine back onto crankshaft. Glue drive shaft in place.

3 Glue crankshaft to radiator on engine side. Dry. Trim end of crankshaft with cutoff blade in a dremel so it sticks out of front of radiator 3/8 in.

4 Glue crank arm to end of shaft. Glue crank handle to hole on bottom of crank arm making sure it stays level until glue sets.

5 Bars of engine mount are made from 1/8 in sq maple and will be glued to crankcase to the chassis rails. Measure distance between these points and make bars to fit. One end of bar has round groove filed in it for better fit to chassis rail. Glue bars from engine to chassis rail with 5-minute epoxy and glue bolt heads to bars.

6 Carburetor pipe is made from 1/8 in maple dowel bent same way as exhaust pipes. Make pipe longer than required and bent 90°. Let dowel dry, then cut the bend until the pipe lines up with carburetor and connector on gas tank. Carburetor sits higher than fuel tank. Ensure dowel is level between two fittings.

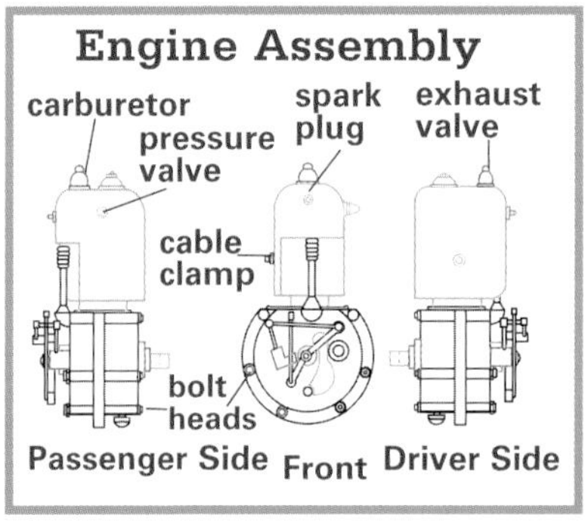
Engine Assembly
carburetor
pressure valve
spark plug
exhaust valve
cable clamp
bolt heads
Passenger Side
Front
Driver Side

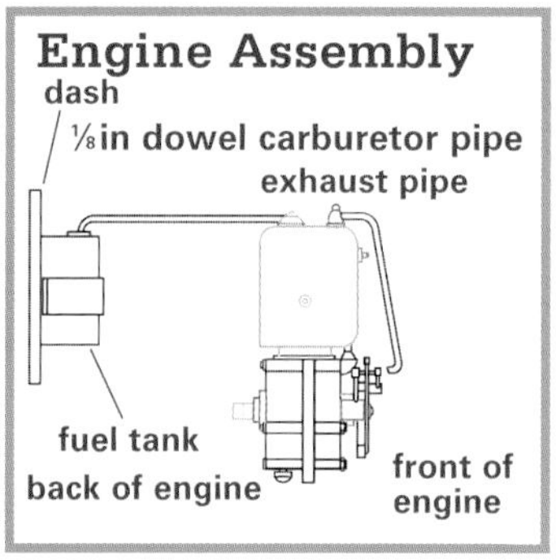
Engine Assembly
dash
1/8 in dowel carburetor pipe
exhaust pipe
fuel tank
back of engine
front of engine

Making Exhaust System

1 Use walnut 3/8 in diameter and long enough to hold in lathe, with a piece sticking out of chuck. Drill 1/8 in diameter hole in one end, then machine to shape. Cut dowel to length, as shown, then place back in lathe and drill 1/8 in hole in other end. Make support brackets from Honduras mahogany 3/8 in x 1/4 in x 3/8 in thick. Drill hole as shown. Sand curve on one end on belt sander and cut piece in half down length in band saw to make 2 supports. Sand edges smooth.

2 Machine pipe connector from 3/16 in maple dowel in lathe (long enough to hold). Make several cuts on a dowel with band saw for exhaust pipe curves. Fill saw cuts with white carpenter's glue, bend dowel to close saw cuts. Place one end of dowel in vice and attach spring clamps on other end to hold saw cut closed. Make sure 1 3/4 in dimension is exact. Make tail pipe angle same way as angle for front chassis rails. Do not assemble any parts until engine is installed.

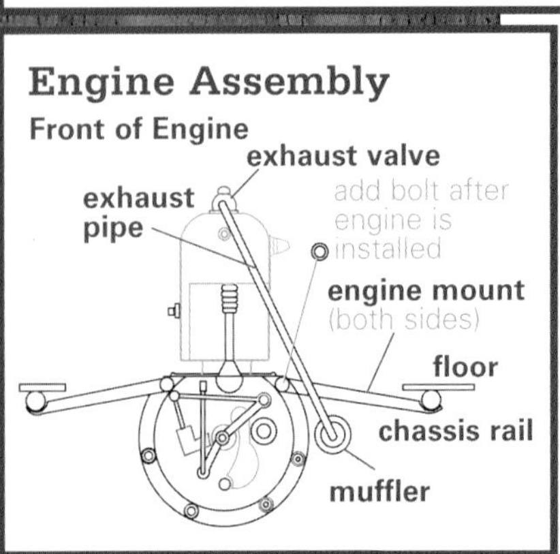
Engine Assembly
Front of Engine
exhaust valve
exhaust pipe
add bolt after engine is installed
engine mount (both sides)
floor
chassis rail
muffler

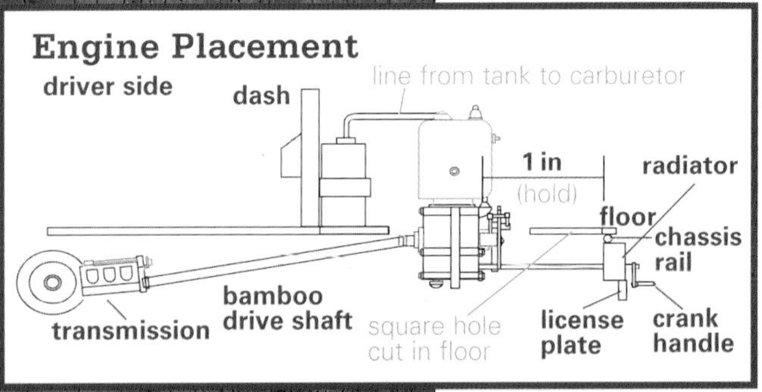
Engine Placement
driver side
dash
line from tank to carburetor
1 in
(hold)
radiator
floor
chassis rail
bamboo drive shaft
transmission
square hole cut in floor
license plate
crank handle

Installing Exhaust System

1 Glue tail pipe into muffler and slide one of supports onto end of connector pipe which is glued into end of muffler.

2 Slide other support over tail pipe and glue 2 supports to tail pipe and connector pipe. Align supports. Place flat edges of supports on flat surface. Dry. Exhaust pipe goes from exhaust valve on top of engine down front of engine passing underneath engine mounts towards back of car.

4 Place muffler assembly on underside of car floor sitting on

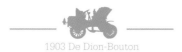

supports. Exhaust pipe lines up with muffler and exhaust valve. Adjust exhaust pipe at valve end on belt sander. Locate muffler just past front fender or beside step in back fender. Trim exhaust pipe on straight 2$\frac{3}{4}$ in part of exhaust pipe. Glue all parts with 5-minute epoxy.

Exhaust Installation

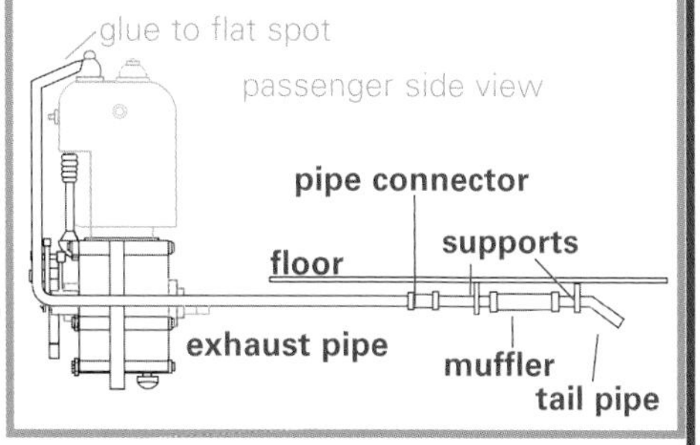
glue to flat spot
passenger side view
pipe connector
floor
supports
exhaust pipe
muffler
tail pipe

Making Engine Cover

1 Use cocobolo 1$\frac{3}{8}$ in x 5 in x $\frac{3}{8}$ in thick and make cardboard pattern of side pieces. Cut out, clamp two together, sand edges.

2 Make top cover from cocobolo 3 in x 1$\frac{1}{2}$ in x 2$\frac{1}{4}$ in wide. Spray wood with marking ink and place on one sidepiece flush with bottom of wood block. Draw line around top edge. Cut on inside of line leaving $\frac{3}{16}$ in thick piece to fit over side pieces. Sand for tight fit. Draw opening on top inside cover. Cut using scroll saw or small saw blade in dremel. Glue (24 hour epoxy) sides to top cover. Dry.

3 Sand cover to shape, as shown, with corners on slight angle wider on top and narrower towards front, coming to point on bottom front corners. Use a drum sander in dremel to sand inside cover to $\frac{3}{16}$ in to $\frac{1}{8}$ in thick. Cut 2 hatch covers $\frac{1}{16}$ in thick, one glued to front of engine cover, one glued over hole cut into cover.

4 Drill 4 holes for round toothpicks in each corner of cover. Cut toothpicks long enough to raise cover over the hole $\frac{1}{16}$ in above main engine cover with toothpicks sticking out of small cover $\frac{1}{16}$ in. See diagram. Machine small knob from $\frac{1}{8}$ in maple dowel spinning in lathe shaped with needle file. Glue to bottom edge of cover on front of engine cover.

5 Make vents from cocobolo $\frac{1}{2}$ in x $\frac{1}{8}$ in thick. Round edges with belt sander. Cut piece into strips (vents) by standing wood on edge and cutting with band saw. Glue vents to side of cover and across front hatch as shown.

6 Glue small dowel $\frac{1}{8}$ in round x $\frac{3}{8}$ in long to top edge of front cover to be hinge for hatch. Make cover rod from $\frac{1}{16}$ in brass rod 4$\frac{1}{4}$ in long. A $\frac{1}{8}$ in brass rod $\frac{3}{16}$ in long with $\frac{1}{16}$ in hole drilled through it makes the pivot. Bend one end of $\frac{1}{16}$ in rod to 90° angle $\frac{1}{4}$ in from one end. Do not cut length of 4$\frac{1}{16}$ in brass rod until cover is glued in place.

7 Drill $\frac{1}{16}$ in hole into cover in front corner on passenger side to place support rod into hole for gluing. Wire-brush cover.

Exhaust

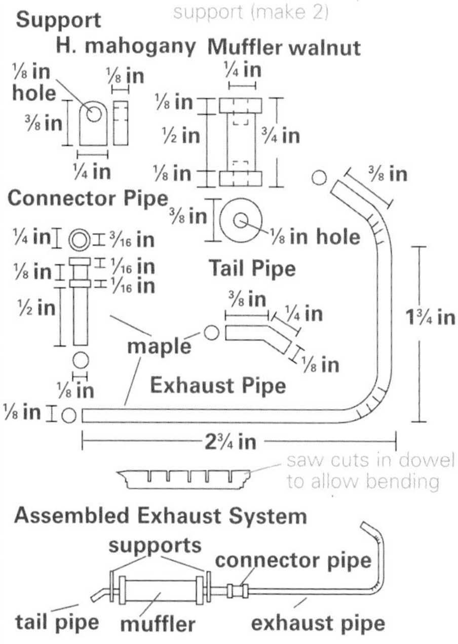
make 1 each except for support (make 2)
Support
H. mahogany
Muffler walnut
1/8 in hole
1/8 in
3/8 in
1/4 in
1/8 in
1/2 in
3/4 in
1/8 in
3/8 in
Connector Pipe
1/4 in
3/16 in
1/8 in
1/16 in
1/16 in
1/2 in
1/8 in hole
Tail Pipe
3/8 in
1/4 in
1/8 in
maple
Exhaust Pipe
1/8 in
1/8 in
1 3/4 in
2 3/4 in
saw cuts in dowel to allow bending
Assembled Exhaust System
supports
connector pipe
tail pipe
muffler
exhaust pipe

Engine Cover cocobolo

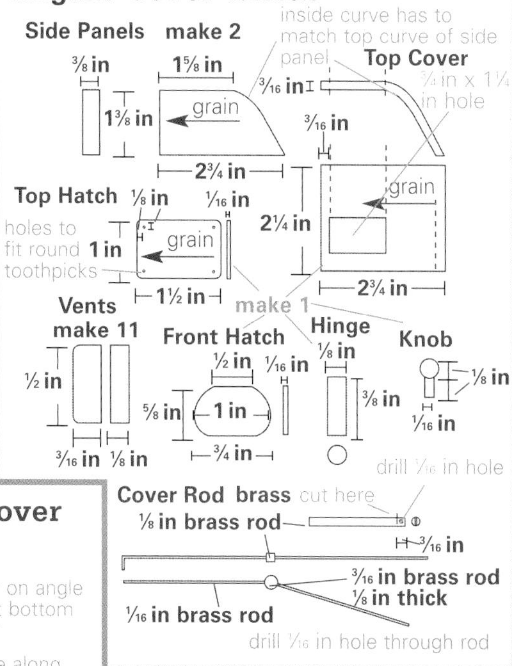
Side Panels make 2
inside curve has to match top curve of side panel
Top Cover
3/8 in
1 5/8 in
3/16 in
3/4 in x 1 1/4 in hole
1 3/8 in
grain
3/16 in
2 3/4 in
Top Hatch
1/8 in
1/16 in
holes to fit round toothpicks
1 in
grain
1 1/2 in
2 1/4 in
grain
2 3/4 in
make 1
Vents make 11
Front Hatch
Hinge
Knob
1/2 in
1/2 in
1/16 in
1/8 in
5/8 in
1 in
3/8 in
1/8 in
1/16 in
3/16 in
1/8 in
3/4 in
drill 1/16 in hole
Cover Rod brass
cut here
1/8 in brass rod
3/16 in
3/16 in brass rod
1/8 in thick
1/16 in brass rod
drill 1/16 in hole through rod

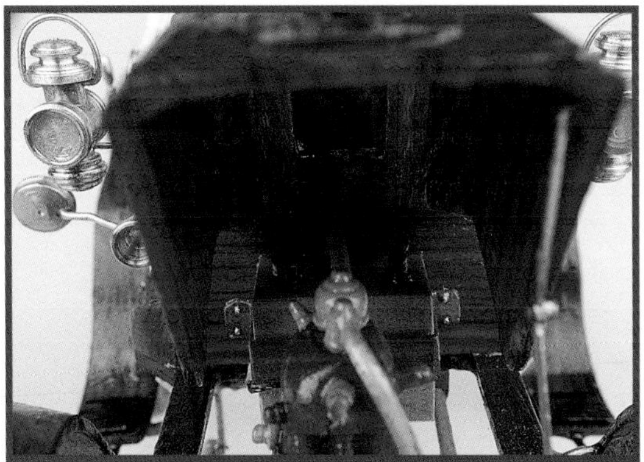

Fuel tank , pressure levers & exhaust pipe joins to top of engine, cover support rod

Assembled Engine Cover

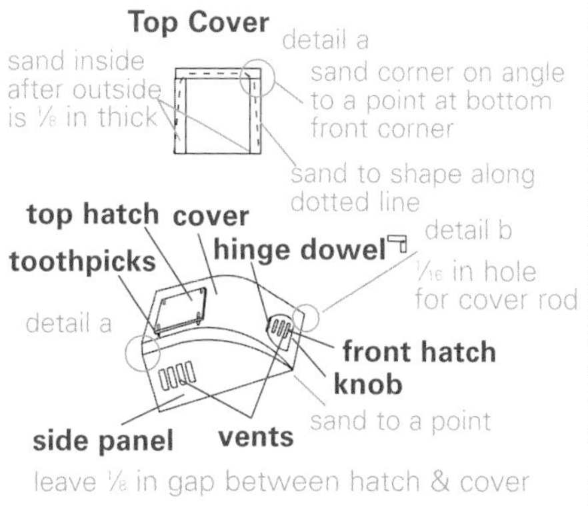
Top Cover
detail a
sand inside after outside is 1/8 in thick
sand corner on angle to a point at bottom front corner
sand to shape along dotted line
top hatch cover
toothpicks
hinge dowel
detail b
1/16 in hole for cover rod
detail a
front hatch
knob
sand to a point
side panel
vents
leave 1/8 in gap between hatch & cover

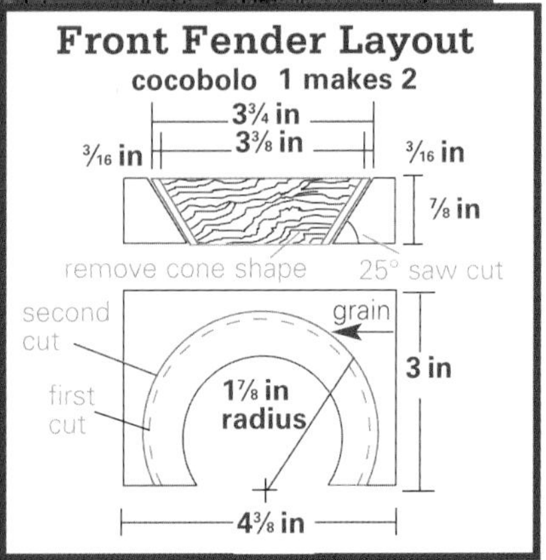
Front Fender Layout
cocobolo 1 makes 2
3¾ in
3/16 in
3⅜ in
3/16 in
⅞ in
remove cone shape
25° saw cut
second cut
grain
first cut
1⅞ in radius
3 in
4⅜ in

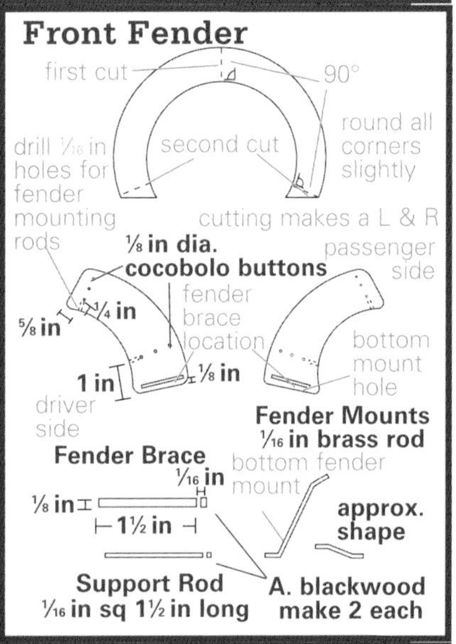
Front Fender
first cut
90°
drill 1/16 in holes for fender mounting rods
second cut
round all corners slightly
cutting makes a L & R
⅛ in dia. cocobolo buttons
passenger side
⅝ in
¼ in
fender brace location
⅛ in
1 in
bottom mount hole
driver side
Fender Mounts 1/16 in brass rod
Fender Brace
1/16 in
bottom fender mount
⅛ in
1½ in
approx. shape
Support Rod 1/16 in sq 1½ in long
A. blackwood make 2 each

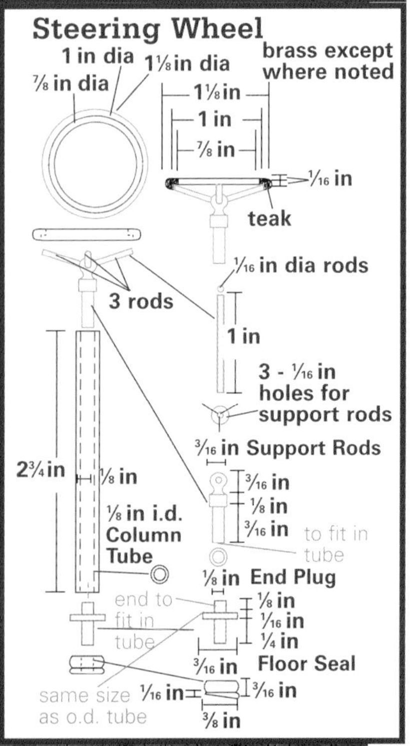
Steering Wheel
1 in dia
1⅛in dia
⅞ in dia
brass except where noted
1⅛in
1 in
⅞ in
1/16 in
teak
1/16 in dia rods
3 rods
1 in
3 - 1/16 in holes for support rods
3/16 in Support Rods
2¾ in
⅛ in
3/16 in
⅛ in
3/16 in
⅛ in i.d. Column Tube
to fit in tube
⅛ in End Plug
end to fit in tube
⅛ in
1/16 in
¼ in
3/16 in
Floor Seal
same size as o.d. tube
1/16 in
3/16 in
⅜ in

Making Front Fenders

1. Spray cocobolo 3⅜ in x 3 in x ⅞ in thick with white stencil ink. Set compass to 1⅞ in radius and draw 3¾ in circle on wood. Draw 3⅜ in circle inside first circle.
2. Set table on scroll saw to 25° angle. Use new blade to make smooth cut inside circle on inside of line. Cut outside circle on outside of line to leave a cone shaped piece wood. Sand smooth with a large drum sander mounted in drill press. Maintain thickness throughout length of curved piece. Cut cone piece in 2 pieces for 2 fenders. Round corners and drill 1/14 in deep holes by hand using pin vice and 1/16 in drill bit into edge of fenders (both the same). Make fender brace and support rods from African blackwood. Glue fender braces in place along bottom edge of each fender. Install support rod after front and back fenders are mounted to car.
3. Make fender mounts from 1/16 in diameter brass rod cut to different lengths and formed to shape. Bend longer rods when fenders are placed on car.
4. Make ⅛ in buttons (rivets) from cocobolo turned to ⅛ in diameter dowel, then sliced into twelve ⅛ in thick pieces. Glue to fenders and sand to 1/16 in thickness when glue dries.

Installing Front Fenders

Place bottom mounting rod in hole in one of front fenders. Place other end into hole farthest away from front of car drilled in edge of floor to mount fenders. Bottom of fender lines up with center of wheel and fender is ¼ in away from wheel which is in middle of fender. Take rod out of fender and bend other rod opposite for other fender. Place fender and rod back on car and measure front fender rod from hole in fender to hole in edge of floor. Ends of rod must be bent to slide into these holes.

Installing Rear Fenders

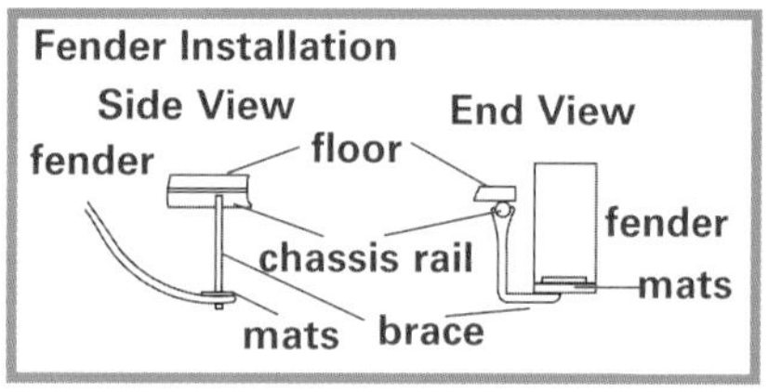
Fender Installation
Side View
End View
fender
floor
fender
chassis rail
mats
mats
brace

1. Glue fenders to body side panels below seat. Step of fender is level with bottom edge of front fender. Glue support rod to front fender brace and glue to underside of rear fender below mat. Keep support rod in middle of 2 fenders. Trim support rod ¼ in long under rear fender.
2. Make L shape brace to attach to chassis under car to underside of rear fender beside mat. Measure distance between chassis under car to the underside of rear fender beside mat. Measure distance between chassis and bottom of rear fender and from chassis to support rod for width of L shaped brace.
3. Make brace by drawing L shape onto maple and cut shape on band saw. Brace is no thicker than 1/16 in and goes from edge of fender to end of support rod that was glued to underside of rear fender. Mount one fender. Glue. Mount other fender.

Making Steering Column

1. Cut ⅛ in brass tube with tube cutter to length shown. Machine end plug from ⅛ in diameter brass rod that fits into brass tube and other end will fit into hole drilled in floor for steering column. Machine steering support from 3/16 in diameter brass rod. Drill 3 holes by hand into this part and deep enough to hold brass rods in place.
2. Cut three 1/16 in brass rods 1 in long and set aside. Solder end plug in place. Place solder paste on joint of parts, use third hand to hold parts, solder together. Place steering support in other end of brass tube with soldering paste on joint. Place 1/16 in rods in holes standing column up on brass rods on a piece of tin. Adjust rods to even space between them and solder in place. Allow to cool.

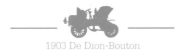

3 Place 1 1/8 in diameter walnut dowel in lathe and cut 1 in diameter step 1/16 in deep in end of dowel, as shown. Bore 7/8 in diameter hole in end of dowel 1/4 in deep. Separate steering wheel ring from rest of wood using a parting tool, stopping halfway through. Use a needle file to round edge of steering wheel. Remove steering wheel from rest of wood.

4 Place steering column on top center of steering wheel with three 1/16 in rods resting on wheel. Cut rods with wire cutters to fit into small step machined into wheel. Clean steering columns with rubbing alcohol. Polish with wire brush in dremel at low speed and no pressure. Glue (sparingly) steering wheel to column with 24-hour epoxy.

5 Make floor seal from African blackwood dowel turned on lathe to 3/8 in diameter x 1 1/4 in thick. Drill 1/8 in hole in center of dowel as shown. Use thread cutting tool for small groove 1/8 in from end of dowel, remove from lathe and sand angle of seal, as shown. Cut to length with band saw or hand saw. Slide seal over end of steering column mounted into floor of car and place steering column on car, leaving 1/2 in from edge of seat. Do not glue in place until levers are added to car.

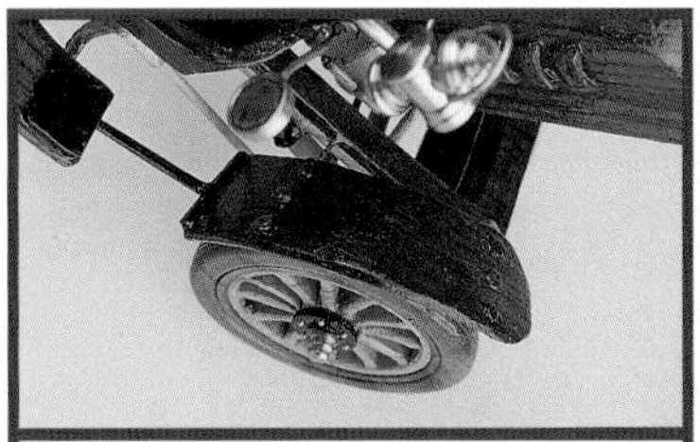
Shows front fender & buttons in fender, support rod

Making Brake Lever

1 Make from brass tube 1/8 in o.d. and 2 in long. Machine handle from brass 3/16 in diameter. Small diameter must fit into tube. Flatten one end of tube with hammer and drill hole large enough for tack pin used to mount brake levers.

2 Solder handle to brass tube. Cool. Use ball peen hammer to flatten handle and rod to 1/8 in thickness.

3 Polish lever with wire brush in dremel at slow speed. Mount lever to car on driver side just ahead of rear fender and above floor into body side panel. Handle of lever is located beside brass rail on seat. Drill hole in body side panel to fit tack pin. Glue (5-minute epoxy) tack pin and lever to car. Install steering column and shift levers.

4 Glue steering column to floor with floor seal fitting over end of steering column. Seal sits flat on floor when steering column is tilted towards seat. Place shift levers into holes in floor and glue (shift lever with 2 handles is glued into hole on right of steering column). Levers touch steering column on both sides. Adjust levers before glue dries.

Brake Lever brass make 1

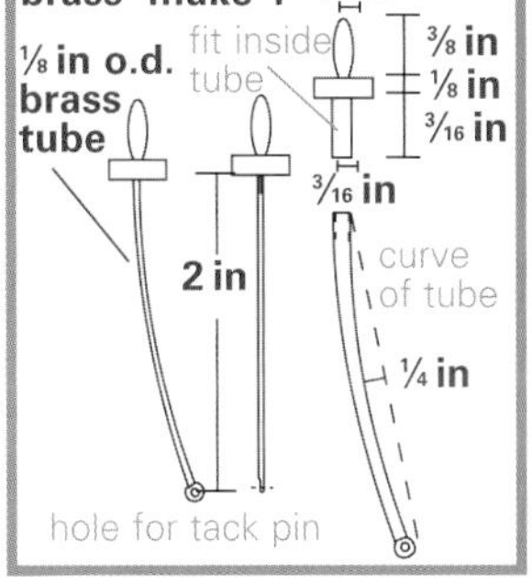
1/8 in
1/8 in o.d. brass tube
fit inside tube
3/8 in
1/8 in
3/16 in
3/16 in
2 in
curve of tube
1/4 in
hole for tack pin

Making Horn

1 Machine horn on lathe from 3/8 in diameter brass rod 3 in long and sticking 1/8 in out of chuck. Shape smaller diameter of horn into bell with needle files. Machine recess in end of brass rod first using boring tool. Make 1/8 in lip around bell. Pull brass rod out of chuck to 1 1/2 in. Use round file to form curve

Horn make 1

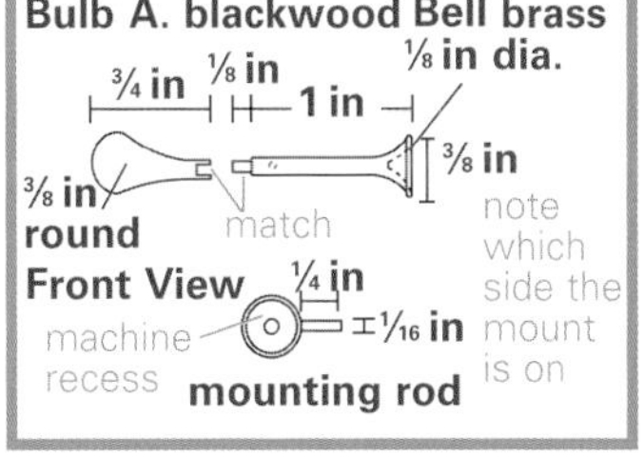
Bulb A. blackwood Bell brass
1/8 in dia.
3/4 in
1/8 in
1 in
3/8 in
3/8 in round
match
note which side the mount is on
Front View
1/4 in
machine recess
1/16 in
mounting rod

Rear Fender make 2 each

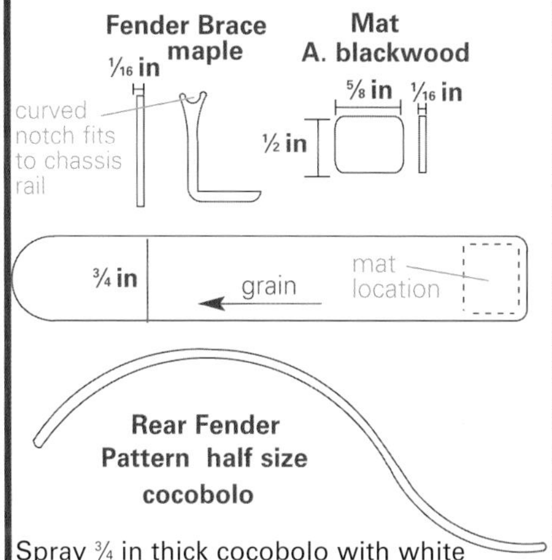
Fender Brace maple
Mat A. blackwood
1/16 in
5/8 in
1/16 in
curved notch fits to chassis rail
1/2 in
3/4 in
grain
mat location
Rear Fender Pattern half size cocobolo

Spray 3/4 in thick cocobolo with white stencil ink and trace (p5) pattern. Cut out on scroll or band saw (1/8 in blade). Leave pattern line for sanding line. Use drum sander in drill press. Sand ends of fenders round. Cut fender mats from African blackwood 1 1/4 in x 1/2 in x 1/16 in thick, then cut in half to make 5/8 in long. Glue mats onto rear fender with 5-minute epoxy.

Making Levers brass

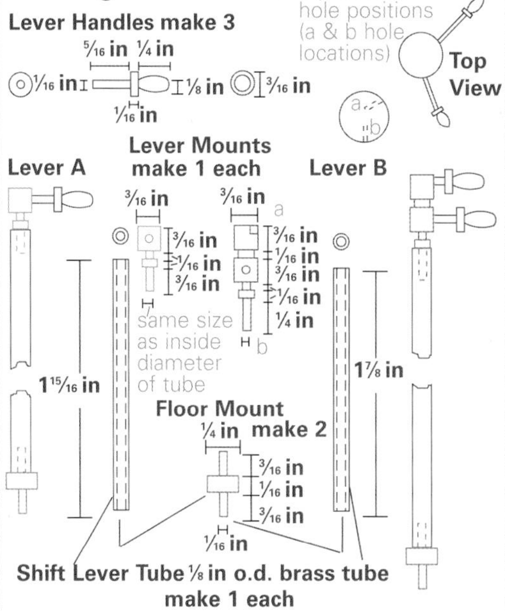
top view of hole positions (a & b hole locations)
Lever Handles make 3
5/16 in
1/4 in
1/16 in
1/8 in
3/16 in
1/16 in
Top View
Lever Mounts make 1 each
Lever A
Lever B
3/16 in
3/16 in
3/16 in
1/16 in
3/16 in
3/16 in
1/16 in
3/16 in
1/16 in
1/4 in
same size as inside diameter of tube
1 15/16 in
1 7/8 in
Floor Mount
1/4 in make 2
3/16 in
1/16 in
3/16 in
1/16 in
Shift Lever Tube 1/8 in o.d. brass tube make 1 each

Cut two 1/8 o.d brass tubes, as shown (not same length). Stubs that go into one end of tube (same for each tube and must fit into holes drilled into floor for these levers). Machine levers from 3/16 in diameter brass rod starting from smaller diameter first to fit into lever supports.

Front view of radiator, engine, front wheels attached to axle

Chassis assembled to floor, muffler & steering box, transmission, crank fits through rod into engine

Side view fenders & break lever, angle of steering wheel

into brass rod from the lip to ⅛ in diameter, as shown.

2 Place parting tool in lathe and machine rest of rod to ⅛ in diameter to match curve of horn. Machine to length, as shown, then cut deeper into rod to form stub to fit into horn bulb (smaller than ⅛ in diameter). Polish bell with steel wool in lathe. Drill ¹⁄₁₆ in diameter hole in ⅛ in diameter part of horn. This is used to solder ¹⁄₁₆ in brass rod to mount horn to side of dash. Cut ¹⁄₁₆ in brass rod ½ in long and solder rod into hole. Clean with rubbing alcohol and polish with wire brush in a dremel.

3 Make bulb from African blackwood ⅜ in diameter x 2 in long. Drill hole in center to match diameter of stub in bell horn. Shape bulb using same method as for bell but do in reverse. Machine end of wood so diameter is bigger than hole drilled in end. Machine this diameter ⅜ in long from end of wood. Form curve with needle file.

4 Use parting tool to cut groove ³⁄₁₆ in deep into wood ¼ in past top of curve. File bulb with needle file until groove and curve meet forming round contour. Remove bulb from wood and glue to end of bell with 5-minute epoxy. Set aside.

Making the Mirror

1 Machine ½ in brass rod ½ in long in lathe. Make recess to hold tin plate. Remove from lathe and drill ¹⁄₁₆ in ¼ in deep hole in end of rod. Place rod in lathe and use parting tool to cut step ¼ in from end of rod. Use needle file to shape back of mirror. Cut ¹⁄₁₆ in diameter brass rod 1½ in long and bend to shape. Mounting plate is made from brass ⅜ in wide and long enough to hold. Drill 3 holes by hand, across width.

2 Cut disk with hollow punch from tin can to fit inside the recess. Place rod into ¹⁄₁₆ in hole drilled into brass rod. Put soldering paste on dull side of tin plate and place into recess. Solder tin and mounting rod at same time. Solder mounting plate in place by placing alligator clip between plate and mirror to absorb some heat. Clean assembly in rubbing alcohol and polish (not tin) with wire brush.

3 Mount horn to car, drill ¹⁄₁₆ in hole ¼ in down from top edge of dash on driver's side with pin vice. Bell of horn will touch dash.

Mirror

make 1 each

¹⁄₁₆ in hole

³⁄₁₆ in

⅜ in

½ in

¹⁄₁₆ in

solder tin disk inside recess to make mirror

Mount
¹⁄₁₆ in brass rod

Mount Plate
³⁄₃₂ in brass shim stock

⅜ in

¹⁄₁₆ in hole
2 tack pin holes

⅛ in

¼ in

³⁄₄ in

¼ in

³⁄₁₆ in

¼ in

Assembled Mirror

tack pin holes

tin plate

driver view

top view

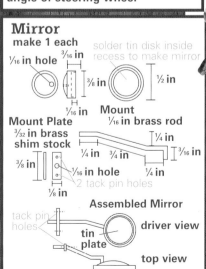

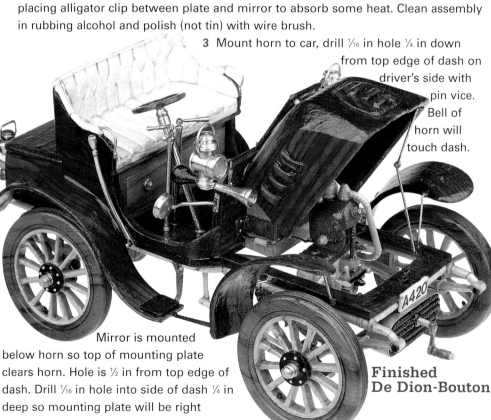

Mirror is mounted below horn so top of mounting plate clears horn. Hole is ½ in from top edge of dash. Drill ¹⁄₁₆ in hole into side of dash ¼ in deep so mounting plate will be right

Finished De Dion-Bouton

against edge of dash. Glue horn and mirror to car with 5-minute epoxy. Dry overnight.

Making Rear Light and Side Lamps

1   Machine body of side lamps from ½ in diameter brass rod sticking out of lathe chuck far enough to machine part. Drill hole through brass rod, as shown, far enough from end so end of rod can be machine cut. Drill ¼ in hole and ¹⁄₁₆ in hole into lamp body (L & R lamps) to solder mounting rods. Machine recess for plastic lens into end of rod using dimensions on diagram. Using parting tool, machine rest of lamp body to shape. Mark distance of lip on back of lamp body from front edge of lamp body to be reference line on brass while spinning on lathe. Machine 2 sides lamp bodies at same time. Repeat for taillight using same diameter rod.

2   Place brass rod in lathe and machine small diameter first. Slide lamp body on this machined diameter through hole to check fit. Turn rod around in lathe, then machine rod to different diameters to form fuel tank on end of burner. Using parting tool cut a groove in bar making sure that edge of groove is total length of burner. Shape groove with needle file. Cut into groove to remove burner from rod. Repeat for all lamp burners.

3   Make vents same way as lamp body starting with recess same size as small diameter on burner. Machine rest of brass rod to shape. Form handles from ¹⁄₁₆ in diameter brass rod using pliers. Make curved handle by wrapping rod around large drill bit then bending ends to shape.

4   Drill small hole under lip of burner to hold handle in place before soldering. Flatten one end of brass tube that fits over mounting rods and drill holes. Cut tube to length. Assemble lamp. Place assembly in third hand to hold parts together and solder entire assembly. Cool. Clean with rubbing alcohol and polish to bright finish. Glue lens (p52, 53) in place with 5-minute epoxy.

5   Cut out rear light lens from red plastic pouch wrenches come in, using hollow punch the size of the recess. Rear light mounting plate is made same way as mounting plate for mirror. Mount just over center line towards driver's side. Drill hole for mounting rod and glue with 5-minute epoxy

6   Place lamp on driver's side to clear horn and above mirror. Mount other lamp in same position. Use tack pins passing through mounts into dash. Glue. Dry.

7   Make mats from ¹⁄₁₆ in thick African blackwood and glue to floor in front of seat. *Note*   One mat is rectangle shape for passenger side, other mat for driver's side is C shape that goes from each side of steering column between under seat panel and steering column.

8   Glue (5-minute epoxy) engine cover across front of dash over engine. Hold in place while glue hardens. Edge of cover is ¼ in down from top edge of dash aligning with square cut floor.

9   Cut support rod to length keeping pivot in middle. Rod goes from hole drilled in corner of engine cover to front corner of sq cut into floor. Bend support rod points toward dash. Glue (5-minute epoxy). Dry 24 hours. Remove excess glue with wire brush in dremel at slow speed and little pressure. Clear coat entire car with urethane clear gloss.

Assembled Side Lamps   Assembled Rear Lamp

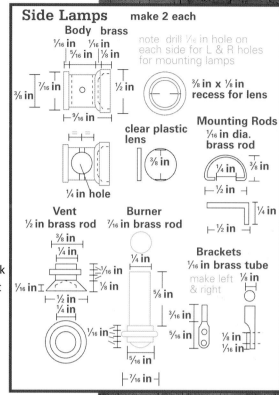

Side Lamps   make 2 each
Body brass
note drill ¹⁄₁₆ in hole on each side for L & R holes for mounting lamps
⅜ in x ⅛ in recess for lens
clear plastic lens
Mounting Rods ¹⁄₁₆ in dia. brass rod
¼ in hole
Vent ½ in brass rod   **Burner** ⁷⁄₁₆ in brass rod
Brackets ¹⁄₁₆ in brass tube
make left & right

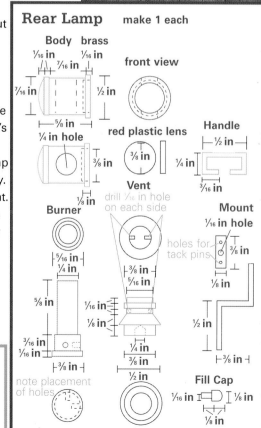

Rear Lamp   make 1 each
Body brass
front view
¼ in hole
red plastic lens
Handle
Vent
drill ¹⁄₁₆ in hole on each side
Burner
Mount ¹⁄₁₆ in hole
holes for tack pins
note placement of holes
Fill Cap

INDEX

Contact for further information (including pattern for small table saw) William Reeves, email reevesd@mts.net